Special Populations in Health Care

D. Miles Burkholder, MBA, LNHA

Nicole Bremer Nash, BA

JONES & BARTLETT
LEARNING

World Headquarters
Jones & Bartlett Learning
5 Wall Street
Burlington, MA 01803
978-443-5000
info@jblearning.com
www.jblearning.com

Jones & Bartlett Learning books and products are available through most bookstores and online booksellers. To contact Jones & Bartlett Learning directly, call 800-832-0034, fax 978-443-8000, or visit our website, www.jblearning.com.

Substantial discounts on bulk quantities of Jones & Bartlett Learning publications are available to corporations, professional associations, and other qualified organizations. For details and specific discount information, contact the special sales department at Jones & Bartlett Learning via the above contact information or send an email to specialsales@jblearning.com.

Special Populations in Health Care is an independent publication and has not been authorized, sponsored, or otherwise approved by the owners of the trademarks or service marks referenced in this product.

Some images in this book feature models. These models do not necessarily endorse, represent, or participate in the activities represented in the images.

This publication is designed to provide accurate and authoritative information in regard to the subject matter covered. It is sold with the understanding that the publisher is not engaged in rendering legal, accounting, or other professional service. If legal advice or other expert assistance is required, the service of a competent professional person should be sought.

Production Credits
Chief Executive Officer: Ty Field
President: James Homer
SVP, Editor-in-Chief: Michael Johnson
SVP, Chief Marketing Officer: Alison M. Pendergast
SVP, Curriculum Solutions: Christopher Will
VP, Business Development: Todd Giorza
Editorial Management: High Stakes Writing, LLC
Editor and Publisher: Lawrence J. Goodrich
Copy Editor, HSW: Karen Annett and Lachina Publishing Services
Development Editor: Gabrielle Nabi
Senior Editorial Assistant: Rainna Erikson
Production Editor: Tina Chen, Lindsay Serra
Marketing Manager: Grace Richards
Manufacturing and Inventory Control Supervisor: Amy Bacus
Cover Design: Scott Moden

Cover Image: **Top row, left:** © jean schweitzer/ShutterStock, Inc.; **top row, center:** © Photodisc; **top row, right:** © Vladimir Melnik/ShutterStock, Inc.; **center row, left:** © absolut/ShutterStock, Inc.; **center row, vertical:** Elderly woman walking with cane: © Hasan Shaheed/ShutterStock, Inc.; **center row, right:** © Blend Images/ShutterStock, Inc.; **bottom row, left:** © Lucian Coman/ShutterStock, Inc.; **bottom row, right:** Photos.com
Composition: Lachina Publishing Services

ISBN: 978-1-28402-561-3

Library of Congress Cataloging-in-Publication Data
Unavailable at time of printing.

6048

Printed in the United States of America
16 15 14 13   10 9 8 7 6 5 4 3 2 1

Brief Contents

Contents

Chapter 2
Comparing Vulnerable Groups 39

Chapter 3
Why Are Some More Vulnerable Than Others? *79*

Chapter 5
Paying for Health Care *149*

Chapter 7
Evaluating the Cost of Care *195*

Chapter 8
Monitoring the Quality of Care 219

Chapter 9
Studying Vulnerable Populations 233

About the Author

D. Miles Burkholder, MBA, LNHA

As Administrator of The Altenheim, Miles Burkholder is responsible for efficiently running all facets of the business. Miles has turned around a 106-year-old 501c(3) private foundation from losing a sizable amount to within Board mandated limits in his 5 years with the company. His department directors nominated him for Kentucky Association of Homes and Services for the Aging—Administrator of the Year in 2011. He has seen the facility receive three straight-zero deficiency surveys from the Office of the Inspector General.

Currently Miles serves on the Finance, Public Relations, and Non-Proprietary Committees with the Kentucky Association of Health Care Facilities. He serves on the Finance, Legislative and Regulatory, and Awards Committees with Leading Age (formerly the Kentucky Association of Homes and Services for the Aging). Miles is a member of The Rotary Club of Downtown Louisville after being a volunteer at Scout-O-Rama for 25 years. He is a member of The College of Health Care Administrators, a twice graduate of The University of Louisville (Accounting and MBA). He is also a Board Member of Goodwill Industries of Kentucky's Cars to Work Program. He is the father of a son, Connor (4), and a daughter, Addison, born in May 2012. He is married to Rachel Wilson Burkholder.

Nicole Bremer Nash, BA

Nicole Bremer Nash has authored multiple books including several from Jones & Bartlett Learning's *The Art and Science of Photovoltaics* series. In addition to research-based authoring, Nicole writes general interest articles for print and Web publishing. She has a Bachelor of Arts in English from Transylvania University (2001), and over 10 years of experience in research and writing. As an advocate and community volunteer, Nicole has a particular interest in women's and children's issues including housing, education, and health care access and quality, and the ways these issues affect individuals' well-being and success.

Nicole is active in her community through advocacy and volunteer work for multiple nonprofit organizations, including Junior League, Women for Habitat for Humanity, and StageOne Family Theatre. Nicole's hobbies include reading, crafting, and conducting science experiments with her family.

Acknowledgments

From D. Miles Burkholder

To my loving wife, beautiful children, and outstanding co-author.
—DMB

From Nicole Bremer Nash

I owe a life of gratitude to my mom, who was once a vulnerable mother with a vulnerable child, and who worked hard to make sure every door was open to me, so I would never have to be a vulnerable adult. Gratitude and love also to my ever-supportive husband, Chris, and our amazing son, Ezra, who both shudder when I begin a new book and smile the most when my books are complete.

Special thanks to Dr. Michael Shaw for being the best, most supportive project manager a writer could ever dream of; and to Karen Annett for her skill, talent, and patience in editing this book. I also appreciate the research help I received from Regan Hunt at Metro United Way (Louisville) for helping me hunt down, access, and comprehend difficult data; and to Medearis Robertson at the Kentucky Fatality Assessment and Control Evaluation (FACE) Program for providing the book with meta-sources and research. Of course, this book couldn't have happened without my co-author, Miles, who works hard every day to address the needs of one of America's most vulnerable and often most ignored populations.

This book is dedicated to all the people who give time, energy, and donations to address the needs of America's most vulnerable people. We would all be worse off without you.

The authors would also like to thank the following peer reviewers for their feedback and helpful guidance:

Quynh Dao Dang, Texas A&M University

Howard J. Eng, The University of Arizona

Patricia Gray, University of Houston Law Center

Fran Henton, Nebraska Methodist College

John Janowiak, Appalachian State University

Martha E. Jennings, Ashford University

Jeanette Pack, Ashford University

Justine Pawlukewicz, NYC College of Technology

Robert Schroeder, Ashford University

Monica L. Vargas, Ashford University

Identifying the Vulnerable

Learning Objectives

After reading this chapter, you should be able to:

- Explain the concept of vulnerable populations.

- Discuss how the theories of common good and individual rights contribute to the creation of public policy in health care.

- Determine how the concept of resource availability relates to one's health.

- Examine the aggregate statistical data on the number and growth of identified vulnerable populations.

- Identify the vulnerable populations in the United States.

Introduction

Two women enter the hospital with pneumonia. They are similar in age, but of different races. One patient has private health insurance; the other is on Medicaid. One patient recovers quickly while the other languishes. What can be surmised from the differences in the two patients? Thinking on this and asking the right questions allows health care providers to create patient care plans that better meet each patient's needs. Providing better health care to all patients requires awareness of environmental factors that may prohibit timely recovery and put the patient at risk for secondary and repeat infections.

Environmental factors such as finances, family, and education all affect a person's **vulnerability**, or risk level. Understanding statistical data on vulnerable populations will help you interpret patient information. This allows easier identification of those who are at risk, so that providers may plan care accordingly. Addressing the needs of at-risk populations leads to faster patient recovery, thereby lowering the cost of patient care.

Lowering health care costs is important for the patient, the care provider, and the whole country. Nonprofit organizations and government agencies work to identify and help at-risk groups. This activity affects both government and organizational policy among health care providers.

This text investigates the statistical data and indicators of vulnerable populations in American health care. It also covers the causes of vulnerability and the prevailing ideologies on dealing with at-risk populations. We will also discuss what is currently being done through policymaking and program implementation to address the needs of vulnerable populations and what the future looks like for at-risk groups. This chapter focuses on identifying vulnerable populations. The relationship between resource availability and health is an important part of recognizing at-risk groups. Finally, we will look at statistical data concerning the at-risk groups identified in the book.

Critical Thinking

The text states, "Addressing the needs of at-risk populations leads to faster patient recovery, thereby lowering the cost of patient care." How does addressing the needs of at-risk populations lead to faster patient recovery?

Self-Check

Answer the following questions to the best of your ability.

1. Asking the right questions allows health care providers to create _____ that better meet each patient's needs.
   a. patient care plans
   b. outpatient clinics
   c. health insurance plans
   d. genetically modified medicines

2. Environmental factors such as finances, family, and education all affect a person's vulnerability, or _____.
   a. mortality
   b. life span
   c. risk level
   d. quality of life

3. Nonprofit organizations and which agencies work to identify and help at-risk groups?
   a. cultural entities
   b. labor unions
   c. local businesses
   d. government agencies

Answer Key

1. **a**   2. **c**   3. **d**

1.1 Social Theory and Public Policy in Health Care

Health is both an individual consideration and a community concern. In other words, an individual makes decisions that directly affect him or herself, and a society makes decisions that affect and manage the society itself. For example, a person may choose to smoke cigarettes, thereby damaging his or her own lungs. However, this action also has an impact on those around the smoker because secondhand smoke has been shown to be a valid health concern. Thus, society may create **public policy**, or laws, that outlaw smoking in public places with the intent of ensuring that one person's decision to smoke does not harm others.

A law that bans smoking in public places is based on the social theory of the **common good**, meaning it is intended to help everybody. The concept of the common good focuses on creating a benefit for the most members of a community. Sometimes the common good is juxtaposed with the social theory of **individual rights**, which is based on protecting personal freedoms. Public controversy often ensues when the common good is perceived to infringe on such individual rights. For example, social theory centered on the common good led to the creation of public policy in the form of a law banning smoking in public places, which results in heated debate among lawmakers and citizens. One side argues that such laws are necessary to protect society; the opposition argues that personal freedom should not be inhibited by the collective citizenry. The United States Bill of Rights is the primary protector of individual liberties in the United States. The argument that personal freedom should not be inhibited by the collective citizenry is primarily based on three amendments:

Prohibiting smoking in public places exemplifies the social theory of the common good, because the mandate is meant to benefit everyone.

- The Ninth Amendment states, "The enumeration in the Constitution, of certain rights, shall not be construed to deny or disparage others retained by the people."
- The Tenth Amendment further protects individual liberties by stating, "The powers not delegated to the United States by the Constitution, nor prohibited by it to the States, are reserved to the States respectively, or to the people."
- The Fourteenth Amendment states, "All persons born or naturalized in the United States, and subject to the jurisdiction thereof, are citizens of the United States and of the State wherein they reside. No State shall make or enforce any law which shall abridge the privileges or immunities of citizens of the United States; nor shall any State deprive any person of life, liberty, or property, without due process of law; nor deny to any person within its jurisdiction the equal protection of the laws."

However, the argument in favor of passing legislation to promote the common good is based directly on the preamble to the Constitution:

Pareto's principle explains why the common good and individual fairness often conflict. In many cases, a small group of people do most of the work, which the majority then benefits from.

- "We the People of the United States, in Order to form a more perfect Union, establish Justice, insure domestic Tranquility, provide for the common defence, promote the general Welfare, and secure the Blessings of Liberty to ourselves and our Posterity, do ordain and establish this Constitution for the United States of America" (Constitution of the United States of America and the Bill of Rights, 1787).

The Constitution and amendments then go on to describe Congress's power to legislate.

Which option is the fair choice? That question plagues American health policy. America dogmatically strives for justice and fairness for all citizens. Social theorists and policy-makers alike refer to the **Pareto principle** when the common good and individual rights are directly at odds. The Pareto principle is the theory that 80% of the outcome is caused by 20% of the effort (Juran, 1994). This is often seen in community involvement situations wherein a handful of people do most of the work while the majority does very little. In social theory, the Pareto principle is often translated to mean that fairness for all does not necessarily create fairness for every individual and that some instances occur wherein fairness for all has negative effects on the common good (Kaplow & Shavell, 2000). Take the case of a communist society wherein all resources are combined then doled out equally among people, regardless of how much each person contributed. Ensuring food for all citizens benefits the common good, but a farmer who worked hard all year to fill the pantry may end up without enough to feed his family for the winter because others were less industrious, so his equal share becomes less than what he worked for.

Social Attitudes Versus Individual Choice

The smoking ban example illustrates how **social attitudes**—which are positive or negative evaluations of people, places, things, events, and the like, and are shared by a majority of the community as a whole—and individual choice are not always in agreement. Social attitudes are the result of generalized, shared ethics in a society. They help shape our overall health environment. For example, positive social attitudes toward cigarettes viewed smoking in public spaces to be perfectly acceptable and even doctor recommended in the early 1900s. The current social attitude toward cigarette smoking has caused the number of cigarette users in the United States to drop below 20% (see Figure 1.1). This in turn has created a drop in tobacco-related illness and death. Negative social attitudes about cigarette use, caused by a collective realization regarding the negative effects of smoke, secondhand smoke, and related illnesses, have positively affected the nation's health.

Figure 1.1: Percentage of adults in the U.S. who use cigarettes

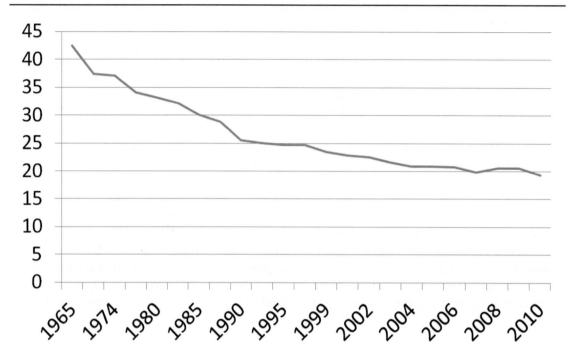

Social attitudes toward cigarette smoking have changed drastically in the last 50 years, causing cigarette use to decline.

Centers for Disease Control and Prevention (CDC). (2011). Trends in current cigarette smoking among high school students and adults, United States, 1965–2010. Retrieved January 9, 2012, from http://www.cdc.gov/tobacco/data_statistics/tables/trends/cig_smoking/index.htm

Social attitudes are part of the collective, or **macro**, influences on our health. Other macro-level influences include messages from the media, such as commercials for fast food. Health policy is often created in response to macro influences on our society's health environment, or the combined collective knowledge created through rigorous study, comprehensive evaluation, and peer-reviewed publication of facts related to the collective public good.

Considering only the macro view does not consider the individual, or **micro**, influences or decisions that we each make about our health. Micro influences on health include whether we choose to walk, bike, or drive to work or school, and which foods we select at the grocery. A debate lingers over whether the micro or macro perspective is more useful when considering health decisions and policy.

Critical Thinking

Can you think of other examples where social attitudes conflict with individual choice? Would abortion (a woman's right to choose) fall into this category? What about medical marijuana?

Self-Check

Answer the following questions to the best of your ability.

1. During which time period did the media and medical professionals promote smoking as "good for your health?"
   a. early 1900s
   b. late 1950s
   c. middle 1970s
   d. early 2000s

2. The *common good* refers to principles and laws intended to help which of the fol-lowing groups?
   a. a few people
   b. a specific group of people
   c. everybody
   d. no one

3. The Pareto principle refers to which of the following principles?
   a. 90% of the outcome is caused by 5% of the effort
   b. 10% of the outcome is caused by 80% of the effort
   c. 100% of the outcome is caused by 100% of the effort
   d. 80% of the outcome is caused by 20% of the effort

Answer Key

1. **a**   2. **c**   3. **d**

1.2 Considerations for Studying Vulnerable Populations

How do we apply social theory to the study of vulnerable populations? First, we must begin by categorizing the influences that affect the health of these groups. The influences are used to determine which social groups in our society are defined as vulnerable populations.

Community and Personal Values

Americans largely associate good health with good personal habits and decisions. This means that culturally, Americans expect each person to take responsibility for his or her health-related habits and actions. Daily exercise, dietary choices, and other behaviors are not heavily regulated by public policy or community values. Each person's own values determine his or her health outcomes.

Of course, we cannot entirely disregard community health values. After all, they do shape public health policy. Community values also affect the community's investment in resources and opportunities that impact health, from regulating pollution levels to ensur-ing the availability of fresh produce. Community-based health policies help bridge the gap between microlevel personal choices and macrolevel governmental thinking. Most public policy decisions grow, not from massive governmental thinking, but from grassroots efforts, like the previously discussed smoking ban(s). These grassroots efforts are evidence of the power of individuals to affect public policy.

The Louisville, Kentucky, Farm to Table program offers a good example. Two movements were simultaneously growing in the Louisville community. One movement, led by local farmers and entrepreneurs, focused on expanding access to locally farmed foods within the community; the other movement, led by parents and school cafeteria employees, focused on improving the nutrition of school lunches. When these two groups combined efforts, the Farm to Table program was altered, and creating avenues to getting locally farmed foods into school cafeterias became an important goal throughout the community. As the community at large increased program participation, the local city government became involved with programs and grants to increase the scope of the Farm to Table program.

Access to Resources

From a macro perspective, we see that the distribution of resources within a community has a direct impact on health risk. Resource distribution often correlates with social status, social capital, and human capital. Though American society tries to equalize the distribution of resources through social welfare programs, it is no secret that individuals gain or lose access to opportunities and resources depending on their social status, social ties, and ability to invest in their own potential.

Social Status

An individual's place in society, called **social status**, is attributable to personal characteristics, opportunities, and rewards. Personal characteristics such as age, gender, ethnicity, geographic location, education level, and income result in social rewards like social power, or a lack thereof. Age affects a person's wellness (e.g., elderly people are usually more susceptible to chronic illness than young adults) as well as a person's need to depend on others for his or her well-being (e.g., children depend on adults for medical care).

Gender is also an important factor in health and level of health risk. Women are more susceptible to certain cancers, for example, but are more likely to seek medical care. Men are more susceptible to work-related health

Courtesy of 123RF Limited/123RF

Opportunities, rewards, and personal characteristics can be attributed to an individual's social status.

Courtesy of Brand X Pictures/Thinkstock

Minorities are less able to take advantage of the social rewards that diminish risk levels; thus, ethnicity and race are oft-studied factors in social status and health risk.

risks, as they traditionally hold more physically demanding jobs. The emotional differences between men and woman also affect vulnerability. Statistically, women are more likely to suffer the ill consequences of eating disorders, whereas it can be said that men are socially trained to eat more red meat and maintain a more robust physique, decisions which come with their own sets of health risks.

Ethnicity and race are two of the most studied factors in social status and health risk because minorities historically have less access to the social rewards that limit risk levels. Lower-class urban neighborhoods with a high number of minority residents often lack representation in social politics and suffer for it with higher levels of air and water pollution, which increase the level of health risk for all residents. Furthermore, poverty can breed crime, and the stress of living in a high-crime area also negatively affects a person's health. Stress can manifest physically by presenting as complaints such as headaches. Stress can also increase the likelihood of negative health behaviors, such as cigarette and alcohol use. Limited access to resources, including fresh vegetables and medical care, increases the burden. Low-income areas are commonly populated with fast-food restaurants that serve high-fat foods, whereas more affluent areas often have more grocery stores and farmers' markets. Additional factors such as migrant status further increase a person's vulnerability. Risk factors do not stand alone. An elderly minority female has different risk factors than an elderly Caucasian male.

Social Capital

Social capital is the measurement of personal relationships in an individual's life. The number, type, and reliability of interpersonal relationships greatly influence a person's vulnerability and health risk. For example, a single mother is less likely to spend a day in bed, resting and recovering from an illness, than a mother who has a

Courtesy of Hemera/Thinkstock

Health risk depends on several factors, including the quantity and quality of a person's interpersonal relationships.

9

partner or someone reliable who can care for the children. Working parents are better able to maintain viable employment if grandparents and other relations are available to help with child care.

The ability to work creates opportunities and other social rewards. An upwardly mobile career path grants access to money and insurance to help pay for doctor visits and medicine. The opportunity to meet people and grow friendships at work adds to a person's support network. A strong, healthy support network directly influences psychological and physical well-being, lessening a person's health risk. Hospitals and rehabilitation facilities have found that patients who have reliable support systems enjoy faster recovery times and spend less time recuperating in the medical center in favor of convalescing at home with the assistance of a robust, developed support system. Reducing the length and frequency of hospital stays reduces the risk of secondary and recurrent infections.

Human Capital

Human capital is the amount of investment in a person's potential. Low-income individuals often have low human capital, while higher-income individuals enjoy investment in their potential in the form of education, opportunities for advancement, and even better access to higher-quality health care. The more investment made in a person's potential, or future, the more that person will be able to contribute to society in a positive way.

Data on various subjects including education, wage earnings, and health care access indicates gaps in human capital based on gender, age, and ethnicity. Poor-performing schools are more common in low-income neighborhoods, females are sometimes passed over for advanced training and managerial positions, and minorities often suffer a lack of social resource allocation. In all of these examples, failure to invest in people's potential negatively influences their long-term outcomes. Poorly educated children are less likely to attend college, the disenfranchised female will lose work productivity, and the neighborhood that needs public resources to fix streetlights will see an increase in crime.

Outside influences are not the only way to invest in human capital. Individuals invest in their own potential by working hard at school and work and by organizing communities to create the change they want. Conversely, investment in human capital can be negatively impacted by a collective lifestyle perspective. The collective lifestyle perspective dictates behavior based on social constructs, or ideas, about the way people "like me" should behave (Barnes, Hall, & Taylor, 2010). Middle-class mothers may perceive that smoking is unacceptable among their peers and so give up smoking. Conversely, adolescents in low-income areas may perceive that smoking makes them more accepted among their peers and so take up the unhealthy habit.

Critical Thinking

Do you have a support network? Can they help with family needs such as child care or transportation? Are they supportive of your education goals?

Health Indicators

The World Health Organization (WHO) is an international organization that coordinates health-related efforts around the globe. The WHO definition of health goes beyond the mere absence of illness, proposing that "health is a state of complete physical, mental, and social well-being and not merely the absence of disease or infirmity" (World Health Organization [WHO], 2012).

From this definition of health, we can see where values and resources are directly linked to well-being. The WHO definition indicates that health exists in varying degrees, based on a number of recognized indicators. Indicators of physical health are considered the measurements of the body's wellness, such as bodily illness and disability. Mental health indicators measure emotional issues such as stress and mental illness. The WHO definition also includes social well-being, based on indicators such as relationships with others. Figure 1.2 illustrates the health continuum.

Figure 1.2: The health continuum

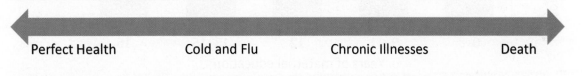

| Perfect Health | Cold and Flu | Chronic Illnesses | Death |

Health is not simply the absence of disease. A person's degree of health exists on a spectrum, fluctuating throughout life.

Health is measured along a continuum, with great health at one end and death on the opposite end. Minor ailments fall nearer the perfect health end of the continuum, with more severe needs nearer the death end.

The WHO definition of health clearly includes physical, mental, and social components. Physical health deals with the body and bodily functions, mental health includes brain functions such as thought and emotions, and social health includes interpersonal relationships with others. Physical health is measured by patient perception, doctor opinion, and clinical testing. Another way to measure health is based on a patient's abilities to perform activities of daily living (ADLs). Basic ADLs include personal hygiene and being able to dress oneself, feed oneself, walk with or without assistance, and use the restroom (Weiner, Hanley, Clark, & Van Nostrand, 1990).

Patient perception of well-being cannot be overlooked when measuring health. An important part of patient perception of well-being involves the concept that people alter their behavior when they perceive that they are unwell. Staying in bed and eating chicken soup are two common "sick role" behaviors. Perception is a key tool in measuring both mental health and social health, as people interpret stressors and relationships differently.

Patient perception, doctor opinion, and clinical testing are standard ways of measuring individual health status but do not offer a larger picture of community health status. Community health status is measured with statistics of the rates of occurrence of illness, disease, and death within a recognized group. This data, such as that shown in Figure 1.3, is used to influence public policy and the distribution of public resources.

Figure 1.3: U.S. infant mortality rates per 1,000 live births, by maternal education and race

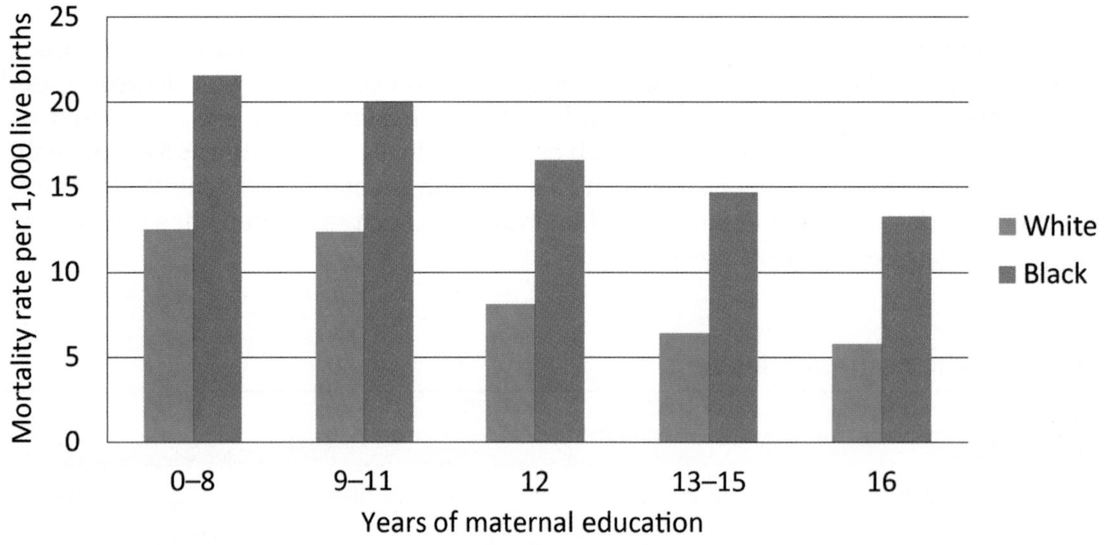

Mortality rates for children born to white mothers is much lower overall than for children born to black mothers; however, both races see a significant decrease in infant mortality as the mother's number of years of completed education rises.

Singh, G. K. & Yu, S. M. (1995). Infant mortality in the United States: Trends, differentials, and projections, 1950 through 2010. American Journal of Public Health, 85*(7). Retrieved January 12, 2012, from* http://www.ncbi.nlm.nih.gov/pmc/articles/PMC1615523/pdf/amjph00445-0063.pdf

---

Critical Thinking

Where does your current total health fall on the health continuum? Can you think of a time when your health measured nearer the negative end?

Do you feel that patient perception is a reliable method of measurement for use in global decisions regarding heath issues?

Courtesy of iStockphoto/Thinkstock

In groups exposed to certain risk factors, negative life events can cause more adverse reactions than in groups not exposed to those same factors.

Risk Potential

The data on infant mortality and maternal race and education in Figure 1.3 also illustrates the concept of **relative risk**, or risk potential. Relative risk is the potential of imperfect health in groups exposed to risk factors, such as drug use, in relation to the potential of imperfect health in groups not exposed to the same risk factors.

The concept of relative risk embodies the **differential vulnerability hypothesis**, which theorizes that some people have more adverse reactions than others to negative life events. Studies of the differential vulnerability hypothesis have found that members of low socioeconomic status groups experience higher levels of anxiety, stress, and emotional duress when faced with negative events and information than do persons of higher socioeconomic status. Considering the factors that contribute to health and well-being (social status, social capital, and human capital), we can ascertain that a deficiency in these factors is a likely cause of the higher levels of mental duress in stressful situations experienced by members of low socioeconomic groups. For example, a wealthy person who receives a speeding ticket is less likely to be concerned about how he or she will pay the ticket than a person on a fixed income. For the latter, paying a ticket strains an already tight budget that must pay for food and shelter. Without reasonable levels of social status, social capital, and human capital, where is the extra money to come from?

Critical Thinking

Why do you think members of low socioeconomic status groups experience higher levels of anxiety, stress, and emotional duress when faced with negative events and information than do persons of higher socioeconomic status?

Public Policy

The World Health Organization works to affect public health policy and practices on a global scale. In the United States, public health policy is created by local, state, and federal politicians. Many organizations influence the policies as they are created. Some organizations or groups that influence public health policy in this country include the following:

- Health insurers
- Lobbyists

- Planned Parenthood of America
- Health care providers
- The American Public Health Association
- The Centers for Disease Control and Prevention
- The Public Health Initiative
- National Association of Public Boards of Health
- Public Health Foundation
- The World Health Organization
- American Medical Association

The list of groups influencing public health policy in the United States goes on and on, but one thing is important to note: There is a community of these organizations. Though Americans primarily take the micro perspective on good health, believing that individuals should be personally responsible for healthy lifestyle choices, the macro perspective is ever present.

Individuals belong to communities, from the neighborhood level to the international community, and every group in between. The community perspective of health care policy emphasizes the creation of a social support system that cares for vulnerable people and populations. Government regulations control the distribution of resources that can strengthen a vulnerable community and positively affect the level of vulnerability to at-risk populations.

Critical Thinking

With so many organizations having an influence on public health care policy, do you think it is possible for one person to make a difference?

Self-Check

Answer the following questions to the best of your ability.

1. The distribution of _____ has a direct impact on health risks.
   a. clinics
   b. money
   c. resources
   d. government

2. The WHO is which of the following?
   a. A rock band formed in the 1960s
   b. World Health Organization
   c. Woman's Health Organization
   d. Workers Health Organization

3. Government regulations control the distribution of _____.
   a. personnel
   b. hospitals

    c.   resources

    d.   ambulances

Answer Key

1. c   2. b   3. c

1.3 Statistical Data on the Population Totals and Growth Trends of Identified Vulnerable Populations

Public policymakers and health care researchers rely on statistical data from governmental or academic studies to inform decision makers on necessary changes to resource allocation. Many organizations perform studies that provide statistics and other data, but the most influential American organization on the subject of public health is the National Center for Health Statistics (NCHS) (2012). The NCHS is part of the Centers for Disease Control and Prevention (CDC). It collaborates with numerous organizational members of the health community in every community across the nation to survey and identify health problems and vulnerable populations in the United States. The result of these studies is the national Healthy People objectives list, which specifies the nation's most pressing health needs and indicates ways to address them and fund programs for doing so. The Healthy People health objectives list is updated every 10 years.

Considerations in Studying Data

It is difficult to get definitive data on any given population. Variations in how studies are conducted, the communities in which they are conducted, and the type of respondents all contribute to incomplete and inaccurate data compilation. Add to these hurdles the fact that vulnerable populations overlap, and it is nearly impossible to create a perfect picture of the total number of America's vulnerable populations, their relative risk profiles, and their needs.

Different data sources, including vital statistics counts of deaths and births, patient perception of illness, health agency records, and clinical diagnoses reports, provide differing estimates of individual needs within groups. It is difficult to compare needs across groups, and studies may be biased. Increases and decreases in some statistics are subjective due to influences of social, or in some cases medical, ethics. For example, a rise in reports of child abuse may not indicate an increase in actual child abuse but instead may indicate a shift in social ethics that has made people more likely to report child abuse incidents.

It is also difficult to compare data across groups because different indicators are used to measure statistics. Resource needs for the chronically ill are often based on clinical records measuring physical limitations. These measurements are based on clinical information, physician recommendations, and patient perceptions of pain and illness. Statistics on family abuse are based on case reports. It is understood that many abuse cases go unreported, but the number of unreported cases is unknown. Needs assessments of other vulnerable populations are based on varying evidence of poor health and functioning. The Public Health Data Standards Consortium promotes standardization of health and community statistical studies and data in an effort to make the data more accessible and meaningful.

Connections Between Vulnerable Groups

The last few decades have seen interesting changes in the population numbers of vulnerable groups. The number of Americans living with HIV and AIDS has risen drastically since the virus was first recognized by the CDC in the 1980s. In fact, the number of people with HIV/AIDS doubled in almost every measured area of residence from 2004 to 2008, as shown in Figure 1.4.

Figure 1.4: Reported number of people living with HIV/AIDS by area of residence

■ Reported AIDS cases
2004–2008

■ Persons reported living with
AIDS (as of December 2008)

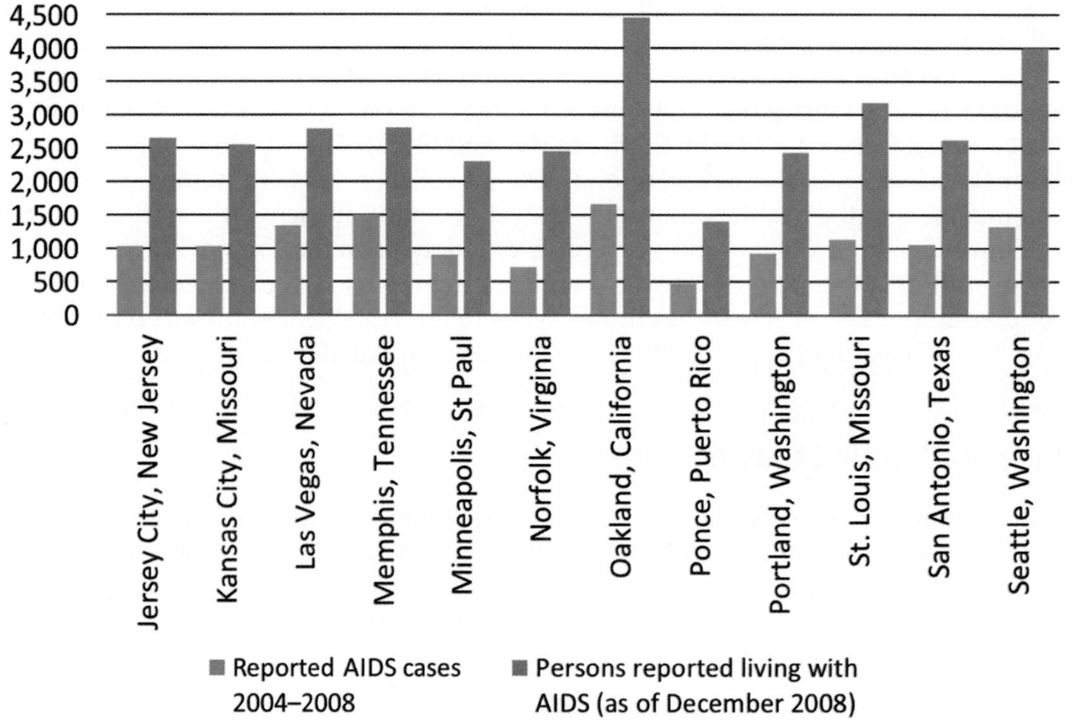

Reported AIDS cases rapidly increased nationwide from 2004 to 2008.

Center for Disease Control and Prevention. (2008a). Reported AIDS cases and persons reported living with AIDS, by area of residence, 2004–2008 and as of December 2008—eligible metropolitan areas and transitional grant areas for the Ryan White HIV/AIDS Treatment Extension Act of 2009. Retrieved from http://www.cdc.gov/hiv/surveillance/resources/reports/2010supp_vol17no1/pdf/2010_hiv_aids_ssr_vol17_n1.pdf#page=8

This data does not include unreported cases, which is a problematic inconsistency in the data measurement. An unknown number of unreported cases complicate resource allocation for this vulnerable population.

HIV/AIDS affects the homeless population at an estimated 3.4%, a higher rate than the general population at 1% (National Coalition for the Homeless [NCH], 2007). Homelessness is difficult to define and track because it is often a transitory situation. The homeless population is measured primarily based on shelter occupancy and street counts, which can vary depending on a range of factors, starting with weather.

Migrants and migrant workers often make up a significant percentage of the homeless population. Statistics on migrants obtaining legal permanent resident status in the United States are easily tracked by the Department of Homeland Security (2010). Unauthorized immigrants are difficult to track because they avoid the immigration system.

This selection of vulnerable populations illustrates how intermingled the groups are. At-risk mothers and infants can be homeless, living with HIV/AIDS or other chronic illnesses, immigrants, or all three. Alcohol and substance abuse is found in all populations, not only vulnerable ones. Chronic illnesses are prevalent among the homeless population and the elderly. Population-specific data better illustrates this point.

Courtesy of Tony Baggett/iStockphoto

The homeless population is affected by HIV/AIDS at a rate three times greater than the general population.

Critical Thinking

Title II of HIPAA (Health Insurance Portability and Accountability Act) has "administrative simplification" provisions and requires national standards for electronic health care transactions. It also sets forth stipulations ensuring privacy and security of health records. Considering how many populations fit in many areas of "at risk," do you believe HIPAA will help or interfere with research involving these special populations?

Self-Check

Answer the following questions to the best of your ability.

1. The most influential American organization on the subject of public health is the
   a. National Center for Health Statistics (NCHS).
   b. AFL/CIO Labor Union.
   c. United States Congress.
   d. Pharmaceutical political lobbyists.

2. Which group promotes standardization of health and community statistical studies and data in an effort to make the data more accessible and meaningful?
    a. National Institute of Mental Health (NIMH)
    b. Centers for Disease Control and Prevention (CDC)
    c. Public Health Data Standards Consortium
    d. Department of Health and Human Services (HHS)

3. Statistics on migrants obtaining legal permanent resident status in the United States are tracked by which organization?
    a. Department of Homeland Security
    b. Department of Defense
    c. Department of Health and Human Services (HHS)
    d. Various state organizations

Answer Key

1. **a**   2. **c**   3. **a**

1.4 Defining Vulnerable Populations in American Health Care

A person's vulnerability to negative health outcomes increases as the level of risk exposure increases. Everybody is vulnerable at some point in his life, though some people's level of vulnerability is rarely very high. Vulnerable populations are those groups of people who are exposed to many risk factors, such as inadequate access to fruits and vegetables, alcohol use, tobacco use, and inadequate housing. The WHO defines risk factors as

> any attribute, characteristic or exposure of an individual that increases the likelihood of developing a disease or injury. Some examples of the more important risk factors are underweight, unsafe sex, high blood pressure, tobacco and alcohol consumption, and unsafe water, sanitation and hygiene. (WHO, 2012)

Individuals and communities that lack resources, social status, social capital, and human capital are referred to as "vulnerable populations." The most prominent vulnerable populations in America are as follows:

- vulnerable mothers and children
- abused individuals
- chronically ill and disabled people
- people diagnosed with HIV/AIDS
- people diagnosed with mental conditions
- suicide- and homicide-liable people
- people affected by alcohol and substance abuse
- indigent and homeless people
- immigrants and refugees

This list represents vulnerable American groups with the highest population numbers and risk factors. These groups appear to be growing quickly and thus putting an increasing strain on America's resources. The macro perspective social theory of public policy recognizes that mitigating risks for vulnerable populations must include reform at the community level. These interventions include programs that include access to housing, food, and health care by geographically locating such resources where there were previously few. The micro perspective social theory of public policy focuses on reforming the resource delivery system on the individual level. These interventions include programs that educate schoolchildren on proper nutrition and pay for immunizations for Medicaid recipients. Public policy strategists struggle to keep up with increasing demands on both the community and individual levels.

Allocating resources to at-risk groups is complicated by the fact that they do not exist in independent bubbles. The problems of these groups are intertwined. Alcohol and substance abuse can be a factor with abusive individuals and high-risk mothers and infants; suicide is a problem among homeless people; and people living with HIV are chronically ill and so have many of the same resource needs as that group. As at-risk populations grow and their problems become more intertwined, the country struggles to find solutions for a lack of needed resources and resource delivery.

Vulnerable Mothers and Children

Many factors can contribute to a pregnancy being termed "high risk." Maternal health in terms of preexisting medical conditions—unhealthy weight; medication use; nutrition; alcohol, tobacco, and substance use—and domestic security can all have negative effects on the unborn baby. Ethnicity has also been shown to be a factor in fetal and maternal health and will be discussed specifically in a later chapter. Though high-risk maternity has a different meaning for different populations, the population of vulnerable mothers and children is marked by inadequate medical care; negative health-related behaviors on behalf of the mother; teenage pregnancy; and infant drug addiction, prematurity, and low birth weight.

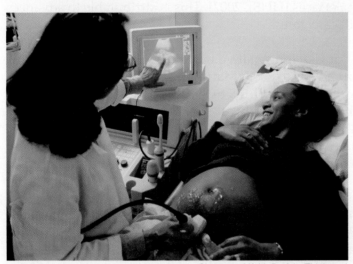

Courtesy of Keith Brofsky/Thinkstock

Maternal health, whether good or poor, has a significant bearing on the health of the unborn baby.

Inadequate medical care during pregnancy leads to higher rates of infant mortality, premature birth, and low birth weight. Infant mortality is caused by many factors, including undeveloped and improperly developed organs, malnutrition (sometimes caused by poor maternal nutrition while in utero), and drug addiction. Premature birth is marked by a gestational age of less than 37 weeks. Low birth weight is considered to be anything under 5.5 pounds. Proper prenatal care can mitigate the risks of these negative outcomes by helping the mother ensure proper habits and nutrition throughout the pregnancy. The earlier the mother receives regular prenatal care, the lower the risk of negative outcomes for both her and the baby. But many vulnerable women do not receive early prenatal care: The total percentage of mothers seeking health care during the first trimester of pregnancy was 83.2% in 2006 (Henry J. Kaiser Family Foundation [KFF], 2012a). There is a direct correlation between a lack of prenatal care and infant mortality.

The United States has the highest infant mortality rate among developed nations (Mac-Dorman & Mathews, 2008). The infant mortality rate in the United States has hovered around 6.5 deaths per 1,000 births for a decade. Although socioeconomic status plays a large role in infant and maternal mortality rates, the number leaves much to be explained. Non-Hispanic blacks had the highest 2005 infant mortality rate, at 13.63 per 1,000 live births, and Cubans living in the United States had the lowest 2005 infant mortality rate, at 4.42 per 1,000 live births.

The total infant mortality rate in the United States declined slightly from 2005 to 2007, with a total rate of 6.86 infant deaths per 1,000 live births in 2005, and 6.75 infant deaths per 1,000 live births in 2007 (Mathews & MacDorman, 2011). It is estimated that the rate will further decline to 5.98 infant deaths per 1,000 live births in 2012 (U.S. Central Intelligence Agency [CIA], 2012a).

Maternal mortality rates are also linked to early, quality prenatal health care. Maternal morbidity was high in the early 20th century, at a rate of 607.9 maternal deaths per 1,000 live births. The rate dropped to 12.1 maternal deaths per 1,000 live births in 2003 (U.S. Department of Health and Human Services [HHS], 2007). This is attributable to advances in medical science and better health care access.

Teen mothers are among the most at risk for negative outcomes. The rate of live births in the United States declined 3% from 2008 to 2009 (Martin et al., 2011). The nation saw a peak in teen births in 1991. The decline in teen births to 39.1 per 1,000 total live births in 2009 is 37% below the 1991 peak of 61.8, and the lowest in seven decades. The teen birthrate declined fairly steadily from 48 live births per 1,000 teen females ages 15 to 19 in 2000, to 34 live births per 1,000 teen females of the same age group in 2010 (Centers for Disease Control and Prevention [CDC], 2012a).

The decline in teen births may be a contributing factor to the decline in preterm deliveries and low birth weight infants. Both 2008 and 2009 saw declines in preterm deliveries both before 34 weeks gestation and at 34–36 weeks gestation. The 2009 total preterm birthrate was 12.18% of all births in America. The preterm birthrate dropped only slightly to 11.99% in 2010 (Hamilton, Martin, & Ventura, 2011). The low birth weight rate in the United States has been steadily increasing since the 1980s. The low birth weight rate in 1989 was 7.05%. By 1999, the rate had increased to 7.62%. Final data for 2009 showed the low birth weight rate to be 8.16%. It is notable that African Americans have a disproportionately high incidence of low birth weight babies, though the incidence rate for this group has remained fairly steady, ranging from 13.61% in 1989, to 13.23% in 1999, to 13.61% in 2009. Hispanics also remained fairly consistent at 6.18% in 1989, to 6.38% in 1999, to 6.94% in 2009. Caucasians, however, have experienced a considerable increase in low birth weight infants. In

1989, Caucasians had a low birth weight rate of 5.62%. That number rose to 6.64% in 1999 and rose again to 7.19% in 2009 (Martin et al., 2011).

Critical Thinking

There is a difference of 9.21 per 1,000 infant mortality deaths between non-Hispanic blacks and Cubans. There is a roughly equal chance of low income and lack of medical access in both of these populations. What contributing factors might explain the difference?

Abused Individuals

Children, the elderly, and female partners and spouses are the individuals most vulnerable to abuse. Abuse comes in many forms, most prominently neglect, physical abuse, emotional abuse, and sexual abuse. Data on abuse is often unspecific regarding the type of abuse being discussed, mostly because different forms of abuse often occur simultaneously.

Many public agencies exist to deal with the problem of domestic abuse and to protect the vulnerable. The U.S. Administration for Children and Families tracks data on abuse within families. The number of reported abuse cases has increased over the last few decades. But the data is skewed by social norms. It is believed that a contributing factor to the increase in reported abuse cases is due to a social ethic that used to hide and ignore abuse, and now recognizes that it is not the victim's fault and that abuse must be investigated. Even so, the data indicates that child abuse and neglect are on the rise.

Courtesy of Hemera/Thinkstock

Two methods are used to count child abuse incidents, taking into consideration the fact that the same child may be the victim of multiple incidents in a given year.

Child abuse cases are counted in two ways. The number of incidents counted is known as the **duplicate victim rate**; the number of victimized children counted is known as the **unique victim rate**. Two separate rates are tabulated to account for the fact that the same child may be reported multiple times in a year. The duplicate victim rate in 2010 was 10 in 1,000 total children in the U.S. population. The unique victim rate was 9.2 per 1,000 children in the United States. This shows that the data collection methods are working, as the difference between the unique count and the duplicate count is small. Of the unique victims from 2006 to 2010, 75% had not been previously reported. In 2010, 81.3% of reported abused children were victims of their parents. A significantly lower 13% were victimized by people who were not their parents (U.S. HHS, Administration for Children and Families, Administration on Children, Youth and Families, Children's Bureau, 2011).

Child abuse statistics show a definite age factor, with abuse reports shrinking in number the older the victim. In 2010, 34% of child victims were infants to 3 years old, 23.4% were 4–7 years old, 18.7% were 8–11 years old, 17.3% were 12–15 years old, and 6.2% were 16–17 years old (see Figure 1.5).

Figure 1.5: Child abuse by age

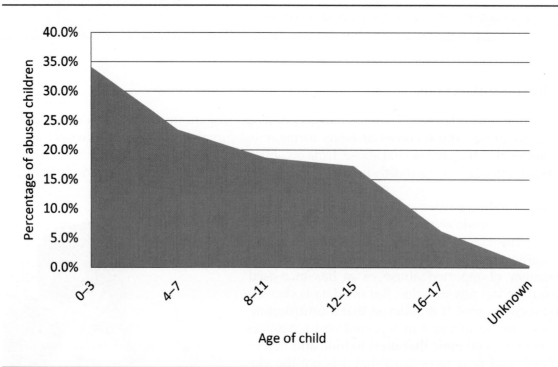

Child abuse report rates decline as the age of the child increases.

U.S. Department of Health and Human Services (HHS). (2010). Retrieved from http://www.acf.hhs.gov/programs/cb/pubs/cm10/cm10.pdf

Just as the young are vulnerable because they cannot defend themselves, so are the elderly. It is estimated that only 1 in 14 elder abuse incidents is reported, and only 1 in 25 incidents of elder financial exploitation is reported each year. Self-neglect, when a person does not attend to physical needs such as nutrition and bathing, is also a factor in elder abuse. Data from 1996 shows 450,000 seniors were abused by others, and an estimated 100,000 seniors neglected their own care (U.S. Administration on Aging, National Center on Elder Abuse, 2005).

A Closer Look: Elder Abuse Estimates

Courtesy of Simon Bourne/ iStockphoto

An estimated 2.1 million older Americans experience some kind of abuse during their elder years.

The American Psychological Association (APA) (2012) estimates a staggering number of elderly abuse cases, suggesting that 2.1 million older Americans experience some kind of abuse during their elder years. Consider this scenario:

Shortly after her 87th birthday, Beth, suffering from the effects of degenerative arthritis and chronic heart disease, moved in with her adult daughter, Laura. This living arrangement caused stress between them. With her financial worries, her 25-year-old son also living at home, and her husband's job always at risk, Laura has lost her temper numerous times. She has called Beth names and has even gone as far as blaming her mother for ruining her tranquility and home life with her family. This has made Beth feel like a prisoner in Laura's home, isolated from the life she knew, as well as frightened and worthless.

Or take the case of Diane, 78, who lives at home with assistance from a home health nurse and a certified nurses' aide. They visit her daily to care for and assist her with activities of daily living. She also depends on home health care assistance with home-based routines and to give her someone from the outside world to talk with. In the beginning, her nursing assistant was extremely helpful and sweet, but recently the assistant has begun ignoring requests, snapping at Diane, and has even come close to knocking her over while cleaning or vacuuming. Diane believes the assistant is bumping her deliberately, but she is afraid to say anything for fear of losing her link with the outside world, so she doesn't confront her nursing assistant.

Neglect is the most common form of elder abuse; 36.7% of the perpetrators are adult children of their victims (U.S. Administration on Aging, National Center on Elder Abuse, 1997). Statistics show that females were significantly more likely to be the victims of elder abuse, at an incidence rate of 67.3%. Neglect can manifest as the intentional failure to meet the health-related needs of an individual, but it can also involve failing to meet the household necessities of an individual. A survey of states' Adult Protective Services departments shows a marked increase in the number of reports of elder abuse, investigated cases of elder abuse, and substantiated reports of elder abuse from 2000 to 2004 (U.S. Administration on Aging, National Center on Elder Abuse, 2006). Whether the increases are due to expanded public awareness of the problem of elder abuse, or due to an increased number of elderly in the community, or due to an actual increase in elder abuse incidents is uncertain.

Financial exploitation is another form of mistreatment suffered by the elderly, and it can come in many forms, from the deliberate misuse of a legal relationship (power of attorney, guardianship, conservatorship, or trustee) to the embezzlement of funds under false pretenses (for example, the taking of government-issued checks or assistance).

Next we turn to a discussion of partner or spousal abuse. Child and elder abuse are more likely to be reported than spousal abuse, but family violence affects all members of a household. An estimated 30% to 60% of people who abuse their domestic partners also abuse children in the household. Approximately 16,800 homicides occur in the United States every year as a result of domestic violence. If these numbers seem low, there is reason for it because domestic partner abuse is one of the most underreported crimes in the nation (National Coalition Against Domestic Violence [NCADV], 2007).

Even with a lack of consistent reporting, trends show that domestic violence is declining. Reporting might be on the rise, at an estimated 60% of incidents reported between 1998 and 2002. The National Crime Victimization Survey (1998–2002) attempted to remedy the reporting gap by surveying members of different populations in the United States. The survey had a limited scope but some interesting findings. In 1993, the estimated victim rate was 5.4 domestic abuse victims per 1,000 U.S. residents. That number fell to 2.1 in 2002. Domestic abuse accounted for 11% of all violent crimes from 1998 to 2002. The majority of domestic abuse offenders are male, and the majority of victims are female. Domestic violence by intimate partners including current and past spouses, boyfriends, and girlfriends constituted over a quarter (26%) of all nonfatal violent crimes against women in 2009. In that same year, domestic violence constituted only 5% of all nonfatal violent crimes against men (National Center for Victims of Crime, 2011). Of the perpetrators in domestic violence cases in federal court, 67% are younger than age 40, and 72% are Caucasian (Durose et al., 2005). Although domestic abuse may be declining, many factors are unchanged.

Critical Thinking

This chapter is concerned with a discussion of the health care needs of special populations. We have already talked about high-risk mothers, infant mortality, and households affected by substance abuse; these populations are particularly vulnerable to negative health outcomes. Why do you think abused individuals would also be categorized as a "special population"?

Chronically Ill and Disabled People

Chronic illness refers to those illnesses that are usually not fully recovered from once a person has them. Diabetes, HIV/AIDS, and emphysema are all examples of life-altering chronic illness. Chronic illnesses can create disabilities, though disabilities also include physical impairments to bodily function that interfere with activities of daily living. Disabilities and chronic ailments have a negative effect on lifestyle, and cost the country millions of dollars per year in health care and other resources. The Centers for Disease Control and Prevention show that chronic disease is the cause of 70% of U.S. deaths every year. Although chronic disease affects our community on the macrolevel, many causes of chronic illness are directly related to individual lifestyle choices. Cigarette use is linked to cancer of the lungs, throat, and other organs; habitual binge drinking causes cirrhosis of the liver; and lack of aerobic exercise leads to diabetes, obesity, and heart disease.

Heart disease was responsible for 26.6% of all registered deaths in 2005. Chronic lower respiratory diseases accounted for 53%, and diabetes was the cause of 3.1% of deaths in 2005. There has been little change in causes of death for age-adjusted death rates in the last few decades. As Figure 1.6 shows, heart disease rates have declined only slightly each year, and hypertension rates are on the rise after a small decline in the 1980s (Kung, Hoyert, Xu, & Murphy, 2008).

Figure 1.6: Leading causes of death by age-adjusted rates

- Diseases of heart
- Cerebrovascular diseases
- Malignant neoplasms
- Chronic lower respiratory diseases

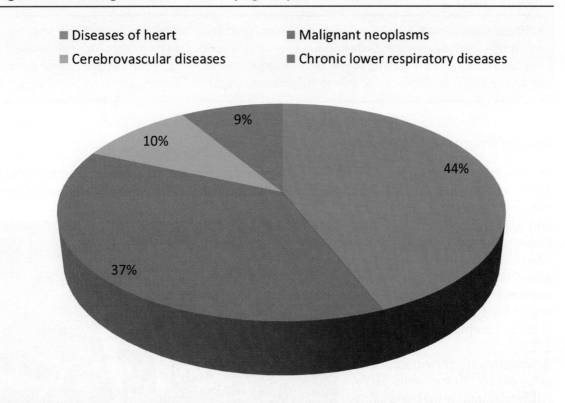

The pie chart shows age-adjusted death rates for select leading causes of death over the last five decades.

Center for Disease Control and Prevention. (2010). Retrieved from http://www.cdc.gov/nchs/data/nvsr/nvsr56/nvsr56_10.pdf

The prevalence of chronic disease is tracked by the CDC's Behavioral Risk Factor Surveillance System. This ongoing telephone survey collects anonymous information directly from patients about their chronic illnesses and quality of life. Data collected in 2009 shows a correlation between respondents who answered that their general health is fair or poor and many chronic illness risk factors such as cigarette use. According to the U.S. Department of Health and Human Service's Healthy People 2020 initiative, almost one-half of all American adults reported at least one chronic illness.

Noninstitutionalized people over age 65 report the most limitations of activity due to chronic illnesses at a rate of 32.6%. Youth under age 18 had the next highest rate in 2006, at 7.3%, and adults ages 18 to 44 reported limited activity at a rate of 5.5% (U.S. Department of Health and Human Services, Healthy People 2020, 2012). The CDC reports that asthma is one of the most common chronic illnesses in school-age children, with 5.6 million children with asthma reported in 2007. Asthma prevalence puts a strain on schools, the health care system, and community resources.

Critical Thinking

Although many chronic diseases are related to personal lifestyle choices such as cigarette smoking, which can cause lung cancer and other serious respiratory diseases, asthma in school-age children does not seem to be related to lifestyle choice. What factors might be causing/influencing such a large population to be afflicted with a chronic disease at such a young age?

People Diagnosed With HIV/AIDS

Human immunodeficiency virus (HIV) prevalence has increased rapidly since the 1980s. Public education about HIV and other sexually transmitted diseases (STDs) has helped mitigate the number of HIV and AIDS patients in the United States. However, in 2011, the African continent was still struggling with rapidly increasing numbers, even as the rest of the world tried to send resources to combat the epidemic.

Courtesy of Dan Moore/iStockphoto

The number of HIV and AIDS patients in the United States has decreased as a result of public education about HIV and other sexually transmitted diseases.

Antiretroviral pharmaceuticals help people living with HIV/AIDS maintain a higher quality of life and prolong their expected life span. These therapies are expensive, and Americans have struggled to let go of antihomosexual prejudice that blocks public policy that would help HIV/AIDS patients receive needed medical treatment. The number of people living with HIV/AIDS has increased steadily since 1978 and is now estimated at 490,696 people in the United States in 2008. The number of new HIV/AIDS infections per year in the United States has remained under 200,000, with 2011 numbers estimated at 50,000 new infections each year (CDC, 2012a).

Although HIV/AIDS has spread to all American populations, the most affected population is African American homosexual and bisexual men. In 2009, this group made up 61% of all new HIV infections. Statistics for 2008 show this group accounting for 49% of the total number of Americans living with HIV/AIDS. Heterosexuals represented 27% of new HIV infections in 2009 and 28% of the population living with HIV/AIDS in 2008. HIV infections are on the rise among Latinos, with the 2009 estimate of new infections showing that Latino men are two and a half times more likely than Caucasian men to contract the disease (CDC, 2012a).

In 2001, black non-Hispanics represented the highest rate of AIDS-related deaths with an estimated 8,041. White non-Hispanics were second with 4,501 estimated AIDS-related deaths. Hispanics were third with 2,882 estimated AIDS-related deaths in 2001 (CDC, 2012a). In 2008, the total estimated number of HIV/AIDS-related deaths for the United States was 17,374. Numbers from 2009 indicate that people age 40 to 44 years old had the highest number of new HIV/AIDS diagnoses at an estimated 5,689. Adults age 35 to 39 years old had the highest total number of people living with HIV/AIDS at an estimated 234,575 (CDC, 2012a).

From 1999 to 2007, the rate of HIV-related deaths declined for people 45 to 64 years of age and people 18 to 44 years of age (see Figure 1.7). HIV-related deaths for children under age 17 remained steady. HIV-related deaths for people age 65 and over increased slightly through 2006 before declining in 2007.

Figure 1.7: Rate of HIV-related deaths by age group

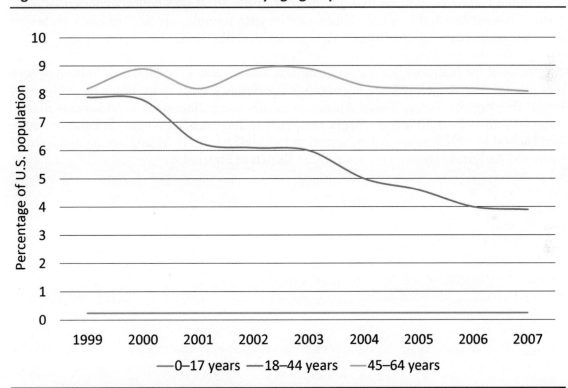

The number of HIV-related deaths for people between the ages of 45 and 64 fluctuated some between 1999 and 2007, but a significant, steady decrease in HIV-related deaths was seen in people 18–44 years of age.

U.S. Department of Health and Human Services (HHS). (2010). Retrieved from http://www.ahrq.gov/qual/nhqr10/Chap2a.htm

People Diagnosed With Mental Conditions

Diagnoses of mental illness include psychosis, neurosis, depression, obsessive-compulsive disorder, bipolar disorder, schizophrenia, and other ailments connected with mental faculties. Mental disabilities include cognitive disorders and mental retardation. Nearly 50% of Americans surveyed claim to have experienced a mental health problem at one time or another. Estimates indicate that one-quarter of the adult population experiences some form of mental health disruption within a given year, though only 5.8% of cases are severe or debilitating (National Institute of Mental Health [NIMH], n.d.).

A portion of the National Survey on Drug Use and Health's (NSDUH) definition of serious mental illness includes the substantial interference with daily life. The 2010 study found that approximately 5% of American adults were diagnosed with serious mental illness. Women were 3.1% more likely to have this diagnosis than men (Substance Abuse and Mental Health Services Administration [SAMHSA], 2011). Young adults age 18 to 25 years old had the highest incidence rate, as shown in Figure 1.8.

Figure 1.8: Incidence rates of mental illness by age in America in 2010

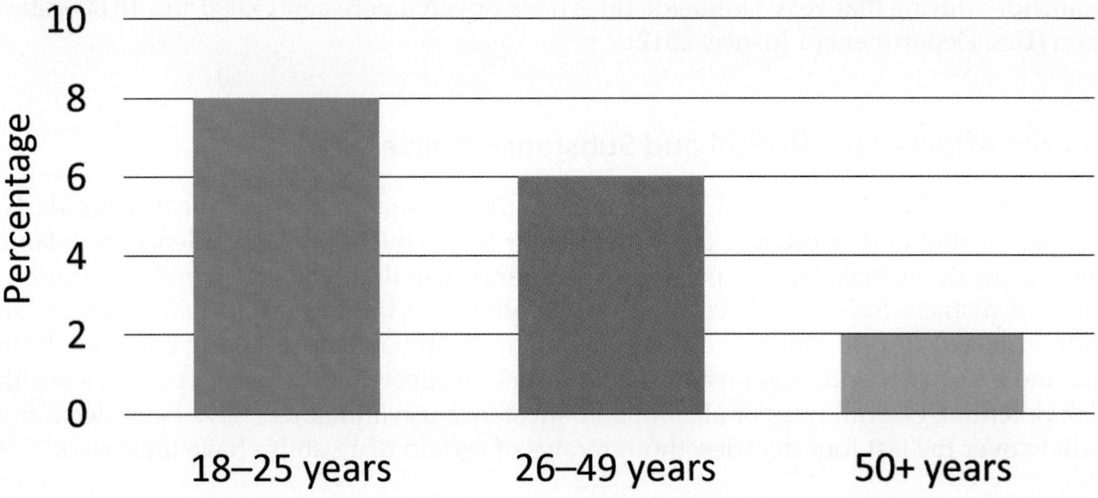

Diagnosis of mental illness occurs most frequently in young people, age 18–25.

National Institute of Mental Health (NIMH). (2010). Prevalence of serious mental illness among U.S. adults by age, sex, and race. *Retrieved from* http://www.nimh.nih.gov/statistics/SMI_AASR.shtml

The use of mental health services by adults increased from 12.8% in 2004 to 13.4% in 2008. Among adults age 18 and over, 13.7% used mental health services in 2010 (National Institute of Mental Health [NIMH], 2012). Increased use of mental health services indicates a positive trend in access to those services; however, the increased suicide rate indicates an increased prevalence of mental illness in the population. The positive trend in services might be due to the negative trend in illness rates and not actually indicative of better resource access.

Suicide- and Homicide-Liable People

Suicide and homicide can be driven by the same social factors. A sense of being stuck in a hopeless situation leads people to a wide range of negative outcomes. Community resource programs that mitigate needs for safety, food, shelter, and education have a large influence on homicide rates in the communities where they function.

Suicide rates have increased, from 11.08 suicides per 100,000 people in 2004 to 11.26 suicides per 100,000 people in 2007 (NIMH, n.d.). In 2010, 1 million adults reported making plans to commit suicide, and 1.1 million adults actually attempted suicide (SAMHSA, 2011).

Homicide refers to both **murder** and **manslaughter**. Murder is the term given to the purposeful, malicious killing of another person. Manslaughter is the killing of another person due to negligence. In other words, intentionally causing a death, even if in the heat of the moment, is murder, whereas causing a death by hitting another car because you were texting while driving is considered manslaughter.

The prevalence of homicides in the United States increased during the early and mid-1990s. The total number did not fall below 18,000 until 1998 when data showed 16,974 homicides during that year. Homicide rates have hovered between 15,000 and 18,000 since then (U.S. Department of Justice, 2012).

People Affected by Alcohol and Substance Abuse

According to the 2010 National Health Survey, 51% of legal adults use alcohol regularly. Simple alcohol and substance use differs from both abuse and dependence. *Substance abuse* indicates a maladaptive pattern of substance use that leads to significant impairment or distress. *Substance dependence*, on the other hand, indicates addiction, where an individual can develop tolerance, withdrawal, or compulsive drug-taking behavior. Both use and abuse/dependence can have negative health effects and increase a person's health risk potential. Overall rates of alcohol and substance use and abuse have been declining slowly over the last four decades, though rates of certain drug abuse have increased.

The country has experienced a small decrease in nonmedical drug use among all surveyed groups from 2002 to 2008. This is a positive change, as the 1990s saw an increase in illicit drug use for children ages 12 to 17. Marijuana use among high school seniors was 33.7% in 1980 and then declined for a period through 1991. In 1995, marijuana use rose drastically to 21.2% and has declined only slightly since, to 20.6% in 2009. Cocaine use among high school seniors followed a similar trajectory. In 1985, the rate of cocaine use among this vulnerable age group was 6.7%. Since then, it has hovered between 1% and 2%, with a 2009 rate of 1.3% (see Figure 1.9) (U.S. Department of Health and Human Services, 2011a).

Figure 1.9: Substance abuse in the past month among persons 12 years of age and over

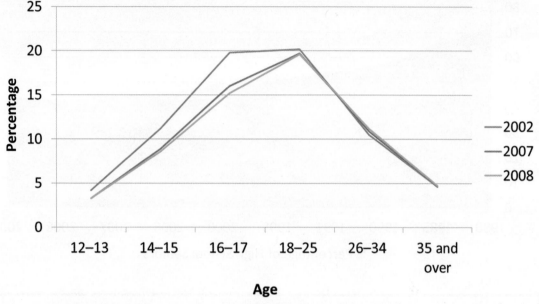

Illicit drug use has declined only slightly for the age groups between 12 and 25, but the rate has remained almost constant for the age groups 26 and over.

Center for Disease Control and Prevention. (2010). Retrieved from http://www.cdc.gov/nchs/data/hus/hus10.pdf#061

In 2010, 50.9% of legal adults reported regular alcohol use, and 13.6% of respondents reported occasional alcohol use. There were 14,406 alcoholic liver disease deaths in the United States in 2007, and 23,199 nonaccident and nonhomicide alcohol-related deaths (CDC, 2012a). Figure 1.10 shows that alcohol use declined overall among high school seniors, with 72% in 1980 and 43.5% in 2009. Hard data is not available as to the reason for this decline, but it is thought to be due to more strict enforcement of laws regulating access to alcohol and community-based prevention programs.

Figure 1.10: Alcohol use among high school seniors

■ Percentage of High School Seniors

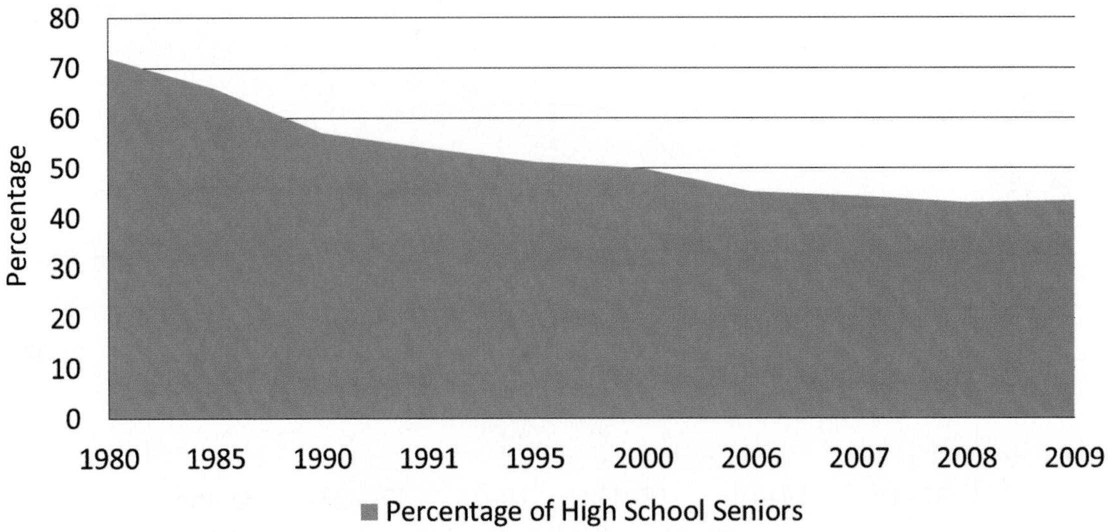

Overall, alcohol use among high school seniors has declined over the last three decades.

Centers for Disease Control and Prevention (CDC). (2012a). Retrieved from http://www.cdc.gov/nchs/data/hus/hus10.pdf#062

Emergency room reports provide many statistics on alcohol and drug abuse in the United States. These reports are made via the Drug Abuse Warning Network (DAWN), through the U.S. Department of Health and Human Services, Substance Abuse and Mental Health Services Administration. There were 4.6 million drug-related emergency department visits across the nation in 2009. Of these, approximately 50% were related to side effects of medications that were taken correctly. The rest included 27.1% related to nonmedical use of prescription drugs; 21.2% of DAWN-reported cases involved illegal drugs; and 14.3% involved drugs and alcohol combined (National Institute on Drug Abuse [NIDA], 2011a).

Critical Thinking

The Drug Abuse Resistance Education (DARE) program was founded in 1982 as an effort by law enforcement to educate adolescents about the hazards (both health and lifestyles) of illicit drug use. As discussed earlier, there has been a measurable decrease in illicit drug use by adolescents. Do you believe that programs like DARE have had an effect on this reduction? If not, what other factors do you believe may be responsible?

Indigent and Homeless People

Homeless people have an extremely high risk for negative outcomes. Homicide, suicide, mental illness, chronic illness, and acute illness all plague the homeless population. Hunger and exposure to the elements are the immediate concerns government and community groups work to alleviate in the homeless population. Creating positive, permanent outcomes for America's homeless takes resources and an understanding of the people in need of aid.

Courtesy of Richard Thornton/Shutterstock

Of the more than half a million people who are homeless on a given night, a growing percentage of that number are families.

In 2009, an estimated 643,067 homeless people were both in shelters and on the streets on a given night. The Department of Housing and Urban Development (HUD) estimates that homeless numbers held steady from 2009 to 2010, but that the number of homeless families has increased in relation to the number of homeless individuals (U.S. Department of Housing and Urban Development [U.S. HUD], 2011). HUD's *2010 Annual Homeless Assessment Report to Congress* found a decline in long-term homelessness, credited largely to the Homelessness Prevention and Rapid Re-Housing Program.

Immigrants and Refugees

Immigration to the United States has increased in fits and starts since the year 1820, with some years seeing less immigration than others. Migrants obtaining legal permanent resident status in 2010 totaled 1,042,625 (U.S. Department of Homeland Security, 2010). Both legal and illegal migrants and refugees present unique challenges to America's social welfare system.

Language barriers strain resource delivery to the migrant population. Educators have developed English as a Second Language (ESL) programs to address the educational needs of migrant and refugee children. Health care organizations purposefully seek bilingual employees who communicate well with patients. Differences in ethical and social norms sometimes prohibit migrants from seeking assistance for housing, health care, and other needs.

The United States office of Citizenship and Immigration Services oversees all legal immigration to the country. Programs exist for the naturalization of foreign-born adopted children, work visas, marriage, citizenship through naturalization, and for those seeking asylum. Legal immigration through the appropriate channels better enables resource delivery to migrant populations. However, legal immigration does not automatically give the foreign-born person the same access to publicly funded health care programs. Special programs exist for aiding refugees. Refugees are different from immigrants because they are forced to flee their home country, as opposed to immigrants who come and leave freely. The federal Office of Refugee Resettlement (ORR) provides critical resources for refugees seeking asylum in the United States.

Critical Thinking

In the United States, people hold very different attitudes toward immigrants and refugees. These attitudes range from the belief that illegal immigrants drain our resources and bring those that prey on them, such as drug dealers and con artists, to peaceful neighborhoods to the belief that by providing the needed resources, the common good will improve. Do you perceive that there is a benefit to providing these resources?

Self-Check

Answer the following questions to the best of your ability.

1. The ongoing telephone survey that collects anonymous information directly from patients is known as
   a. Survey Says.
   b. CDC's Behavioral Risk Factor Surveillance System.
   c. System Support Network.
   d. Satisfaction Survey.

2. There are an estimated _____ new HIV infections every year.
   a. 75,000
   b. 20,000
   c. 38,000
   d. 50,000

3. Diagnoses of mental illness include
   a. hypertension.
   b. urinary tract infection.
   c. obsessive-compulsive disorder.
   d. diabetes.

Answer Key

1. b   2. d   3. c

> **Case Study:** Macro Perspective Versus Micro Perspective: The Patient Protection and Affordable Care Act of 2010
>
> We have seen all of these principles of social theory in the debate over the Patient Protection and Affordable Care Act of 2010 (PPACA) (One-Hundred Eleventh Congress, 2010). The PPACA was signed into law by President Barack Obama and was his signature legislative project. Both President and First Lady Obama dedicated themselves to improving the health and access to health care of all Americans. The primary focus of the PPACA is to limit the power of the private health insurance companies to deny claims and coverage, to improve affordability of health care, and to expand the qualifications for Medicaid.
>
> The Pareto principle that the common good actually has a negative effect on some is at the heart of the debate. One side argues that reforming America's health care system is vital for the public good. The opposition argues that the reforms called for in the PPACA will cost the collective a great deal but will benefit only a few. A similar but slightly different argument given is that a few will be forced to pay for the collective. Both of these arguments are based on the concept that the common good (in this case, reform of the health care system) is not good for all.
>
> Wrapped up in the economic concerns over the PPACA is the issue of individual rights versus the common good. Americans worry that a single-payer system would take away individuals' rights to select their own doctors and dictate their own course of health care. This concern is based on the macro versus micro dichotomy, as public policy works on a macro scale but greatly alters our micro influences.

Chapter Summary

Any society that wants to call itself modern must recognize the populations most at risk of negative outcomes and provide resources to help create positive outcomes for these vulnerable groups. Doing so adds to the health and economic viability of the community. But an "all for one, and one for all" model does not always work on a large scale. Resource allocation must be done thoughtfully to create the most positive outcomes for the most people. Statistical data on vulnerable populations helps inform public policy decisions that equalize fairness as much as possible while providing for those in need. At a pivotal point in America's history, following a recession that saw many people lose health care access, recognizing who is vulnerable and how to help them is key for improving the chances of positive outcomes for individuals and the community as a whole.

> **Critical Thinking**
>
> Why is it important for society to help ensure that the health care needs of the special populations described in this chapter are met? Are the methods of data gathering that are described able to provide enough information to enable well-informed and intelligent decisions by policymakers?

Self-Check

Answer the following questions to the best of your ability.

1. For over a decade the infant mortality rate in the United States was
   a. 7.3 deaths per 7,000 births.
   b. 6.5 deaths per 1,000 births.
   c. 1.8 deaths per 3,100 births.
   d. 4.2 deaths per 4,000 births.

2. Marijuana use among high school seniors was
   a. 15.3% in 2003.
   b. 21.8% in 1987.
   c. 100% in 1936.
   d. 20.6% in 2009.

3. An estimated _____ elderly neglected their own care in 1996.
   a. 100,000
   b. 2,300
   c. 42
   d. 7 million

4. Statistical data on vulnerable populations helps inform public policy decisions that equalize fairness as much as possible while providing for those in need.
   a. True
   b. False

5. The CDC show that chronic disease is the cause of what percentage of U.S. deaths?
   a. 30%
   b. 50%
   c. 70%
   d. 85%

6. Overall rates of alcohol and substance use and abuse have been declining slowly over what period of time?
   a. the last year
   b. the last four decades
   c. the last four years
   d. the last century

Answer Key:

1. b   2. d   3. a   4. a   5. c   6. b

Additional Resources

Visit the following websites to learn more about the topics covered in this chapter:

Louisville, Kentucky, Farm to Table program

http://www.louisvilleky.gov/healthyhometown/farmtotable/

World Health Organization

http://www.who.int/en/

The Centers for Disease Control and Prevention

http://www.cdc.gov/

Web Exercise

Choose one of the special populations mentioned in this chapter and research the problems and suggested solutions about how industry will meet the needs of these populations. Write a two-page paper with the following information:

- population selected and why you chose that group
- the barriers they face in accessing health care
- proposed solutions to help remove or to remove those barriers
- your thoughts on whether or not the solutions suggested are valid and an explanation of your position

Select at least three reputable websites that explain your group's problems in accessing health care and the proposed solutions. These websites must be reputable and reliable (no public editing such as Wikipedia or blogs). Your paper must meet APA standards. The final product will be double-spaced, Times New Roman 12-point font, with appropriate grammar and correct spelling. Be sure to include the websites you visited.

Key Terms

common good Social theory based on reciprocity and doing good for all society members.

differential vulnerability hypothesis The theory that some people have more adverse reactions than others to negative life events.

duplicate victim rate The number of child abuse incidents counted.

human capital The amount of investment in a person's potential.

individual rights Social theory based on individuals' choices and freedoms.

macro influences Larger social and environment influences on our lives.

manslaughter Killing another person due to negligence.

micro influences Personal decisions and influences on our lives.

murder The purposeful, malicious killing of another person.

Pareto principle The theory that 80% of the outcome is caused by 20% of the effort.

public policy Laws, regulations, and other government activities that dictate how society should function.

relative risk The potential of imperfect health in groups exposed to risk factors in relation to the potential of imperfect health in groups not exposed to the same risk factors.

social attitudes Positive or negative evaluations of people, places, things, and events that are shared by a majority of the community as a whole.

social capital The measurement of personal relationships in an individual's life.

social status A person's place in society as created by personal characteristics, opportunities, and rewards.

unique victim rate The number of victimized children counted in child abuse cases.

vulnerability A person's risk level, based on factors such as environment, education, resources, and finances.

Comparing Vulnerable Groups

Learning Objectives

After reading this chapter, you should be able to:

- Explain the difference between curative and preventive approaches to health care.

- Identify common factors among vulnerable populations.

- Examine age as it relates to the concept of vulnerability.

- Determine the ways in which gender contributes to vulnerability.

- Discuss how culture and ethnicity affect vulnerability on both personal and population levels.

- Explain the relationship between education and income levels, and vulnerability.

Introduction

The United States boasts one of the most robust health care systems in the world. It is statistically credited with the longer healthy lifetimes enjoyed by a majority of the American population. Advances in medical science and technology certainly improve medical interventions, but a recent change in the philosophy of medical care is credited with improving the population's health on a macro level. As the cost of health care in America soared during the 1990s and 2000s, the health care community's focus shifted from curative care to preventive medicine.

Curative medicine focuses on curing existing diseases and conditions. In contrast, **preventive medicine** works by educating the community on healthy lifestyle habits, such as regular exercise, nutritious food choices, and abstention from smoking. The idea is to prevent or forestall disease rather than wait until someone falls ill before providing treatment; however, living healthy lifestyles is still a personal choice. Studies indicate that preventive health care reduces morbidity, and that a preventive approach not only thwarts diseases that are associated with unhealthy choices, such as diabetes, heart disease, and cancer, but also creates strong immune systems to fight common illnesses like flu and cold viruses. Furthermore, people who do not get sick are more productive workers because they do not have as many sickness-related absences. This point is particularly important when considering vulnerable populations. For many people, especially those in the most at-risk groups, workdays lost to illness means days without pay. Financial instability detracts from a person's social status, which is a nonmaterial resource that contributes to vulnerability. Less social status means less access to community resources, such as health care and fresh foods. Lack of resource access leads to more illness, and so the cycle continues.

Many individuals have limited access to health care, which includes the inability to access medical clinics for reasons of proximity, the lack of insurance coverage, and financial constraints such as inability to pay for medical treatments. Preventive medicine focuses on educating people before they become ill, but resource accessibility restricts preventive medicine programs and responsive health care programs from reaching the most at-risk populations. Evidence of this is seen in data on topics like breast cancer diagnosis, where African American women have a higher mortality rate due in part to diagnosis at later stages. Just as determining who is vulnerable is vital to resource allocation, comparisons must be made between vulnerable groups in order to provide the right access at the right time to the right group. From this point, reactionary health care can lead to reinforcement of the principles of preventive health care, and sustainable lifestyle choices can be made to improve overall health.

Critical Thinking

Which methodology do you prefer, curative or preventive medicine? Why?

Self-Check

Answer the following questions to the best of your ability.

1. Preventive medicine reduces illness and disease by
    a. providing members of the community with vaccines.
    b. educating the community on healthy lifestyle habits.
    c. providing medicine to the community to cure specific diseases.
    d. researching cures to diseases.

2. What is the focus of curative medicine?
    a. educating the community on healthy lifestyle habits
    b. providing healthy lunches at schools
    c. distributing condoms and clean needles to the community
    d. curing existing diseases and conditions

3. Comparisons are made between vulnerable groups in order to
    a. provide the right access at the right time to the right group.
    b. provide the right vaccine to the right person.
    c. provide the best diet recommendations based on need.
    d. find the correct cure.

Answer Key

1. **b**   2. **d**   3. **a**

2.1 Common Factors

At each stage in the life cycle, different populations experience vulnerability differently. Infants, for example, who rely almost entirely on others for their physical and emotional needs, are more vulnerable than adolescents, who have achieved a certain measure of independence. Gender is also a factor when comparing vulnerability; because of the power differential between the two groups, men and women experience vulnerability in different ways. A person's cultural heritage or ethnicity is also a variable in terms of determining his or her level of vulnerability, as well as education and income level. It should be noted that subgroups within population groups also experience differing levels and types of vulnerability. Many people who are at risk for poor health outcomes fall into multiple categories: For example, a woman may also be homeless. In this sense, because she belongs to two vulnerable groups (she is a woman, and she is also a member of the homeless population), she is doubly vulnerable.

Vulnerable populations are often compared using statistical data. Studies frequently use four categories, or factors, to compare statistical trends across populations:

- age
- gender
- culture and ethnicity
- education and income levels

These factors allow researchers to compare groups within vulnerable populations as well as across vulnerable populations. Figure 2.1 illustrates cross-comparison data by race and age.

Figure 2.1: Cross-comparison of mortality by race and age

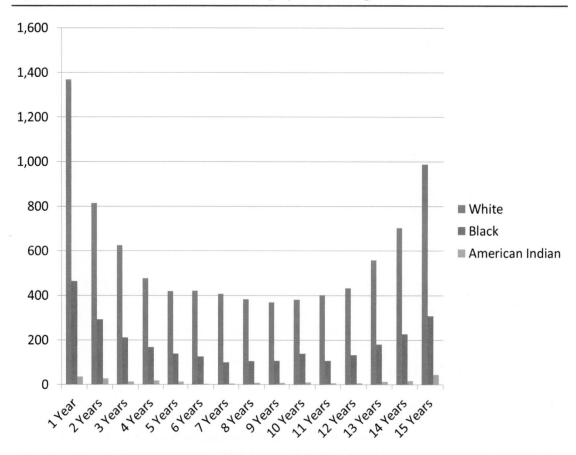

Mortality risk in juveniles is highest from ages 1 to 3, decreases during the elementary years, and then rises again at the start of adolescence.

Center for Disease Control and Prevention. (2010). Retrieved from http://www.cdc.gov/nchs/data/dvs/MortFinal2007_Worktable310.pdf

---

Critical Thinking

What vulnerable groups do you belong to? Describe the group and its vulnerability.

Self-Check

Answer the following questions to the best of your ability.

1. Studies frequently use four categories, or factors, to compare statistical trends across populations. Which of the following categories is not used?
   a. age
   b. gender
   c. education
   d. citizenship

2. Different populations experience vulnerability differently.
   a. true
   b. false

3. What information is used to compare vulnerable populations?
   a. Citizenship
   b. Marital status
   c. Statistical data
   d. Occupation

Answer Key

1. **d**   2. **a**   3. **c**

2.2 Comparing Vulnerable Groups by Age

According to the U.S. Census Bureau, the median age in 2000 was 35.5. As the baby boomer generation reaches age 65, the median age in America will continue to rise. In fact, it is projected to be 39.1 in 2035 and then to decline very slowly in subsequent years as the baby boomer generation passes away (U.S. Census Bureau, 2012a).

Age is a crosscutting factor in all vulnerable populations. People experience vulnerability differently depending on age. Infants and children are among the most vulnerable of all populations because they rely entirely

Courtesy of Monkey Business/Fotolia

A person's age affects the type and extent of the vulnerability they face.

on others to provide for their physical and emotional needs. Adolescents and adults are less vulnerable because they are able to affect their circumstances and provide for some of their own needs. As older adults near the end of their lives, they once again become vulnerable as they rely on others for help with daily activities. Because they are more susceptible to chronic illnesses than people in other age groups, the elderly also have an increased need for medical care. Statistical data use appropriate, study-specific age ranges to help identify needs within vulnerable populations.

Vulnerable Mothers and Children

As discussed in Chapter 1, premature birth and low birth weight put infants at increased risk of health problems and death. Although factors such as ethnicity, education, and income levels do factor into the risk of low birth weight; maternal age is also closely linked to low birth weight risk. Mothers 10 to 14 years of age have the highest prevalence of low birth weight infants. Maternal age over 40 places second on the risk chart. Mothers between the ages of 25 to 29 years old show the least risk for having low birth weight babies.

The prevalence of low birth weight occurrences in mothers under age 15 may partially be due to the reluctance of those mothers to seek appropriate prenatal care. Lack of a high school diploma is also tied to low birth weight, and mothers under age 15 have typically not completed high school. Mothers with unplanned pregnancies who negatively view their conditions also seek prenatal care later in the pregnancy. The urge to hide the pregnancy is common among mothers under age 15 (Kiely & Kogan, n.d.). Factors like education and attitude affect mothers in all age groups and are particularly prevalent in younger mothers.

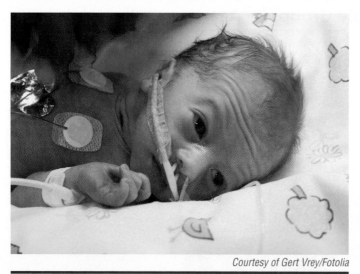

Courtesy of Gert Vrey/Fotolia

Ethnicity, education, income levels, and maternal age all factor into the risk of low birth weight risk.

It should be noted that the United States experienced a significant decline of nearly 30% in teen births from 1991 to 2005. In 2006 and 2007, the United States saw a small increase of 5% in teen births, but then the downward trend resumed in 2008 and 2009. These declines have occurred across all ethnic groups, signaling widespread positive attitudes about teen pregnancy prevention (Centers for Disease Control and Prevention [CDC], 2012a).

Over the same time period, more live births occurred to women of advanced maternal age, due in part to advances in reproductive technologies. The occurrence of multiple births increases with maternal age. While many reproductive technologies are known to carry a slightly increased risk of multiples, a woman's aging eggs also increase this risk.

Multiple births and complications (such as those resulting from an aging body that lacks as much elasticity as it did in youth) contribute to the increased rate of low and very low birth weight babies among mothers over age 40 (Martin et al., 2012).

Abused Individuals

Children and elderly people are more likely to suffer abuse than teens, young adults, and middle-aged adults. Children under the age of 3 years have the highest victimization rate (34%), with the rates decreasing as age increases. The reported abuse rate among children ages 4 to 7 is 23.4%. The rate for children ages 8 to 11 is 18.7%, followed by 17.3% for children ages 12 to 15. The abuse rate declines drastically from there to 6.2% for children ages 16 and 17. The rate of reported child abuse has declined steadily since 2006. This decline is due in part to states' alternative response programs and a decline in the number of Child Protection Services (CPS) investigations (U.S. Department of Health and Human Services, 2011b).

Elder Abuse

Adults over the age of 65 are particularly susceptible to abuse because the effects of aging often create a need for assistance with the activities of daily living. In fact, prevalence of abuse directly correlates with increased age.

Elder abuse takes many forms, including neglect, physical harm, and exploitation. As Figure 2.2 illustrates, neglect is the most commonly reported form of elder abuse. Verbal abuse and physical abuse follow in that order, with sexual abuse showing the lowest prevalence rate.

The U.S. National Center on Elder Abuse estimates that approximately 450,000 people over the age of 60 are victimized annually. Estimates are based on state numbers of reported and investigated incidents of abuse. It is unknown how many incidents actually occur each year because the majority of elder abuse takes place in private residences by victims' family members. Real rates of occurrence are suspected to be as high as five unreported incidents for each reported incident (U.S. National Center on Elder Abuse, 2005). Reports of elder abuse have increased significantly over the last few decades. This is likely due to America's aging population and a shift in the social attitudes of the current elderly population that encourages the reporting of abuse.

Figure 2.2: Rates of elder abuse by type

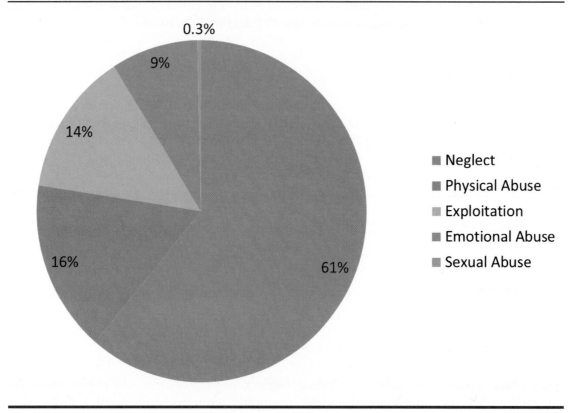

- Neglect
- Physical Abuse
- Exploitation
- Emotional Abuse
- Sexual Abuse

0.3%
9%
14%
16%
61%

Neglect accounts for the largest percentage of elder abuse.

Center for Disease Control and Prevention. (2010). Retrieved from http://205.207.175.93/HDI/TableViewer/chartView.aspx.

Domestic Violence

Women age 20 to 24 experience the highest prevalence of domestic abuse among adults; in fact, 85% of domestic abuse victims are women. Males under the age of 18 account for 10.7% of family violence assault victims. Approximately 62.4% of domestic violence offenders are over the age of 30. The percentage of spouse abuse offenders over age 30 is 73%. About 50% of abuse offenders who are in nonspousal relationships are in the 18 to 29 age range. This data signifies an age gap between domestic partner abuse victims and their offenders (Durose et al., 2005).

Chronically Ill and Disabled People

Chronic diseases are long-lasting and often incurable, as opposed to acute diseases, like the common flu, that are usually easily and quickly recovered from. Many chronic diseases are closely linked to disability and death. As the body ages, it deteriorates and chronic illnesses set in. Asthma is the most common chronic disease in children, and many children limited by asthma grow up to be only minimally affected by the disease. Other childhood diseases, such as diabetes, cystic fibrosis, congenital heart problems, and obesity, often have lingering effects that considerably impact health in adulthood. Disabilities that occur in childhood, such as losing the use of a limb, rarely change in adulthood.

Arthritis and osteoporosis are common in the 65 and over population, and both can seriously limit a person's mobility, quality of life, and activities of daily living. Obesity is classified as a chronic disease and is closely correlated with a propensity toward diabetes. Adults ages 65 to 79 had the highest incidence of diabetes diagnoses, but 2009 numbers show the population aged 45 to 64 years had the highest rate of new diabetes diagnoses (U.S. Department of Health and Human Services, CDC, and National Center for Health Statistics, 2012).

Cancer affects all age groups, but persons age 65 to 84 have the highest incidence rates overall. Children under age 20 have the highest rate of bone and joint cancers. Adults age 55 to 64 have the highest occurrence of cancers involving the eye and ocular orbit. Overall, cancer patients age 75 to 84 have the highest morbidity rate (U.S. Department of Health and Human Services, 2012).

People Diagnosed With HIV/AIDS

Children ages 13 to 14 have the lowest incidence of HIV diagnosis, with an estimated 21 total new HIV diagnoses for this age group in 2009. Adults ages 20 to 24 had the highest number of new HIV diagnoses in 2009 with an estimated total of 6,237 new diagnoses. People ages 13 to 29 years old comprised 39% of all new HIV diagnoses in 2009, the majority of which were ages 20 to 24 years old. The numbers are slightly different for new diagnoses of AIDS. In 2009, the Centers for Disease Control and Prevention (CDC) estimated 13 total new AIDS diagnoses for children under age 13 and 58 new diagnoses for teens age 13 to 14. Adults age 40 to 44 had the highest number of new AIDS diagnoses in 2009, at an estimated 5,689. In 2008, only seven children under age 13 diagnosed with HIV/AIDS died in the United States. Advances in antiretroviral drugs are prolonging the healthy life span enjoyed by HIV/AIDS patients. Public education programs on avoiding HIV are proving worthwhile as the rate of new HIV/AIDS diagnoses in the United States declines (CDC, 2012).

People Diagnosed With Mental Conditions

One common health problem that many HIV patients develop is HIV-associated dementia (HAD). Many elderly persons are affected by similar dementia conditions, including Alzheimer's disease. **Serious mental illness (SMI)** is any mental disorder that significantly interferes with daily life. Serious mental illnesses range in type, onset, and severity. The category includes mental illnesses such as bipolar disorder, major depression, and schizophrenia. Even including Alzheimer's disease in that category, the population age 50 and over has the lowest occurrence of SMI. Young adults ages 18 to 25 have the highest occurrence rate (National Institute of Mental Health [NIMH], 2012c). Even though a young adult may be diagnosed with a mental illness, this is a chronic condition and the person will still have the same diagnosis over the age of 50 and beyond. Symptoms may be controlled by medication but these patients are not "cured." Age of onset is an important factor for all mental disorders: One-half of the total number of mental health conditions begins under age 14 (NIMH, 2012b).

Suicide- and Homicide-Liable People

Suicide is linked to mental conditions. The National Institute of Mental Health (NIMH) found that people over age 65 are disproportionately liable to complete suicide. Of the general population, 11.3 people per 100,000 people committed suicide in 2007; persons 65 and older had a suicide rate of 14.3 suicides per 100,000 people. In contrast, suicide is the third leading cause of death for teenagers and young adults ages 15 to 24 (NIMH, 2012b).

Homicide offender and victimization rates by age are very similar, indicating that most homicides take place against the offenders' peers. Young homicide victims are more likely than those in other age groups to know their offenders. Young adults ages 18 to 24 have the highest homicide rate, a trend that has held steady for many decades, even as overall homicide rates have declined. The 1980s and 1990s saw a considerable increase in homicide rates in the 18 to 24 age group, while homicide rates in other age groups declined (U.S. Bureau of Justice Statistics, 2012).

Infanticide is the killing of children age 5 and under. Parents have the highest offender rate. Caucasians had the highest number of infanticide victims between 1976 and 2005, but African Americans had the highest per-capita incidence rate. Infanticide is most common in children under 1 year of age, and the risk of infanticide declines with age (NIMH, 2012c). Studies have found that most occurrences are by the mother. Domestic violence is often a contributing factor, as are poverty, mental illness, and substance abuse (Friedman & Resnick, 2007). Various factors contribute to the decrease in risk as a child ages. Stronger emotional bonds with parents may help decrease infanticide risk. Additionally, children become more social as they age, which may also increase safety.

Eldercide is the killing of persons age 65 and older. It accounts for about 5% of all homicides. The elderly are more likely than any other age group to be killed during the committing of a felony. Elder males are more likely than elder females to be eldercide victims. Eldercide rates have declined since 1976 from 5.4 eldercide victims per 100,000 people ages 65 and older, to 1.9 eldercide victims per 100,000 people ages 65 and older in 2005 (U.S. Bureau of Justice Statistics, 2012).

People Affected by Alcohol and Substance Abuse

Alcoholism is overuse of and dependence on alcohol. One of the earmarks of alcoholism is frequent **binge drinking**, measured as five or more drinks per occurrence. Adults report fewer binge drinking episodes per month than underage drinkers. College-age young adults between 18 and 20 report the highest level of binge drinking episodes in a month at a rate of 72%. Teenagers aged 15 to 17 are

Courtesy of Aaron Amat/Fotolia

According to a 2009 survey, individuals as young as 12 sought treatment for drug and alcohol abuse.

second, with a binge drinking reported rate of 65% (U.S. Department of Justice, 2002). Figure 2.3 shows the relationship between binge drinking episodes and age.

Figure 2.3: Binge drinking among youth and adult drinkers during last 30 days

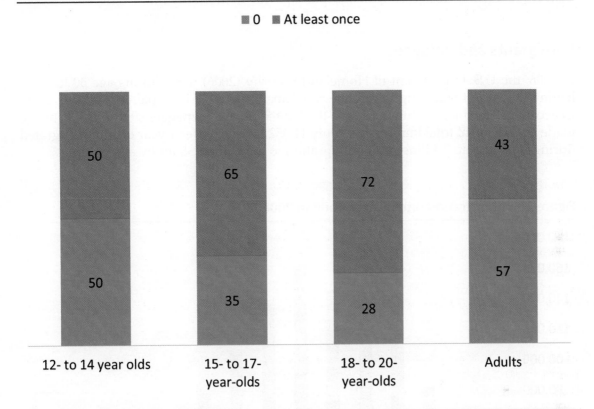

Teenagers report more binge drinking episodes than adults.

U.S. Department of Justice. (2002). Retrieved from http://www.udetc.org/documents/Drinking_in_America.pdf

Substance abuse statistics in the United States indicate that children as young as 12 show a need for substance and alcohol abuse treatments. In 2009, 9.3% of the population age 12 and over sought treatment for substance and alcohol abuse (National Institute on Drug Abuse [NIDA], 2012). In 2003, people ages 18 to 25 had the highest incidence of illegal, or illicit, drug use. That rate dropped from 60.5% in 2003 to 56.6% in 2008. The age group of 26- to 34-year-olds had the highest illicit drug use rate of 58.2% in 2008, but 18- to 25-year-olds had the highest rates of current drug use of 19.6% in 2008 (NIDA, 2012).

Indigent and Homeless People

During the global recession caused by the collapse of the worldwide banking system in the early 2000s, the number of homeless families and children increased, though estimates are based on shelter reports and timed counts, and as such, it is difficult to estimate by exactly how much. From October 2009 to September 2010, children under the age of 18 accounted for 59.3% of the total number of counted homeless persons. Most homeless children enter shelters with their family units. Many homeless families are headed by mothers. This might be because 23.2% of homeless, indigent persons during the year were ages 18 to 30, a common age range for new maternity. People ages 31 to 50 who contribute significantly to the United States workforce accounted for 16.2% of the homeless population. Homelessness decreases with age, perhaps due to mortality rates.

Immigrants and Refugees

In 2006, the U.S. Department of Homeland Security (2006) listed adults age 30 to 34 as having the largest incoming immigration numbers, at 164,751 people. Adults ages 25 to 29 accounted for 146,551 immigrants to the United States. Teenagers 15 to 19 years of age made up 111,132 of total immigrants. Only 11,352 infants under 1 year of age immigrated during 2006. Figure 2.4 illustrates immigration to the United States by age group.

Figure 2.4: Immigration rate by age group in 2006

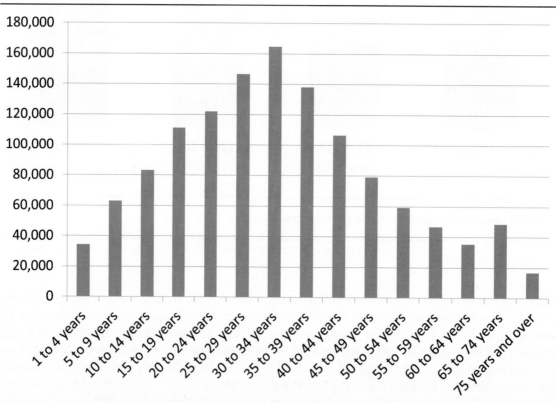

Most people who immigrate to the United States do so between the ages of 25 and 40.

U.S. Department of Homeland Security. (2006). Retrieved from http://www.dhs.gov/files/statistics/publications/LPR06.shtm

Critical Thinking

Do the age groups in these categories surprise you? Did the fact that people over age 65 had a higher suicide rate than other groups surprise you? Or are you surprised that college-age young adults between 18 and 20 report the highest level of binge drinking episodes in a month at a rate of 72%? Explain your reaction.

Self-Check

Answer the following questions to the best of your ability.

1. Mothers in what age range have the smallest risk of having low birth weight babies?
    a. 10–14 years of age
    b. 25–29 years of age
    c. 31–36 years of age
    d. 43–46 years of age

2. According to the U.S. National Center on Elder Abuse, approximately how many people over age 60 are victimized annually?
    a. 150,000
    b. 350,000
    c. 450,000
    d. 1,000,000

3. Children in what age range have the lowest incidence of HIV diagnosis?
    a. 1–4 years of age
    b. 5–9 years of age
    c. 10–12 years of age
    d. 13–15 years of age

Answer Key

1. **b**   2. **c**   3. **d**

2.3 Comparing Vulnerable Groups by Gender

Men and women experience vulnerability differently. Women are more likely to be the victims of domestic abuse and are more likely to head homeless family units. Men are more likely to experience violence. Men and women also experience health issues at differing levels. Even within an identified vulnerable population, men and women have different needs.

Vulnerable Mothers and Children

The condition of pregnancy puts mothers at risk for negative health outcomes, though most pregnancies end with healthy mothers and infants. Mothers with other risk factors, such as poverty and ethnicity, experience more problems both during and after pregnancy. A discussion of high-risk mothers and babies based on gender focuses on infants, as the mothers are obviously women.

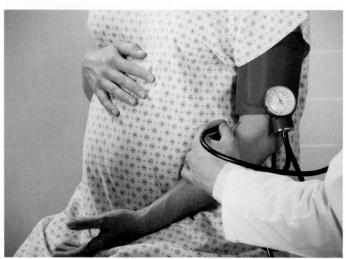

Courtesy of Comstock/Thinkstock

Pregnancy puts women at risk for developing health problems, but women already in at-risk groups have an even greater predisposition to experiencing problematic pregnancies.

The total United States population in 1980 was 226,546,000 people. Out of that number, 110,053,000 were male, and 116,493,000 were female. In 2010, the total American population consisted of 151,781,000 males and 156,964,000 females. Thus, the trend of more females than males in the total population has continued. This is particularly interesting because slightly more males than females are born into the population each year. In fact, there were more male live births than female births in the United States for nearly three straight decades. In 2008, there were 105 males born for every 100 females. The data therefore indicates that males have a higher mortality rate overall than females (U.S. Census Bureau, 2012b).

Female babies have a longer life expectancy at birth of 80.6 years, in contrast to their male counterparts, who have an at-birth life expectancy of 75.7 years. The infant mortality rate for males is 6.72 deaths for every 1,000 males born. This is higher than the infant mortality rate for females, which is 5.37 deaths for every 1,000 females born (Central Intelligence Agency (CIA), 2012b).

Abused Individuals

According to the National Coalition Against Domestic Violence (n.d.), men are statistically more likely to be domestic violence offenders. In fact, females account for 85% of all intimate partner abuse victims. Male children who witness domestic violence are statistically more likely to become domestic violence offenders in their adulthood.

Child Abuse

Although more men are domestic violence offenders, more women abuse children. In 37.2% of child abuse cases, women were the sole, or independent offenders—compared with 19.1% of independent male offenders. Male children are statistically less likely to be victims of child abuse, at 48.5% of all child abuse cases, whereas female children accounted for 51.2% of child abuse cases (U.S. Department of Health and Human Services, 2011b).

Elder Abuse

As mentioned, there are slightly more women than men in the American population. This makes it difficult to

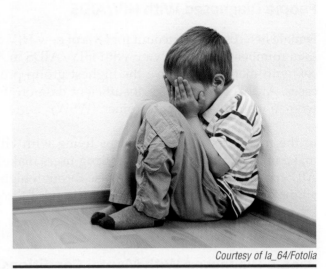

Courtesy of la_64/Fotolia

Male children account for 48.5% of child abuse cases.

determine the precise reason that women make up over half of the total number of elder abuse victims in the United States. It is possible that females may be slightly overrepresented in statistics on elder abuse by gender, partly because of the gap in age expectancy: The life expectancy is 75.7 years for males and 80.6 years for females. As women live longer, there is more opportunity for abuse.

Although women represent a higher incidence rate of elder abuse in nearly all categories, men have a higher rate of elder abuse by abandonment; overall, men have a higher offender rate of elder abuse. However, women represent a slight majority of elder abuse offenders by way of neglect. Similarly, women have a self-neglect rate of 65%, compared with the male self-neglect rate of 35% (U.S. National Center on Elder Abuse, n.d.).

Chronically Ill and Disabled People

According to the Centers for Disease Control and Prevention, in 2007, 20.3% of adult women had chronic illnesses, such as emphysema, and disabilities that make daily activities more difficult. Men had a slightly lower rate of 17.3%. Among the senior citizen population, 7.5% of women require help with activities of daily living, compared with 5.1% of men age 65 and over.

Specific chronic illnesses do not affect men and women at equal rates. Of adults over age 20, 11.8% of the total male population is diagnosed with diabetes, compared with 10.8% of the total female population. Heart disease is more common in the male population, at an occurrence rate of 12.7%. The rate of heart disease in the female population is lower, at 10.6%. Cancer is more prevalent among women, with 8.6% of the female population having had cancer at some point in their lives, compared with 7.9% of men (U.S. Department of Health and Human Services, 2012).

People Diagnosed With HIV/AIDS

Female heterosexuals account for 68% of new HIV diagnoses among heterosexuals. Of the total number of people living with HIV/AIDS in America, 75% are men. Men who have sex with men (MSM) have the highest group prevalence rate of 48% of all HIV/AIDS cases. At this time, there is insufficient data on the causal factors of HIV/AIDS among women who have sex with women (WSW).

In the total number of Americans living with HIV/AIDS, female injection drug users make up 26% and male injection drug users make up 16%. Overall, 72% of female HIV/AIDS patients contracted the disease through high-risk heterosexual activity. Just 13% of all males living with HIV/AIDS contracted it through heterosexual contact (Centers for Disease Control and Prevention, 2008b).

People Diagnosed With Mental Conditions

Overall, men and women report mental conditions at approximately the same rates. Women statistically suffer more *serious* mental disorders than men and have a higher incidence of **internalizing disorders**, or mental health conditions that cause emotional responses, such as anxiety and depression. Men have a higher rate of **externalizing disorders**, which lead to outward activities of destruction, such as drug abuse and antisocial behaviors (Thompson, 2008).

It is believed that social attitudes about gender roles and equality have much to do with the difference in mental disorders experienced by the genders. For example, social pressure about body image is proven to add to a woman's anxiety over her physique, which can lead to eating disorders. Likewise, social pressure over how a man "should" act encourages men to act out in response to anxiety instead of internalizing (NIMH, 2000).

The effects of social pressures on mental conditions explain the difference in condition types between the genders. This theory is furthered by the fact that men and women experience mental conditions that do not have a social component at equal rates. Bipolar disorder and schizophrenia each affect males and females at similar rates, and brain imaging tests have found that the brains of people with bipolar disorder are physically different from those with socially associated conditions such as depression (NIMH, 2012a).

Suicide- and Homicide-Liable People

Males have a higher suicide rate than females. In 2007, suicide was the seventh leading cause of death for men in the United States, and the 15th leading cause for women in the United States. In fact, although women have a higher rate of *attempted* suicides, men are nearly four times as likely as women to actually complete suicide. In addition, men and women choose markedly different methods when they commit suicide (NIMH, 2007). Figure 2.5 shows that men prefer firearms and women prefer poisoning.

Figure 2.5: Suicide method by gender

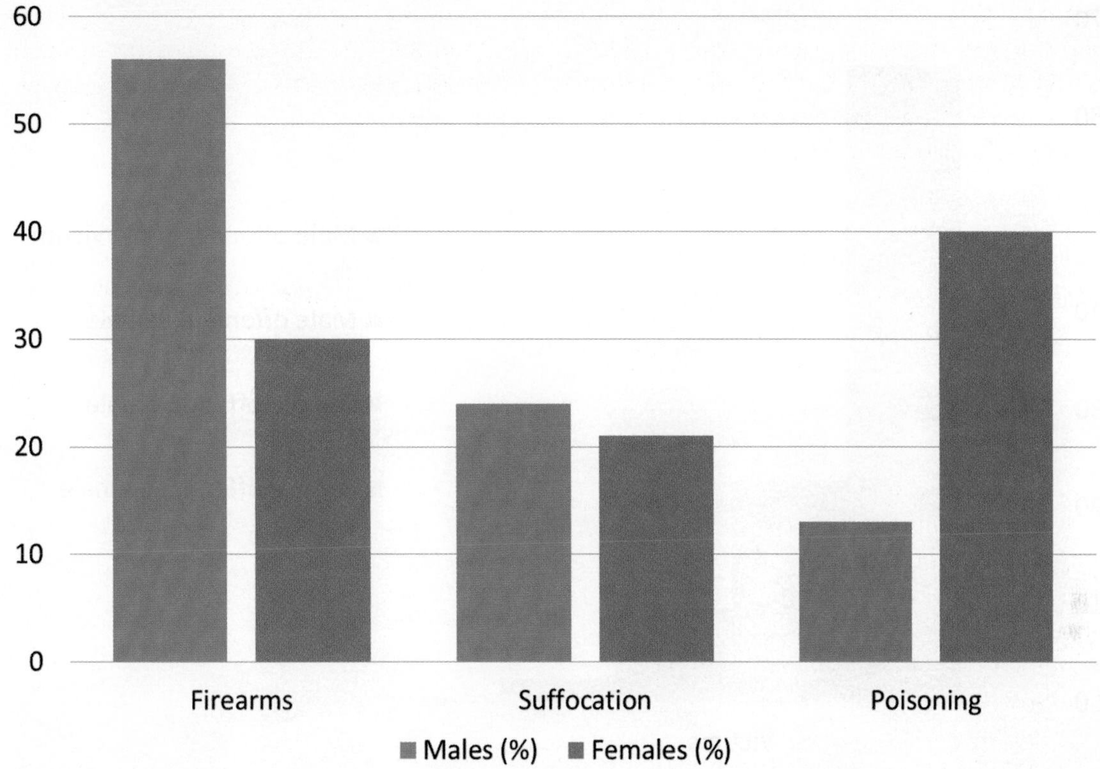

Men and women commit suicide by suffocation at similar rates, but vastly differ in use of firearms and poisoning.

National Institute of Mental Health (NIMH). (2007). Retrieved from http://www.nimh.nih.gov/health/publications/suicide-in-the-us-statistics-and-prevention/index.shtml

Men have significantly higher homicide offender and victim rates than women. Figure 2.6 shows the relationships between offenders and victims by gender. Numbers from 2005 indicated that men are four times more likely than women to be homicide victims. Men are more likely to kill other men, but women kill men at a higher rate than other women. This might be because women are more likely to be victims of other types of violent crimes, especially sex crimes and intimate partner abuse.

Male infants and elders are more likely than their female counterparts to be homicide victims. Females are significantly more likely to be victims of sex-related homicides. Social settings are a significant factor in homicide rates, as illustrated by the fact that 94.7% of gang-related homicides had male victims, compared with 5.3% female victims. Figure 2.6 shows the breakdown of homicide types by gender (U.S. Bureau of Justice Statistics, 2012).

Figure 2.6: Homicide offenders and victims by gender

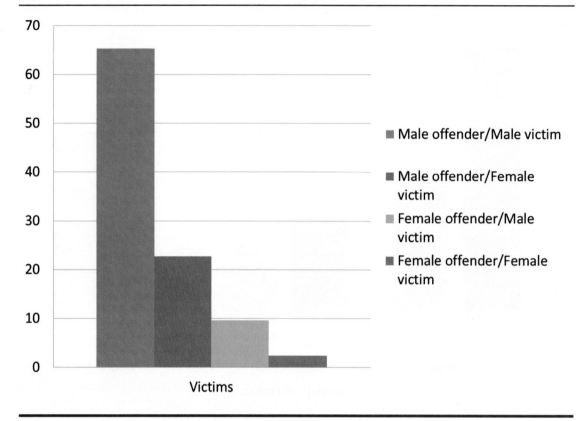

- ■ Male offender/Male victim
- ■ Male offender/Female victim
- ■ Female offender/Male victim
- ■ Female offender/Female victim

Victims

Most murders committed involve a male offender and male victim.

Bureau of Justice Statistics. (2005). Retrieved from http://bjs.ojp.usdoj.gov/content/homicide/teens.cfm

Courtesy of Ryan McVay/Thinkstock

Women report that they drink alcohol less often than men and, when they do drink, tend to consume less than men.

People Affected by Alcohol and Substance Abuse

Women report that they drink less alcohol and drink less often than men. In fact, women are almost twice as likely as men to be lifetime abstainers. Even so, alcohol abuse creates slightly different problems for men and women, and treatment methods thus differ for each gender.

Because women are more likely than men to have multiple, simultaneous addictions to alcohol and different drugs (Office of Substance Abuse Services [OSAS], 2004) and experience more barriers to addiction help via socioeconomics and health care access, they are more likely to seek treatment from general practitioners than from specialized treatment centers; they are therefore less likely to receive appropriate, addiction-specific treatment (Green, n.d.). Furthermore, because most women who seek substance abuse treatment are likely to have suffered physical or emotional abuse, and are more likely than their male counterparts to be of low socioeconomic backgrounds, treatments for women must address the specific issues that contribute to their substance abuse habits. Women seem to respond better to same-gender treatment centers and groups because the male influence affects the way women interact with each other and think about themselves. Therapists have found that all-female support groups often focus on emotional responses to events (such as childbirth), whereas all-male groups often focus on gaming, sports, or other activities. Men in mixed gender groups usually dominate the discussions, leaving the women with a lack of group support.

In general, women have better success and retention rates than men when they receive gender-specific treatments. However, researchers believe this is more about the relationships women build during group therapy programs than about the actual course of treatment (OSAS, 2004).

Indigent and Homeless People

Achieving an accurate count of the number of homeless persons in the United States is difficult. Statistics are based on reports from homeless shelters and counts taken by volunteers over specified periods. From October 2009 to September 2010, reported numbers of people in homeless shelters showed that males accounted for 62% of the total number of sheltered people, and females accounted for 38%. Males are also over-represented, making up 80% of both **transitional** (or short-term) **homelessness** and **episodic** (or frequent) **homelessness** (Substance Abuse and Mental Health Services Administration [SAMHSA], 2011b).

The number of family units experiencing homelessness rose in the early 2000s. Though males account for the majority of sheltered persons on a given night, females account for 77% of adults in sheltered families. Most families using shelters are made up of a mother, or other maternal figure, and two children, with no adult male. The number of homeless families is anticipated to decline to early 2000s levels as the global recession of the early 2000s to early 2010s abates (Substance Abuse and Mental Health Services Administration [SAMHSA], 2011b).

Immigrants and Refugees

Males ages 18 to 34 represented 62% of the unauthorized immigrant population in 2010. In that same year, females dominated the 45 and over age group at 53%. Figure 2.7 shows the breakdown of unauthorized immigration to the United States in 2010 by age group and gender (Hoefer, Rytina, & Baker, 2011).

The gender trends for legal immigrants who gain permanent resident status are the opposite from those of unauthorized immigrants. Of the 1,042,625 people who gained permanent resident status in 2010 to the United States, 471,849 were male, compared with

570,771 females. The ratio of single to married persons in this group differs greatly by gender. Of the 471,849 men, 204,770 were single and 254,333 were married. Marriage was also more prevalent among females, though at a significantly higher incidence rate. Of the 570,771 women, 185,698 were single and 342,625 were married (U.S. Department of Homeland Security, 2011).

Many people immigrate to the United States to improve their lives through employment opportunities. As with most populations, legal immigrant males have a higher employment rate than their female counterparts. Less than half of the total number of new male permanent residents in 2010 were listed as not working, whereas more than half of the number of new permanent resident women were listed as not working. Female homemakers were more than 31 times more prevalent than male homemakers in this same population (U.S. Department of Homeland Security, 2011).

Figure 2.7: Total unauthorized immigration numbers by age and gender, 2010

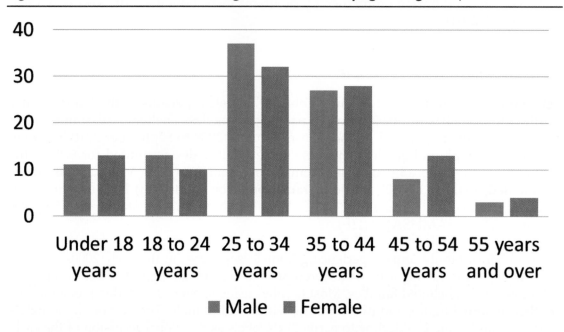

Unauthorized immigration is most prevalent in the 25–34 and 35–44 age groups. Of these unauthorized immigrants, slightly more are men.

U.S. Department of Homeland Security. (2006). Retrieved from http://www.dhs.gov/files/statistics/publications/LPR06.shtm

Critical Thinking

In 2010, the United States Census said that in the general population, there are 5,183 more women than men. Given the fact that 105 male children are born for every 100 female births, how would you explain the difference between more male births and fewer males in the adult general population?

Self-Check

Answer the following questions to the best of your ability.

1. The infant mortality rate for females is _____ deaths for every 1,000 females born.
   a. 1.32
   b. 2.53
   c. 3.57
   d. 4.97

2. The method men commonly use to deal with mental issues is known as
   a. externalizing.
   b. internalizing.
   c. binge eating.
   d. becoming depressed.

3. Women seem to respond better to what type of substance abuse resources?
   a. mental health treatment centers
   b. faith-based treatment centers
   c. same-gender treatment centers
   d. addiction-specific treatment centers

Answer Key

1. c   2. a   3. c

2.4 Comparing Vulnerable Groups by Culture and Ethnicity

Minority groups in the United States are significantly more likely than members of the Caucasian majority to experience poverty due to insufficient health care, poor education, and an unmet need for social capital, human capital, and social status. Marriage/domestic partnership, for example, is just one factor that adds to a person's social capital. Marriage rates among 15- to 44-year-old female Hispanics and female non-Hispanic whites are around 50%, but non-Hispanic black females in this age range have a significantly lower marriage rate, at around 26%. It is interesting to note that across all ethnicities, individuals with bachelor's degrees or above have higher marriage rates than those with no postsecondary education (Goodwin, Mosher, & Chandra, 2010). Community programs often have difficulty meeting the needs of minority groups—an issue that cannot be solved simply by throwing more money at the problem. Nonprofit organizations within the United States might benefit more through cooperation and the sharing of resources, information, and the cessation of duplicate processes and systems.

Vulnerable Mothers and Children

Low income and a lack of health insurance contribute to a lack of early, quality, prenatal care. Minority populations account for a large portion of Americans living in poverty. This fact alone indicates that Hispanic, black, Native American, and other minority race mothers are statistically at a higher risk for poor maternity health outcomes (chronic health issues and low birth weight). During the prime childbearing age range of 15 to 44, marriage rates of female Hispanics and non-Hispanic white populations near 50%. Non-Hispanic blacks have a significantly lower rate. Mothers with paternal support are more likely to seek early and regular prenatal care, which increases their chances for positive outcomes for both mother and baby.

Infant Mortality

Poor prenatal health care increases the risks of infant and maternal mortality. There are approximately 2.5 infant deaths per 1,000 full-term live births in the United States. Out of that number, Asians and Pacific Islanders have the lowest infant mortality rates. Non-Hispanic whites experience infant mortality at 2.29 deaths per 1,000 live births. Non-Hispanic Blacks' infant mortality rate is 67% higher than their white counterparts, with 3.82 deaths per 1,000 births (MacDorman & Mathews, 2011). Prenatal care levels and maternal lifestyle choices are cited as the main reasons for these differences.

Sudden infant death syndrome (SIDS) is the unexplainable death of an infant any time before the first birthday. The 2006 SIDS rate in the United States was 0.53 occurrences per 1,000 live births. Out of that number, Native Americans and Alaska Natives had the highest prevalence, while the SIDS rate for non-Hispanic whites falls in the middle of the spectrum (Mathews, Menacker, & MacDorman, 2003).

Contributing factors to infant mortality include maternal health and low birth weight. Non-Hispanic blacks have the highest low birth weight prevalence at 13.6%. This is significantly higher than other ethnic groups. Hispanics have the smallest prevalence of low birth weight at 6.9%. Non-Hispanic whites fall in between blacks and Hispanics with a prevalence of 7.2% (MacDorman & Mathews, 2011).

Maternal Mortality

The 2007 maternal mortality rate in the United States was 12.7 deaths per 1,000 live births. Non-Hispanic blacks have the highest maternal mortality rate with 28.4 deaths per 1,000 births. This trend continues to plague health care researchers and the non-Hispanic black community as they search for ways to lower it. Non-Hispanic whites have the second highest maternal mortality rate at 10.5 deaths per 1,000 births, and Hispanics have the lowest at 8.9 deaths per 1,000 live births (Xu, Kochanek, Murphy, & Tejada-Vera, 2010).

Courtesy of yurmary/Fotolia

Infants born underweight are especially prevalent in teen pregnancies.

Teenage Mothers

Teenage mothers have special prenatal and postnatal health needs. Teen mothers have a higher rate of low birth weight infants than most other age groups. The teen birthrate in the United States in 2009 was 38 births for every 1,000 teenagers 15 to 19 years old. Figure 2.8 shows the breakdown of teen births by ethnic group. Hispanic teens continue to have the highest teen birthrate, with non-Hispanic blacks having the second-highest prevalence rates (CDC, 2012).

Figure 2.8: U.S. birth rates for women aged 15–19 years by race/ethnicity

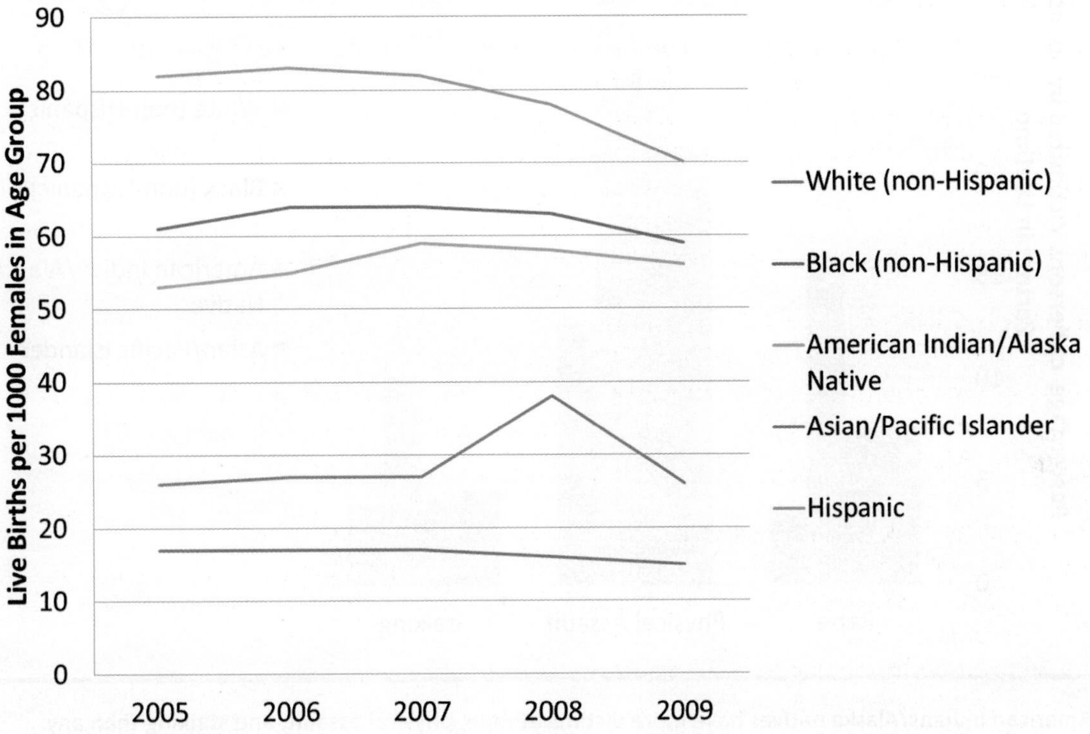

Hispanic and black women have the highest rate of teen pregnancy.

Centers for Disease Control and Prevention. (2010a). U.S. birth rates for women aged 15–19. Retrieved from http://www.cdc.gov/teenpregnancy/LongDescriptors.htm

Abused Individuals

Native Americans and Alaska Natives experience significantly higher domestic abuse rates than any other ethnic group in the United States. However, some researchers believe that factors such as personal interpretation of abuse and cultural attitudes regarding reporting abuse may alter the statistics. Asians and Pacific Islanders have the lowest incidence rate, while Caucasians and African Americans have similar rates in the middle of the spectrum (Tjaden & Thoennes, 2000). Figure 2.9 offers the rates of domestic abuse by ethnic group.

Figure 2.9: Domestic partner abuse rates by abuse type and ethnic group

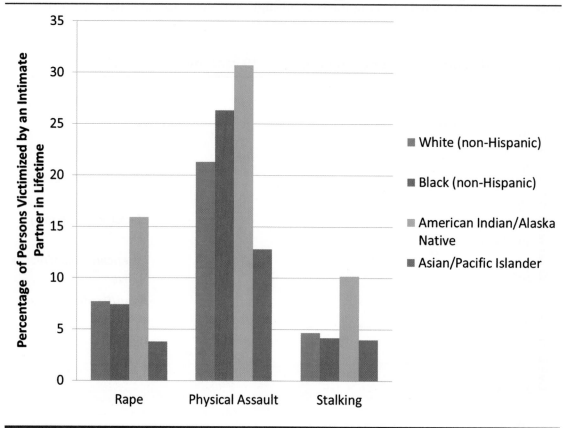

American Indians/Alaska natives have more victims of rape, physical assault, and stalking than any other ethnic group.

U.S. Department of Justice. (2010).

Child Abuse

Though Native Americans and Alaska Natives have the highest domestic partner abuse rates, they have very low child abuse rates. Caucasian children have a higher prevalence of child abuse, at 44.8%, than other ethnic groups in the United States. Child abuse rates for African Americans and Hispanics are close: 21.9% and 21.4%, respectively. Figure 2.10 shows that about half of child abuse offenders are Caucasians. Child abuse offender rates by ethnicity follow the same trends as the victim rates (U.S. Department of Health and Human Services, 2011b).

Figure 2.10: Child abuse offenders by race and ethnicity

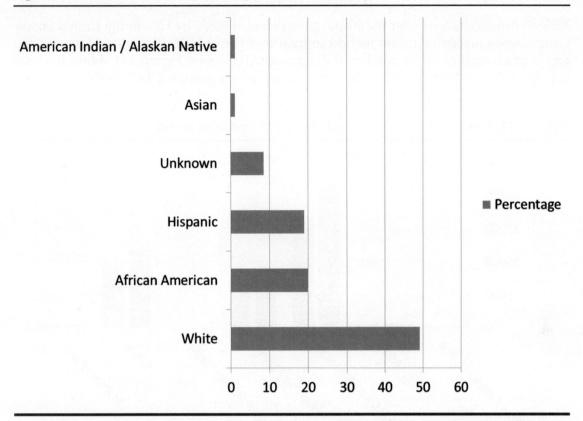

Conversely, American Indians/Alaska Natives make up less than 5% of all child abuse perpetrators, whereas whites make up nearly 50%.

U.S. Department of Health & Human Services. (2010). Retrieved from http://www.acf.hhs.gov/programs/cb/pubs/cm10/cm10.pdf

Elder Abuse

According to the 2004 Survey of Adult Protective Services, 77.1% of reported elder abuse victims are white and 21.2% are African American (U.S. National Center on Elder Abuse, 2006). Whites have the highest prevalence for abuse by neglect, emotional abuse, physical abuse, and financial abuse. Blacks are around 15% more likely to abuse by abandonment (U.S. Department of Health and Human Services, Administration for Children and Families, Administration on Aging, 1998).

Chronically Ill and Disabled People

Hawaiians and Pacific Islanders have the highest prevalence of diabetes, at 23.7%. African Americans have the highest rate of kidney disease, at 2.8%. Native Americans have the highest prevalence of multiple chronic diseases, including ulcers (9.9%), liver disease (2.6%), arthritis (25.5%), and chronic joint symptoms (33%). The difference in chronic disease prevalence among ethnic groups is partially due to genetics, but the effects of socioeconomic situations and lifestyle choices cannot be ignored (Schiller, Lucas, Ward, & Peregoy, 2012).

People Diagnosed With HIV/AIDS

African Americans are by far the ethnic group most affected by HIV in the United States. Caucasians represent a distant second in total number of HIV diagnoses. However, the gap is much smaller in the number of diagnosed AIDS cases. Figure 2.11 shows the relationship between HIV and AIDS cases by affected ethnic groups (CDC, 2008).

Figure 2.11: Estimated diagnosis of HIV and AIDS by ethnic group

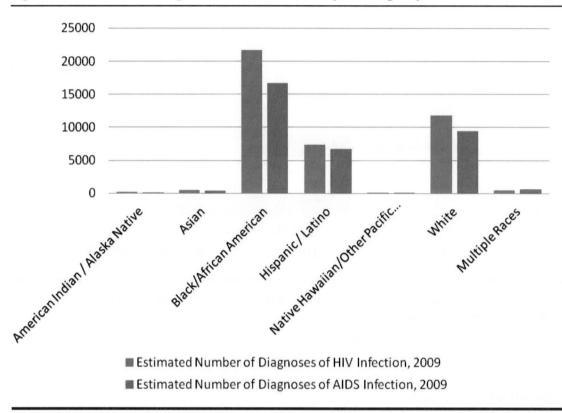

■ Estimated Number of Diagnoses of HIV Infection, 2009
■ Estimated Number of Diagnoses of AIDS Infection, 2009

Diagnosis of HIV and AIDS is extremely low in American Indian/Alaska Natives, Asians, Native Hawaiians, and those of multiple races.

U.S. Department of Health & Human Services. (2010). Diagnoses of HIV infection by race/ethnicity. Retrieved from http://www.cdc.gov/hiv/topics/surveillance/basic.htm#hivaidsrace

U.S. Department of Health & Human Services. (2010). AIDS diagnoses by race/ethnicity. Retrieved from http://www.cdc.gov/hiv/topics/surveillance/basic.htm#aidsrace

People Diagnosed With Mental Conditions

Individuals listed as having family history from more than one race have the highest occurrence of serious mental illness (9.3% overall occurrence rate). Native Americans and Alaska Natives have the second highest serious mental illness rates at 8.5%. The serious mental illness rate for Caucasians is in the middle of the range (5.2% incidence rate), and African Americans are nearer the low end of the spectrum with an incidence rate of 4.4%. Native Hawaiians and other Pacific Islanders have the lowest occurrence of mental illness at a rate of 1.6% (SAMHSA, 2012).

Suicide- and Homicide-Liable People

Native American and Alaska Native males have the highest suicide rate of 27.61 per 100,000 in the population, followed by non-Hispanic white males with 25.96 suicides per 100,000 people of that population. Asian males have the lowest suicide rate among their gender with fewer than 10 suicides per 100,000 population, and non-Hispanic black females have the lowest suicide rate of their gender with approximately 2 suicides per 100,000 people (CDC, 2012b).

Most homicides have the same gender offenders and victims. African Americans have a higher incidence of felony murders, drug-related homicides, and homicides as a result of arguments. Caucasians have higher rates of infanticide and eldercide, and are more likely to involve multiple victims. For suicide, Caucasians use poison at a significantly higher rate than African Americans, though African Americans are only about 15% more likely than Caucasians to use guns (U.S. Bureau of Justice Statistics, 2012).

People Affected by Alcohol and Substance Abuse

According to the Substance Abuse and Mental Health Services Administration, alcohol use is most prevalent among Caucasians with over 50% reporting alcohol use in the past month. Hispanics have the highest rate of binge drinking at 25.1%, though Caucasians have the highest rate of heavy alcohol use. Figure 2.12 illustrates the prevalence of alcohol use by ethnicity and amount (2011b).

Figure 2.12: Alcohol use among persons aged 12 years or older by race/ethnicity, 2010

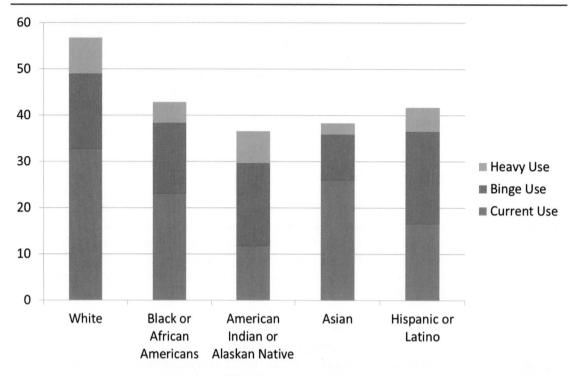

Total alcohol use is similar across non-white races; however, type of use varies greatly within that total.

U.S. Department of Health & Human Services. (2010). Retrieved from http://www.samhsa.gov/data/NSDUH/2k10NSDUH/2k10Results.htm#3.1.4

African Americans have the second-lowest heavy alcohol use rate but the highest rate of illicit drug use with 10.7% reporting having used illegal drugs within the last month. Drug use went up for all groups except Asians during the period from 2002 to 2010 (SAMHSA, 2011b).

Indigent and Homeless People

Understanding the ethnic composition of the indigent population you are trying to serve informs decisions from staffing to programming. In general, the homeless population represents the ethnic makeup of the city in question. For example, Chicago, Illinois, is likely to have a higher percentage of African Americans in homeless shelters than Bowling Green, Kentucky.

The Substance Abuse and Mental Health Services Administration (SAMHSA) uses reports from shelters and temporary housing to count the number and demographics of homelessness in America. According to SAMHSA, a slight majority of all counted homeless persons are non-Hispanic whites, followed closely by blacks. Figure 2.13 illustrates the percentage that each ethnic group represents in the total number of counted homeless persons.

Figure 2.13: Ethnic group representations in the homeless population

- White
- Black or African American
- Hispanic or Latino

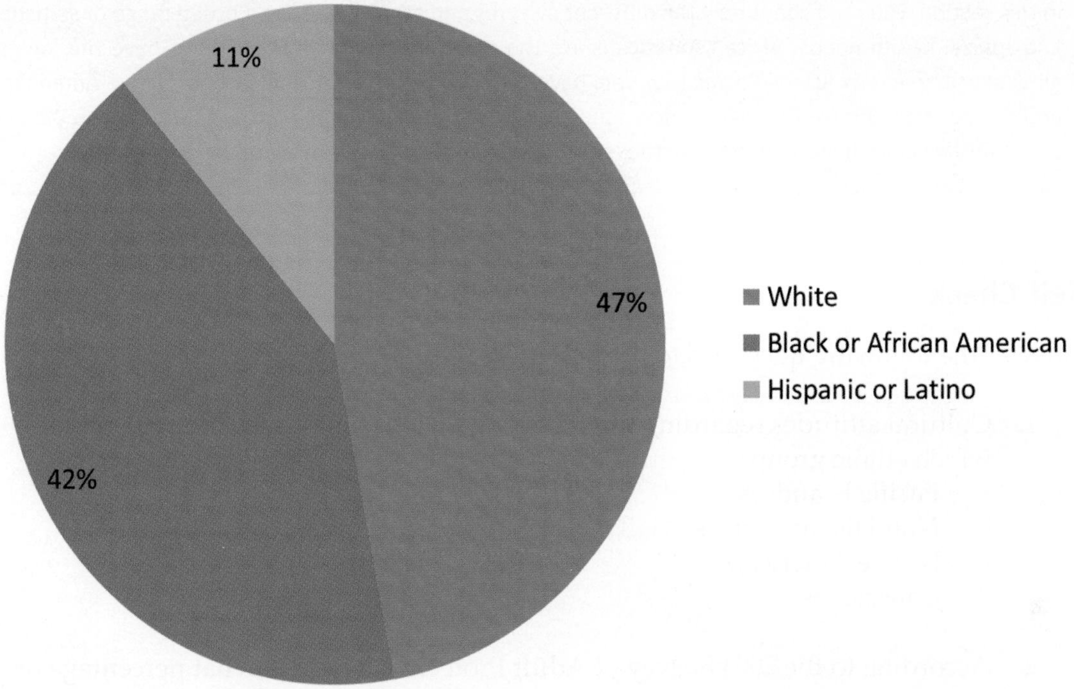

A majority of the homeless population is either white or black, with Hispanics and Latinos making up little more than a tenth of the population.

U.S. Department of Health & Human Services. (2010). Retrieved from http://homeless.samhsa.gov/ResourceFiles/hrc_factsheet.pdf

Immigrants and Refugees

Immigration to the United States is largely based on political and economic strife in other parts of the world. People move to the United States to flee war and poverty, to be with family, and to seek employment and upward mobility. In other words, the ethnic composition of new immigrants to the United States during a certain period largely reflects those areas of the world where political and economic strife is at its highest levels. For example, America experienced a considerable increase in the number of Asians seeking permanent residency after the Vietnam War ended in the 1970s. The 1980s saw an increase in immigrants from the Americas, seeking escape from the guerilla warfare plaguing both Central and South America at the time. In the 1990s, the ratio of immigration by country of origin changed again, this time to people fleeing civil wars in parts of Europe and Africa. Immigrants fleeing Mexico's drug war and Caribbean poverty accounted for the highest numbers of immigrants to the United States in the early 2000s.

Critical Thinking

In this section, you read about how the different cultures and ethnicities span a broad range of statistics and special health needs. African Americans are the most affected by AIDS/HIV but have the lowest alcohol use, whereas Asians/Pacific Islanders have the lowest infant mortality rates. Native Americans and Alaska Natives have the highest domestic abuse but the lowest child abuse rates. Do you believe that cultural values have an impact on these statistics?

Self-Check

Answer the following questions to the best of your ability.

1. Cultural attitudes regarding the reporting of abuse may alter the statistics of which ethnic group?
   a. Pacific Islanders
   b. Non-Hispanic blacks
   c. Native Americans
   d. Caucasians

2. According to the 2004 Survey of Adult Protective Services, what percentage of reported elder abuse victims are white?
   a. 63.9%
   b. 77.1%
   c. 83.2%
   d. 94.7%

3. According to the Substance Abuse and Mental Health Services Administration (SAMHSA), what percentage of persons who use shelters and other homeless services are "other races"?
   a. 4.5%
   b. 15.6%
   c. 27.9%
   d. 49.8%

Answer Key

1. c   2. b   3. a

2.5 Comparing Vulnerable Groups by Education and Income Levels

Education and income are part of the investment in people called "human capital." An evident income, resource, and health gap exists between people who have completed high school or the equivalent and people who have not. Another gap exists between people with high school diplomas and GEDs and people with college educations. The more education a person achieves, the higher that person's earning potential becomes. For example, the average income for households with some high school education but no diploma or GED is $25,604 per year. The number rises significantly to $39,647 with the completion of high school. Figure 2.14 shows the direct relationship between household income and completed level of education. In general, education leads to better, longer-lasting jobs and social relationships.

Figure 2.14: Relationship between education level and household income

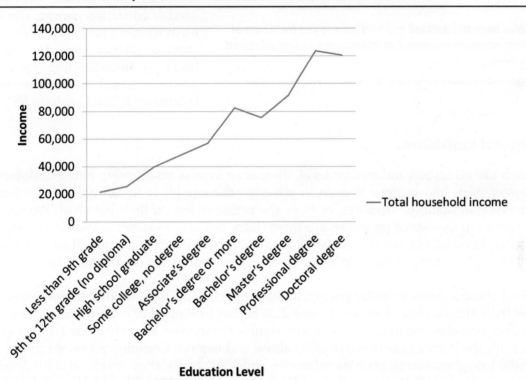

Household income increases as education level increases up to the professional degree level, then decreases slightly at the doctoral level.

U.S. Census. (2009). Educational attainment of householder. Retrieved from http://www.census.gov/compendia/statab/2012/tables/12s0692.pdf

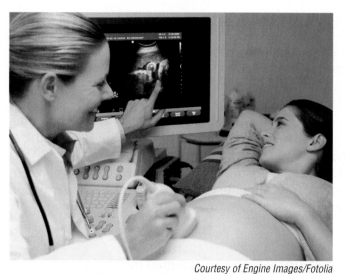

Courtesy of Engine Images/Fotolia

Babies born to educated mothers have lower incidence of infant mortality compared to infants born to less-educated mothers.

Vulnerable Mothers and Children

The rate of Americans failing to obtain needed health care, dental care, and prescription drugs because they are unable to afford them is on the rise. This situation particularly affects mothers and infants during one of the most high-risk times of their lives. There is a direct inverse relationship between infant mortality and maternal education level. Infant mortality rates decline with each level of education gained. The low birth weight rate follows the same inverse relationship. The likelihood of breastfeeding increases with maternal education level (Mathews & MacDorman, 2007).

Abused Individuals

Much like education and income level, there is an inverse relationship between domestic abuse reports and income. Women in poverty are more likely to call upon the police to intervene in domestic disputes, or have the police called on their behalves. Women on government assistance programs are three times as likely to suffer domestic violence as women in middle income brackets. Women in households with an annual income under $7,500 are five times as likely to be involved in domestic abuse (Sampson, 2007).

Child abuse follows a similar pattern to that of partner abuse. Children in households of less than $15,000 annual income have a 22% higher likelihood of experiencing abuse and neglect than children in households with double the income. Poverty alone is not responsible for the higher prevalence of child abuse and neglect. Common problems in impoverished neighborhoods, such as substance abuse, low education levels, and inadequate housing, are also contributing factors (U.S. Department of Health and Human Services, Administration for Children and Families, 2003). Elder adults with an annual income of $5,000 to $9,999 have the highest elder abuse prevalence in all abuse categories (U.S. Department of Health and Human Services, Administration for Children and Families, Administration on Aging, 1998).

Chronically Ill and Disabled People

Poor socioeconomic conditions include inadequate housing, lack of financial income, lack of a strong social support network, and poor access to fresh foods and social services like health care. Although chronic illnesses and disabilities do not necessarily strike people in low socioeconomic situations, the people in those situations are more adversely affected by chronic ailments.

Lack of affordable, accessible health care means that patients of low socioeconomic status are less likely to receive proper care for their ailments. Their quality of life is likely to be more adversely affected than those who have stronger familial ties and personal relationships. Add to these challenges the fact that many people in poverty-stricken areas have the types of jobs that are not flexible or kind about missed work, and the situation becomes even more dire. The American health care system relies on individuals to pay for treatment, and chronically ill and disabled people with low income and education levels are disproportionately affected.

People Diagnosed With HIV/AIDS

As with most health outcomes, HIV/AIDS prevalence increases as education and income decrease. Both African-American and Hispanic populations in low-income areas have an HIV prevalence rate of 2.1%. The HIV prevalence rate for Caucasians in low-income areas is below 2%. These numbers are significant when compared to the overall HIV prevalence rates of these populations. The overall HIV prevalence rate among African Americans is 1.7%. The Hispanic population has an overall HIV prevalence rate of 0.6%; and the Caucasian population has the lowest overall HIV prevalence rate of 0.2%. There are more African Americans and Hispanic people living in poverty than Caucasian people, which does account somewhat for the higher HIV prevalence rates in low-income areas. However, the numbers signify that HIV prevalence rates are higher overall and in each population among the poor (Denning & DiNenno, n.d.).

People Diagnosed With Mental Conditions

A study announced in the July 25, 2011, issue of *BMC Medicine* found that people in France, the United States, the Netherlands, and other first-world countries suffer depression at some point in their lives at a rate of 15% for the entire population, in contrast to people in less affluent countries, who suffer depression at a rate of 11% (U.S. Department of Health and Human Services, 2011b).

Within the United States, mental illness is more commonly associated with poverty than wealth. Poor living situations can induce depression and anxiety, making this type of mental condition more prevalent among low-income populations. People with debilitating mental illnesses often have difficulty maintaining gainful employment. As such, there is a high occurrence of individuals with severe mental illness seeking government aid (U.S. Public Health Service, 1999).

Suicide- and Homicide- Liable People

Both suicide and homicide are linked to exposure to violence and substance abuse. Even if a person does not personally have a history of exposure to violence and substance abuse, if those problems are persistent in the areas they live, then the individual's risk of homicide and suicide increase. Both studies and police report higher levels of suicide and homicide in areas of low socioeconomic standing (Macomber & Pergamit, 2009).

Courtesy of Mitarart/Fotolia

Exposure to violence and substance abuse increase a person's risk of homicidal or suicidal behavior.

People Affected by Alcohol and Substance Abuse

Unlike so many of the topics covered here, where positive outcomes increase as education level rises, alcohol use increases as education level rises. College graduates have a regular alcohol use rate of 69.1%. The regular alcohol use rate for adults who did not finish high school is 36.8%. Young adults age 18 to 22 who are enrolled in college full-time have a binge drinking rate of 44.2%, whereas people in the same age group who are not enrolled in full-time college have a binge drinking rate of 35.6%. Average alcohol use is higher for adults with full-time jobs, but binge drinking and heavy alcohol consumption are higher among the unemployed/underemployed (SAMHSA, 2011b).

Substance abuse decreases with education level. Adults with college degrees have a substance abuse rate of 7.3%. Those who finished high school but did not continue on to college have a substance abuse rate of 8.3%. The rate jumps to 10.6% for those who do not finish high school. Employment level and substance abuse are also inversely related; substance abuse rates increase as employment levels decrease. Adults with full-time employment have a substance abuse rate of 8.9%. The rate for part-time employees is 10.9%. The rate of substance abuse by the unemployed is 15.7% (SAMHSA, 2011b).

Indigent and Homeless People

Homelessness is directly related to poverty. The global recession of the early 2000s caused a rise in unemployment, and the number of homeless persons who all too recently were relatively affluent increased significantly. The recession also created an increase in homeless persons who were underemployed.

Indigence and unemployment often create a cycle that can mire individuals. Without access to toileting and personal grooming facilities, it is difficult to present a clean appearance for job interviews. Organizations such as Dress for Success and government programs exist to help persons who are unemployed and homeless attain employment, through outreach to improve grooming and professional appearance.

Immigrants and Refugees

The Center for Immigration Studies reported in 2002 that 11.5% of the United States' total population was composed of immigrants. At that time, 30% of U.S. immigrants lacked a completed high school education. Immigrants are two-thirds more likely than U.S. natives to live in poverty. The poverty rate for natives in 2002 was 10.6%, whereas it was 17.6% for immigrants. At that time, 24.5% of immigrant families utilized government aid (Camarota, 2002). Figure 2.15 illustrates that the ratios haven't changed much in a decade and that naturalized U.S. citizens have a lower poverty rate than noncitizens (U.S. Census Bureau, 2012b).

Figure 2.15: Poverty rates by U.S. citizenship

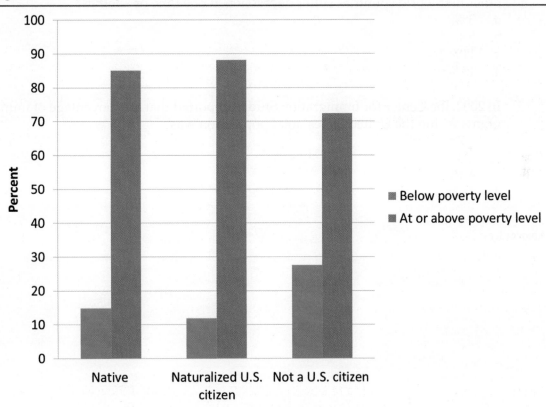

Poverty rates among native and naturalized citizens are similar; however, immigrants are almost three times as likely to live in poverty as American citizens.

U.S. Census Bureau. (2012). Poverty status of population by sex, age, nativity, and U.S. citizenship status: 2009.

Critical Thinking

This chapter discussed the direct relationship between levels of education, income, and health care. Many of the examples showed immediate relationships between these factors. Do you agree with the conclusion that low income is directly related to poor-quality health care?

Self-Check

Answer the following questions to the best of your ability.

1. What percentage of children in households of less than $15,000 annual income experience abuse and neglect?
    a. 22%
    b. 37%
    c. 43%
    d. 79%

2. What percentage of people in France, the United States, the Netherlands, and other first-world countries suffer depression at one time or another?
    a. 3%
    b. 5%
    c. 11%
    d. 15%

3. In 2002, the Center for Immigration Studies reported that the percentage of immigrants within the United States' total population was
    a. 1.7%.
    b. 4.3%.
    c. 9.4%.
    d. 11.5%.

Answer Key

1. a   2. d   3. d

Case Study: Health Care Access for Indigents and Women Blocks Hospital Merger

---

In 2011 a merger was proposed among health care providers operating in Kentucky that would combine Jewish Hospital Healthcare Services, Inc., CHI Kentucky, Inc., Catholic Health Initiatives, University Medical Center, Inc., Jewish Hospital & St. Mary's Healthcare, Inc., Flaget Healthcare, Inc., St. Joseph Health System, Inc., and JH Properties, Inc. The intention of the merger was to create a statewide united health care system (named Kentucky Statewide Network) and consolidate the finances of the organizations to rescue those within the group that were struggling.

Concerns about the merger were raised on the basis that the University of Louisville Hospital, managed by the nonprofit organization University Medical Center, Inc. (UMC), is a publicly owned teaching hospital. As such, the hospital is a public safety net resource, responsible for providing health care access to all persons, including indigents and others who are unable to pay for services. Though all hospitals are legally bound to provide medical care to all people, the merger brought up concerns that financial pressure would limit the hospital from continuing as a public health safety net.

Additional concerns about the merger involved the politically charged and belief-based topic of women's reproductive rights. With the exception of the hospital and UMC, Inc., all organizations involved in the proposed merger were already governed by the Ethical and Religious Directives for Catholic Health Care Services (ERDs). ERDs prohibit certain procedures, including tubal ligations, abortions, and fertility treatments. Under the merger agreement, the publicly funded hospital system and all of its affiliates would also be subject to these restrictions.

Merger proponents claimed that reproductive procedures would be moved off hospital property to other nonaffiliated health care offices. Opponents of the merger argued that the female indigent population would be particularly affected by the new restrictions; as they already lacked health care access, forcing them to go elsewhere for reproductive-related services was both physically and financially restrictive for this vulnerable group.

In the end, Kentucky Governor Steve Beshear refused to allow the merger on Attorney General Jack Conway's (2011) recommendation that the merger be blocked based on accessibility and other concerns regarding the hospital. The merger passed in 2012, without the inclusion of the University of Louisville Hospital and University Medical Center, Inc.

Chapter Summary

It is not enough to talk about vulnerable populations as separate groups with separate problems, risk factors, and needs. All vulnerable groups share many factors, including gender, age, ethnicity, and socioeconomic status. The data helps us to understand what makes these groups vulnerable and who the people we call *vulnerable* are. Poverty is a significant factor for all vulnerable groups because it limits access to resources that have the potential to improve the affected people's quality of life.

Critical Thinking

Vulnerable groups often share many common factors. Do you think there is one single predominant factor that makes groups vulnerable?

Self-Check

Answer the following questions to the best of your ability.

1. What has a significant effect on immigration trends to the United States?
   a. Political and economic strife in other parts of the world
   b. Political and economic strife in the United States
   c. The price of gas in other parts of the world
   d. The price of gas in the United States

2. What is the average income for households with some high school education but no diploma or GED?
   a. $16,454
   b. $25,604
   c. $31,000
   d. $45,650

3. Elder adults with what income level have the highest elder abuse prevalence in all abuse categories?
   a. Under $5,000
   b. $5,000 to $9,999
   c. $10,000 to $19,999
   d. More than $20,000

Answer Key

1. a   2. b   3. b

Additional Resources

Visit the following websites to learn more about the topics covered in this chapter:

Robert Wood Johnson Foundation

http://www.rwjf.org/vulnerablepopulations/

The World Health Organization

http://www.who.int/en/

Urban Institute: Health Policy Center on Vulnerable Populations http://www.urban.org/health_policy/vulnerable_populations/index.cfm

Web Exercise

Choose one of the vulnerable populations mentioned in this chapter, and research the problems and suggested solutions about how industry will meet the needs of these populations. Write a two-page paper with the following information:

- population selected and why you chose that group
- a description of what makes them vulnerable
- the barriers they face in accessing health care
- proposed solutions to assist or remove barriers
- your thoughts on whether or not the solutions suggested are valid and an explanation of your position

Select at least three reputable websites that explain your group's problems in accessing health care and the proposed solutions. These websites must be reputable and reliable (no public editing such as Wikipedia or blogs). Your paper must meet APA standards. The final product will be double-spaced, Times New Roman 12-point font, with appropriate grammar and correct spelling. Be sure to include the websites you visited.

Key Terms

alcoholism Overuse and dependence on alcohol.

binge drinking Five or more drinks per occurrence.

curative medicine Medical practices focusing on curing existing diseases and conditions.

eldercide The killing of persons age 65 and older.

episodic homelessness Recurring, frequent, or ongoing homelessness.

externalizing disorders Mental conditions that lead to outward activities of destruction such as drug abuse and violence.

infanticide The killing of children age 5 and under.

internalizing disorders Mental health conditions that cause emotional responses, such as anxiety disorders and depression.

preventive medicine Medical practice focusing on education and lifestyle choices with the intention of minimizing the risk of illness.

serious mental illness (SMI) Any mental disorder that significantly interferes with daily life.

sudden infant death syndrome (SIDS) The unexplainable death of an infant any time before the first birthday.

transitional homelessness Short-term homelessness.

Why Are Some More Vulnerable Than Others?

Learning Objectives

After reading this chapter, you should be able to:

- Explain social, political, and economic conditions and trends that contribute to the creation of food deserts.

- Evaluate how the population of the United States is changing, and consider how this affects vulnerable populations.

- Analyze how changes in social, political, and economic factors contribute to the vulnerability that represents the haves and have-nots.

- Define social capital and how it is related to health.

- Identify political factors that affect health.

- Recognize economic factors that affect health.

Introduction

Towns and cities have planning and zoning departments within their local government structures. The Planning and Zoning Department is responsible for ensuring that the city infrastructure, including telephone lines, roads, electricity, and water, reaches all necessary areas. It is also responsible for the local codes that keep large retailers like Walmart from moving into residential neighborhoods. Town planning helps minimize traffic on residential streets by creating shopping districts that are near but not in neighborhoods where people live.

Think about how far the nearest grocery store is from your home. Is it within walking distance? If so, how do you transport the groceries home? For many Americans, locating shopping districts outside of neighborhoods creates a need for vehicle transportation from home to the grocer. Many people living in low-income urban housing lack access to cars, and public transportation leaves much to be desired in many cities and is completely absent in many towns. Large retailers need a lot of customers to support the store and a lot of people to staff it. For this reason, many large grocers avoid urban areas and many rural areas where there are not a lot of potential customers nearby, opting instead to set up shop in densely populated suburban areas.

This phenomenon has created a serious problem in many urban areas in cities and small town centers alike. **Food deserts** are residential areas with no readily available access to grocers who carry fresh fruits, vegetables, and meats. Many residents in food deserts subsist mainly on cheap processed foods that they can purchase at mini-marts and gas stations. A diet lacking in fresh healthy foods creates long-lasting health problems. As many food deserts also lack accessible health care, the health of the vulnerable populations in these areas is doubly impacted.

The food desert issue is one of social, political, and economic factors. Socially, these areas have needs, such as access to affordable food, shelter, and clean water, that must be addressed. Politically, it is up to the government to change zoning codes and offer incentives to encourage grocers and health care providers to move into areas in need of access. Economically, it is difficult for retailers and service providers to grow in economically depressed areas. This chapter investigates ways in which social, political, and economic factors increase vulnerability for at-risk populations.

Critical Thinking

Do you live in a food desert? If so, what options do you have for accessing areas with fresh fruits, vegetables, and meats?

Self-Check

Answer the following questions to the best of your ability.

1. Which of the following best describes a food desert?
   a. a physical desert that lacks food
   b. residential areas with no readily available access to grocers who carry fresh fruits, vegetables, and meats
   c. residential areas with no readily available access to water
   d. an economically depressed region

2. Why is it bad to locate shopping districts outside of neighborhoods?
   a. Not everyone has access to transportation.
   b. Locally grown food is more beneficial.
   c. People do not connect as closely with grocers.
   d. People become reliant on junk food.

3. Besides food, what do many food deserts also lack?
   a. gas stations
   b. sanitation
   c. water
   d. health care

Answer Key

1. **b**   2. **a**   3. **d**

3.1 Portrait of the Nation

The population's needs change as the makeup of the population itself changes. The country is evolving as both the country and the populace age. America has long been known as "the melting pot," where many people from different cultures live side by side. Never in the country's history has this been truer than it is today. A more diverse populace has more diverse needs, and it is not surprising that some groups have their needs met more effectively than others.

The U.S. population increased at a rate of 5.3% from 2000 to 2005 (U.S. Census Bureau, 2007). This population growth is attributable to many factors, including more births than deaths, as well as immigration. It is also compounded by the fact that people live longer now than ever before. The baby boomer generation, which includes those individuals born between the years 1946 and 1964, is the largest current generation in the United States. As the baby boomers enter their senior years, America's population portrait is aging along with them. America experienced its highest median age ever at 36.2 on July 1, 2005, and it is expected to increase as the baby boomer generation ages. Average life expectancy is also increasing as medical and health science improves. The average American life expectancy in 1996 was 76 years; it is expected to rise to 82.6 in 2050. The fertility rate is not expected to change much from the current 2.1 births per adult female; therefore, America's population might see a slight decline when the baby boomer generation dwindles with age (U.S. Census Bureau, 2007).

The ethnic makeup of the United States is changing as well. While America's largest race population has historically been Caucasian, census data shows that this population's growth rate slowed to just 1% from 2000 to 2005. In contrast, the African American population experienced a 6% growth rate during this time, which is higher than the national average. The Native American and Alaska Native population grew at 7%. America's Asian population boomed at 20% growth, and the Hispanic population had the highest increase at a rate of 21% (U.S. Census Bureau, 2007). In 2000, Caucasians made up 75.1% of the American population, and African Americans represented 12.3% of the nation's population. By 2010, the percentage of the population identified as Caucasian declined to 72.4%, while African Americans increased to 12.6% of the population. The percentage of the population identified as Asian rose from 3.6% in 2000 to 4.8% in 2010 (U.S. Census Bureau, 2011a). As the population growth rates for minority populations race to catch up with the Caucasian population total, the growth for Caucasians has slowed. This means that Caucasians will not be the majority population in the United States for much longer, and the face of America is becoming increasingly multicultural.

Critical Thinking

The makeup and size of the U.S. population is changing rapidly. What challenges do you predict for the U.S. health care system in the year 2050, assuming that the current trends continue?

Self-Check

Answer the following questions to the best of your ability.

1. What is America's largest race population?
   a. Caucasian
   b. African American
   c. Asian
   d. Hispanic

2. The average American life expectancy is expected to be _____ by 2050.
   a. 76.4
   b. 82.6
   c. 91.3
   d. 88.7

3. In 2010, what percentage of the U.S. population was African American?
   a. 2%
   b. 10%
   c. 10.3%
   d. 12.6%

Answer Key
1. a   2. b   3. d

3.2 How We Live

The makeup of the average American family has changed drastically over the last 40 years. In 1970, 40.3% of the population was married couples with children under age 18. By 2005, this group made up only 23.1% of the population. By 2010, the number of married couples with children under age 18 further declined to 21% (U.S. Census Bureau, 2010). The percentage of married couples without children increased from 53% in 2005 to 58% in 2010 (U.S. Census Bureau, 2012d). The percent of "other family households," composed of single parents, unmarried parents, or extended family households, rose from 10.6% of the population in 1970 to 16.7% in 2005. Populations of men and women living alone have also increased slightly, from 5.6% and 11.6%, respectively, to 11.2% and 15.2%, respectively (U.S. Census Bureau, 2007). Increases were seen in every "other family households" category in the 2010 census, including those with men or women living alone (U.S. Census Bureau, 2012e).

Children under age 18 composed 24% of the 2010 American population (U.S. Census Bureau, 2011b). Although the majority (69%) of children in the United States continue to live with both parents, there has been a significant decline from 85.2% in 1970. The number of children living with one parent continues to favor the mother, at 10.8% of all children in 1970 and 24% in 2009 (U.S. Census Bureau, 2011c). In 1970, 1.1% of children lived with their fathers only. That number rose to 4.8% in 2005 (U.S. Census Bureau, 2007). In 2011, there were 1.7 million single fathers in the United States, representing 15% of all single parents (U.S. Census Bureau, 2012f).

America's changing family structures both contribute to and are affected by the changes in housing, education, and income trends throughout the population. As we will see, the ties between people have significant effects on vulnerability, as social support can help us reach our goals and keep us safe. Where we live and our financial situations also affect vulnerability in terms of resource allocation. Statistically, snapshots of how we live offer insight into the ways in which personal resources—housing, education, and income—limit or increase vulnerability. This understanding allows us to seek ways to address the needs of those most vulnerable.

Courtesy of Dan Barnes/iStockphoto

Almost two thirds of the housing units in the United States in 2005 were separate, single-family units.

Housing

Of the 124.4 million housing units in the United States in 2005, 77.7 million were single-family detached units. Single-family attached units accounted for 7 million housing units. In that year, there were 31 million multifamily units. Owner-occupied homes were the majority, at 62% of all housing units. Renter-occupied units made up 28% of all housing units. The American Housing Survey (AHS) found that owner-occupied units were significantly more likely to be appropriately equipped with housing elements such as safe drinking water, functional plumbing, and cooking appliances.

African Americans are more likely than other ethnic groups to live in housing with severe deficiencies, such as vermin, continuing water leaks, and exposed wiring (10.4%). Hispanics are a close second at 9.2%. Asians and Caucasians live in dwellings with severe deficiencies at rates of 4.6% and 4.4%, respectively (U.S. Department of Housing and Urban Development, 2012).

The U.S. Department of Housing and Urban Development (HUD) works with local housing agencies to provide public housing for low-income individuals and families. HUD estimates that there are around 1.2 million families and individuals living alone that rely on public housing (2012).

Education

Statistics from 2005 show that Caucasians were most likely to graduate from high school, and Asians were a close second (90.1% and 87.6%, respectively). African Americans had a high school graduation rate of 81.1%, while Hispanics were at 58.5% (U.S. Bureau of Labor Statistics, 2012).

The United States experienced a record number of individuals with bachelor's degrees and higher in 2004 and 2005. The Asian population led in postsecondary education completion with 50.2%. Caucasians were a distant second at 30.6%. The gap is smaller between Caucasians and African Americans, who had a 2005 postsecondary education rate of 17.6%. Hispanics had the lowest rate at 12% (U.S. Bureau of Labor Statistics, 2012).

Income and Poverty

It is important to consider inflation and the rise in the cost of living when comparing income across decades. **Real median income** is middle average income level for the United States, adjusted for inflation. America's real median income increased slowly from $35,379 in 1967 to $46,326 in 2005 (U.S. Census Bureau, 2007). Figure 3.1 shows the real median income disparity across America's most prominent ethnic groups.

Figure 3.1: Real median income disparity across ethnic groups

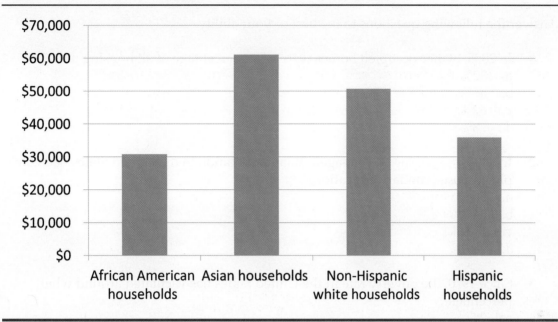

There is a significant disparity between the real median incomes of Asian households and African American households.

U.S. Census. (2010). Retrieved from http://www.census.gov/population/www/pop-profile/files/dynamic/MoneyIncome.pdf

African American households had the lowest median income ($30,900). Asian households had the highest ($61,100). The median for non-Hispanic white households was $50,800. The median for Hispanic households was $36,000 (U.S. Census Bureau, 2007).

Since 1970, the poverty rate in the United States has vacillated around the 12% mark. The number of people living in poverty is significantly higher than the poverty rate and experiences greater variances. The number of Americans living in poverty was lowest during the 1970s, staying around 25 million. By the early 1990s, that number had risen to nearly 40 million people. In 2005, an estimated 37 million Americans were living in poverty (U.S. Census Bureau, 2007).

Critical Thinking

College graduation rates have increased steadily since the 1970s but so, too, have poverty rates. What do these trends tell us about access to education and poverty? Based on what you read, do you see a relationship between income and education?

Self-Check

Answer the following questions to the best of your ability.

1. In 2005, owner-occupied homes were what percentage of all housing units?
    a. 32%
    b. 45%
    c. 62%
    d. 78%

2. In 2005, _____ of the college-aged Asian population in the United States had completed postsecondary education.
    a. 50.2%
    b. 64.3%
    c. 78.9%
    d. 98.6%

3. Since 1970, the poverty rate in the United States has vacillated around what percentage?
    a. 2%
    b. 12%
    c. 23%
    d. 30%

Answer Key

1. **c**   2. **a**   3. **b**

3.3 Social Conditions: Social Capital

Lucinda and Brad are nurses at a large, urban children's hospital. One of their cancer patients, a 9-year-old named Josh, took a turn for the worse and was rushed into surgery to stop internal bleeding. At the end of Lucinda and Brad's work shift, Josh still had not awoken after surgery, and doctors were concerned that he would not make a good recovery. Both nurses left work exhausted and with heavy hearts for a patient they were fond of. Lucinda went home to her toddler and husband. Brad went home to an empty apartment.

Recall from Chapter 1 that social capital is the measure of interpersonal relationships that people have with others; to phrase it differently, social capital is the support network of family and friends who take care of us when we are ill and hug us at the end of a bad day. In the example, Lucinda has more social capital than Brad because Lucinda is able to escape the trials of a bad day at work by enjoying the company of her child and husband through family activities like eating dinner together or playing a game.

Having people to call on to lend a hand when we need assistance is important to every person's physical and emotional well-being. Patients with strong support networks are more likely to recuperate faster and have shorter hospital stays. Parents with family nearby are more likely to enjoy an occasional night out knowing that their children are well cared for in their absence. Caring friends and family can offer shelter or financial help when times are tough. Studies have found that people in at-risk populations generally have less social capital than those who are not generally part of vulnerable populations.

Vulnerable Mothers and Children

Many American children have parents who work outside the home. For working parents, child care is a necessity and can be difficult to maintain. Think back to your childhood. What did you do during the day before beginning primary school? Who did you stay with? Did your parents or guardians pay for that care, or were you cared for by a family member who did not charge for the service? When you fell ill, was a parent able to take off work to stay home with you?

Many people in vulnerable populations lack the type of job stability that allows them to take off work whenever they might be needed at home. This is particularly problematic for single parents. It is difficult to maintain a healthy work-life balance without a strong, supportive social network to fill the gaps left by an absent parenting partner. Single parents who can call on friends and relatives to keep their sick children so they can go to work are more likely to maintain long-term employment.

A look at employment rates of unmarried mothers by race supports the theory that Caucasians are more likely to have more social capital than their peers (Ciabattari, n.d.). Figure 3.2 shows that Caucasian single mothers are more likely to be employed than those of other ethnic groups.

Figure 3.2: Employment rates and ethnicity among single mothers

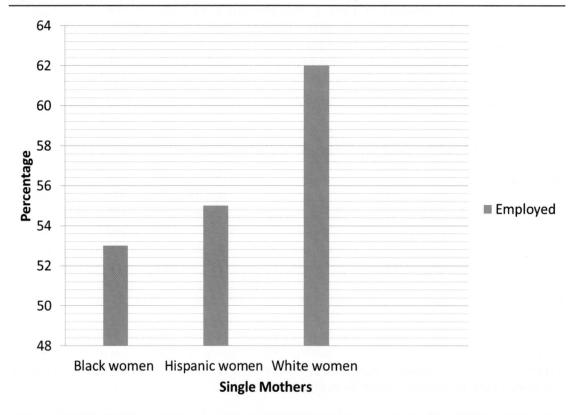

Black and Hispanic single mothers are less likely than their white counterparts to be employed.

U.S. Department of Labor Statistics. (2004). Retrieved from http://www.upjohninst.org/publications/wp/05-118.pdf

Social capital can also affect a person's health care choices. Married mothers are over three times more likely than unmarried mothers to receive prenatal care early and often. Caucasian adults are the group most likely to seek prenatal care during the first trimester. Studies show that Caucasian women are also the ethnic group that rates highest in social capital. A strong, supportive network of friends and family is more likely to encourage a healthy pregnancy and positive attitude than a weak, unsupportive group. In this way, a person's social capital can have a negative effect by discouraging early prenatal care and having negative opinions about the pregnancy. For example, a pregnant 17-year-old in her senior year of high school may feel that her friends no longer want her around, and perhaps that her parents don't want to talk about the pregnancy. This isolating situation may lead the young mother to make unhealthy choices in diet, medical care, and perhaps even in drug use as she strives to act as if she is not pregnant in order to fit in with her peers and pacify or rebel against her parents.

Abused Individuals

One of the earmarks of abuse is withdrawal from friends and family. Abusers often alienate their victims by harassing, bullying, or physically abusing them when they attempt to build or maintain personal relationships. Abuse victims often allow themselves to become isolated out of shame and a reluctance to be found out. Child abuse victims often have a tendency to isolate themselves from adults such as teachers as well as from their peers. Isolation is also a significant factor in the difficulty of reporting elder abuse, as many abused elders have been removed from their homes and away from friends due to physical needs.

Chronically Ill and Disabled Persons

People with strong relationships with others are more likely to maintain healthy lifestyle habits. For example, married men are more likely to eat healthier and get more exercise than

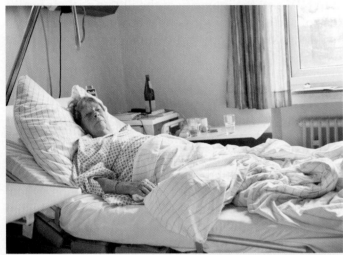

Courtesy of Silvia Jansen/iStockphoto

It can be difficult to preserve social relationships when one suffers from a chronic illness or disability.

their unmarried peers. Women with strong friendships often encourage each other to take time for themselves, keep their bodies healthy, and stay physically fit. The physical rewards of quality relationships mitigate the risk for chronic illness.

Chronic illness and disability can diminish a person's social capital by making it difficult to maintain relationships. A marriage or domestic partnership may suffer if one member is unable to fully participate in the relationship due to chronic illness. Chronic diseases and disabilities can make it difficult for a person to leave home to engage in civic groups and activities or to travel with friends. This can be particularly true with degenerative diseases like multiple sclerosis (MS). MS causes dysfunction of the nervous system, and symptoms can range from shaking to paralysis of the limbs. A 47-year-old woman with MS may once have enjoyed dinners out with friends and romantic weekends away with her partner, but find it increasingly difficult to leave the house as the disease progresses. Missing the fun may add to her feelings of isolation, which contribute to her loss of social capital when she feels disconnected from her friends and partner. When a chronically ill or disabled person is no longer able to engage in activities with friends and family, that person loses social capital as those relationships weaken.

Persons Living With HIV/AIDS

During the 1980s, HIV was stigmatized as a "gay men's" illness. Many families abandoned members upon learning of their HIV positive status, leaving them to rely solely on friends and themselves for help and support as they combated the disease. Though society now knows that HIV affects people of all races, ages, genders, and behaviors, the stigma attached to HIV has only slightly dissipated, in part because men who have sex with men (MSM) are still the demographic with the highest HIV infection rate. Education programs within the lesbian, gay, bisexual, and transgender (LGBT) community focus on lowering the rate of infection, while specialized community health programs work to provide emotional support and help obtain appropriate care for people living with HIV/AIDS.

Though treatments are available to lengthen the life expectancy of HIV/AIDS patients, the disease is fatal. Death usually follows a prolonged period of serious illness, during which the patient's medical care is both costly and time consuming. Many HIV positive children are born to low-income mothers who lack both the financial and social support resources to care for the children. HIV positive adults often lose much of their social support due to both the stigma attached to HIV and the intensity of the illness as their health fails. These factors contribute to a loss of social capital for people diagnosed with HIV/AIDS, which makes dealing with the disease significantly more difficult.

Persons Diagnosed With Mental Conditions

Our relationships with other people help define us. People who lack social capital report higher stress levels and more symptoms of depression and other mental illness than peers with fulfilling social networks. The disruption of the family unit is associated with mental conditions that can last an entire lifetime. Many mental conditions, such as depression, have the negative effect of causing sufferers to withdraw from family and friends. Often, the more a person withdraws, the worse the illness becomes. Maintaining close personal ties is closely associated with mental health. Consider the earlier example of the pregnant 17-year-old. In addition to the stress of being pregnant and a teenager, she also now has the stress of feeling alienated from her friends at a time when her friends should be boosting her self-esteem. All the added stress combined with the loss of close friendships puts her more at risk for developing depression.

Suicide- and Homicide-Liable Persons

Suicide was the 10th leading cause of death in the United States in 2007 at a rate of 11.3 per 100,000 people (National Institute of Mental Health [NIMH], 2007). Risk factors for both suicide and homicide include abusive families, firearms in the home, substance abuse, and mental disorders. The risk of suicide is significantly increased for those who have a family history of suicide.

Bullying increases a young person's suicide risk. This is particularly true for adolescents who identify as LGBT. However, a strong support network of family, friends, and teachers lessens a young person's suicide risk by providing the victim of bullying with the emotional support necessary to maintain his or her positive self-esteem. This is true for people of all ages and in all situations, not only adolescent bullying victims. Feeling valued by others and having somebody to turn to protects against suicide risk factors. More important, a person who is suicidal may have friends who can advise him or her to seek professional help. They may encourage him or her, for example, to contact the National Suicide Prevention Lifeline (1-800-273-TALK), which is available toll free, 24 hours a day.

Courtesy of Mehmet Dislsiz/Fotolia

In 2007, suicide was the 10th leading cause of death in the United States. Risk factors and a disconnect from social interactions and support can increase a person's likelihood of committing suicide.

Loss of close relationships and loved ones, in addition to loss of independence, can cause depression leading to suicide in the elderly.

Homicide rates are similarly associated with a lack of social capital. Disconnection from other people, combined with the trials of economic depression, creates a deficit of social trust that leads to violent crime. Gangs prey on members' needs for social ties and acceptance and encourage violent behavior as a means to earn respect. Low-income areas have a higher rate of familial dysfunction, creating a social situation wherein gangs can thrive and increasing the homicide rates in these areas.

Persons Affected by Alcohol and Substance Abuse

Social capital is closely linked to alcoholism and substance abuse. Evidence exists that a predisposition to alcoholism may be at least partially passed genetically from parent to child. Children who grow up in households where adults abuse alcohol, smoke cigarettes, or use illicit drugs are significantly more likely to do the same in their adulthoods.

Social capital is also linked to substance abuse in terms of emotional and physical support gained from close personal relationships. Many people turn to alcohol and illicit drugs as a coping mechanism to deal with adversity when their needs are not otherwise met. The people who contribute social capital can also be a strong force in overcoming alcohol and drug addictions.

Indigent and Homeless Persons

Social isolation and lack of social capital are earmark characteristics of indigent people. The lack of close social ties contributes directly to the condition of homelessness, as well as to the many risk factors, such as alcoholism and poverty, that can create homelessness. Many teenagers who report homelessness cite abusive living situations as the reason for leaving home. Some of these teens stay for short periods of time with various friends and relatives but never stay in one place for very long. Many others end up in the streets because they lack the social capital to find places to stay, meaning nobody is willing to take them in, care for them, and keep them safe.

Surveys of sheltered homeless report that many adults experiencing homelessness also experienced homelessness or **transient homelessness** in childhood. Transient homelessness is a state of being homeless but staying with friends or family for short periods of time before moving on. The social isolation of indigent people also contributes to difficulty in counting and tracking homelessness in America. Much of the information gathered on the homeless in America comes from surveys of sheltered homeless individuals.

Immigrants and Refugees

Immigrants often leave behind friends and family to come to America. Once here, they must establish new social networks in order to rebuild social capital. Though many informal groups exist to help immigrants connect with others from their home countries, America's immigration policies are a roadblock to building such social networks. As we will discuss in later chapters, many immigrants and refugees live in low-income housing because once they are on American soil, they find a dearth of government resources to help them establish new lives. Additionally, America's social attitudes toward foreign nationals are often isolating.

The mental distress that many refugees experience from having lived through events such as guerrilla warfare that caused them to seek refuge outside their home countries also makes it difficult for them to establish new, meaningful relationships. Many legal immigrants move to the United States to find that they cannot practice their professions in the United States due to licensing regulations (as is often the case for physicians and attorneys). Illegal immigrants face similar challenges, as they attempt to stay under law enforcement's radar. The mental stress of losing income can lead to loss of self-respect and the perceived loss of the respect of one's peers. In addition to legal barriers and barriers to resources, immigrants to America must also overcome language barriers and differing customs to build social capital and the benefits that come with it.

Critical Thinking

How would you rate your social capital? Think about who you would turn to if you found yourself in a predicament. Who could you talk to? Who would you go to for emotional—or even monetary—support?

Self-Check

Answer the following questions to the best of your ability.

1. Which ethnic group is most likely to seek prenatal care during the first trimester?
   a. African American
   b. Asian
   c. Pacific Islander
   d. Caucasian

2. What activity increases a young person's suicide risk?
   a. bullying
   b. Facebooking
   c. dating
   d. drug use

3. Surveys of sheltered homeless report that many adults experiencing homelessness also experienced homelessness at what stage of life?
    a. childhood
    b. early adolescence
    c. early adulthood
    d. infancy

Answer Key

1. **d**   2. **a**   3. **a**

3.4 Political Conditions: Social Status

Social status can improve with higher amounts of social capital and human capital. It can also decline if the same factors decline. A person with a high level of education, reasonable wealth, steady employment, and strong family and friend connections has more social status than a low-income individual with little education and no wealth.

Social status is also tied to age. The very young and the very old hold less social status in our society because they are dependent on others for help with daily living. Race also affects social status, for both socioeconomic reasons and the history of discrimination as well as discriminatory attitudes that still exist in American culture. Gender is tied to social status in much the same way that race is. African Americans were formally given the right to vote by the 15th Amendment in 1870, whereas women did not receive that right until the passing of the 19th Amendment in 1920. This fact alone shows that gender and politics are strongly intertwined.

Vulnerable Mothers and Children

Social status plays a fundamental role in the lives of high-risk mothers and infants. African Americans had the highest rate of teen pregnancy until 2005, when the teen birthrate among the Hispanic population bypassed that of African Americans. Figure 3.3 illustrates recorded teen birthrates by race.

Figure 3.3: Teen births by ethnicity

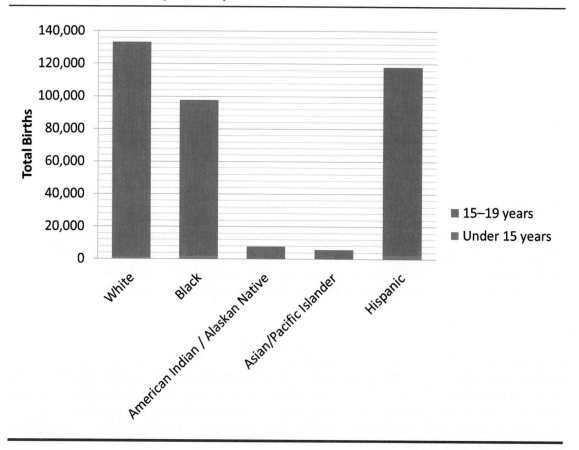

While white, black, and Hispanic teens have similarly high rates of teen pregnancy, American Indian/ Alaska Native and Asian/Pacific Islander teens each give birth to less than 10,000 children each year.

Center for Disease Control and Prevention. (2011). Retrieved from http://www.cdc.gov/nchs/data/nvsr/nvsr60/nvsr60_01.pdf#table15

African Americans have the highest rate of **gestational hypertension**, or high blood pressure during pregnancy (Centers for Disease Control and Prevention [CDC], 2012a). This might be due to a genetic predisposition, but lifestyle choices linked to area of residence cannot be ignored. Many food deserts are in urban areas populated by low-income African Americans, many of whom are high-risk mothers. Unemployment; unsafe housing and neighborhoods; lack of access to fresh fruits, fresh vegetables, and lean meats; and lack of health care access are also all likely contributors to the high fetal mortality rate among African American women. Lack of social status and lack of human capital are closely linked in the lives of high-risk mothers and babies.

Abused Individuals

Abuse is about power and the roles people play within relationships. As discussed, the very young and very old lack social status partly because they depend on others for their daily care. This puts them at a distinct disadvantage within the social structure of any relationship, most especially those with caregivers.

Social workers and clinicians report a significant trend in intimate partner abuse wherein the victim is somehow of lesser social status than the offender. The difference in status may result from financial inequality (for example, the victim is financially dependent upon the abuser) or even from a difference in education levels. Many reports indicate that social ideology about the woman's role in the household (tend the home and children, obey the man), the

Courtesy of Goodshoot/Thinkstock

Society's endorsement of strict gender roles and the way children should behave may contribute to the unbalanced power dynamic that make abusive situations possible.

"right" way for men to act (strong, in control, and domineering), and the way children should behave (seen-not-heard, obedient) contributes to the power disparity that allows for abusive situations to occur.

Chronically Ill and Disabled Persons

The most severely disabled children rely heavily on help from adults to achieve basic activities of daily living, and many continue to do so into adulthood. Chronically ill and disabled adults may find it difficult to maintain employment. The U.S. Census Bureau reports that 9.9% of people ages 16 to 64 in the noninstitutionalized population reported disabilities in 2009 (U.S. Census Bureau, 2007). Of the population reporting disabilities, 17.8% were employed in 2011, compared with 63.6% of the population with no reported disabilities in the same year (U.S. Bureau of Labor Statistics, 2012).

Vulnerable populations are at increased risk for negative outcomes regarding chronic illness and disability. Lack of health care access and the living conditions associated with poverty put vulnerable groups at increased risk for developing chronic illnesses and disabilities. Lack of social and human capital makes it more difficult for them to cope with long-term ailments. In this way, the very young and very old who suffer chronic conditions are particularly vulnerable.

Courtesy of Peeter Viisimaa/iStockphoto

A large number of the people living with HIV/AIDS are minorities. This may be due to the fact that injectable drug use, prevalent in low-income, minority-populated areas, is the second leading cause of HIV/AIDS infection.

Persons Diagnosed With HIV/AIDS

HIV is more prevalent in low socioeconomic urban areas than in neighborhoods with higher levels of education and income. Injection drug users have the second highest HIV/AIDS incidence, and injection drug use is rampant in America's economically depressed areas. The number of minorities living with HIV/AIDS is due to the prevalence of minorities in economically depressed urban areas, as well as the higher rate of injectable drug use among many young minorities. As low-income urban neighborhoods have higher numbers of minority residents, lack of access to preventive education programs and health care increases the HIV/AIDS transmittal rate among the socially and economically disadvantaged.

Persons Diagnosed With Mental Conditions

Childhood events help shape mental health later in life. Children dealing with poverty, family disruption, abuse, chronic illness, or minority group status are more likely to exhibit symptoms of mental illness. Many symptoms of mental conditions first appear in adolescence, a time when young people's bodies and minds are rapidly changing. The Administration for Children, Youth, and Families reports that single mothers raising children in poverty have a particularly high incidence of mental illness due to the stressors associated with their situations.

While situational stressors resulting from social status can induce mental illness, so too can mental illness reduce a person's social status. Withdrawal from friends and family can cause a loss of social capital that contributes to a loss of social status. Maintaining employment can be impossible in cases of severe mental illness. Loss of income and dependency on others for financial support reduces a person's social status.

Suicide- and Homicide-Liable Persons

Social status based on race, gender, education and income levels, and power directly influences violence. Intimate partner abuse is based on the power differences between those in the relationship. Children and the elderly have less social status than people ages 20 to 65, who are more likely to be abusers. Disadvantaged minority groups have higher suicide and homicide rates than members of higher social standing.

Hispanics' moderate suicide rates are attributed to a communal respect for family. Hispanics with risk factors, including substance abuse, mental conditions, low human capital, and broken families, have higher suicide and homicide rates than those with few risk factors.

Suicide and homicide in Alaska Native and Native American communities are associated with broken communities and the disintegration of their traditional cultures and family structures. These communities are plagued with the effects of systemic economic depression. Suicide and homicide risks for this ethnic group include mental illness, family violence, and substance abuse.

Persons Affected by Alcohol and Substance Abuse

Adolescents experience increased risk for experimenting with alcohol and other substances because, at this developmental stage of life, they are testing boundaries and are eager to fit in with their peer group. Adolescents with risk factors, including family violence, poor educational opportunities, and poverty, are significantly more likely to try and to continue use of alcohol, cigarettes, and illicit drugs. The effects of these substances on developing brains add to the likelihood of continued use and considerably negative outcomes.

Courtesy of Digital Vision/Thinkstock

The pressure of adhering to societal gender roles and entertaining an embellished sense of self contributes to a person's likelihood to use alcohol and drugs.

The elderly occupy a similar rung on the social status ladder as adolescents. Though alcoholism and substance abuse rates are lowest among the elderly, access to habit-forming prescription drugs increases their risk of substance abuse. Separation from family and friends, loss of intimate partners and independence, and the depression associated with leaving a lifelong home contribute to alcoholism and substance abuse by the elderly.

Social status associated with gender and ethnicity also contributes to alcohol and substance abuse. Individuals may be influenced by cultural norms to use certain drugs or alcohol, such as Native Americans who use peyote for religious purposes. Similarly, expected gender roles and idealized concepts of self contribute to a person's likelihood to use drugs and alcohol.

Indigent and Homeless Persons

The global economic recession of the early 2000s saw many middle-class Americans lose their jobs and slip into poverty. As people struggled to stay in their homes, a mortgage crisis erupted, fueled by illegal and unethical lending and foreclosure practices. The strain on America's low-income housing programs increased, while government spending on social welfare programs decreased. Becoming unemployed and losing a home creates a loss of social status that affects most aspects of one's life.

Homeless children are particularly vulnerable to deficiencies in health care and poor nutrition. They are also more likely to experience mental distress and have many unexcused school absences. These factors hinder a child's ability to gain a meaningful and complete education, contributing to low human capital later in life.

Like the number of homeless family units, the number of unaccompanied youth is also growing. Counting both those who are part of homeless family units and unaccompanied homeless youth, estimates put the annual number of children experiencing homelessness for at least one night around 1.6 million (Paquette, 2010). Many unaccompanied homeless youth are runaways, but a great many have been expelled from their homes or family units by adults. A majority of these young homeless are fleeing severe mental, physical, and sexual abuse. Abuse is also a driving factor in the homelessness of women and minorities. Once homeless, women become particularly vulnerable to drug abuse, assault, unwanted pregnancies, adverse pregnancy outcomes, and negative health outcomes. Homeless women and children's particular vulnerability creates an even greater social status deficit for these individuals, which greatly increases their risk of disease.

Immigrants and Refugees

Even well-educated immigrants to America experience a loss of social status due to language barriers, cultural differences, and negative social attitudes regarding immigration and particular ethnicities. The loss of social capital caused by leaving one's home country also contributes to a loss of social status. Many refugees find it difficult to subsist in a country where very few people grow their own food and build their own shelter, especially when they come from regions where the ability to do so was the foundation of social status and life. Refugees fleeing wars in Somalia and Liberia often find it difficult to transition to a lifestyle where food comes wrapped in plastic and everybody wants an enormous house.

Female refugees are particularly vulnerable, as many are uneducated and do not speak English at all. Refugee women and children often suffer severe emotional distress caused by the brutality from which they are fleeing. Depression as well as language and education barriers make it difficult to build new relationships and access programs and resources that ease the strain of building a life in a foreign place. As many refugees come from impoverished regions, they often arrive with serious health care needs. The American health care system is particularly difficult to navigate if you do not speak its language.

Critical Thinking

Mental illness, family violence, and substance abuse are contributing risk factors of suicide in Alaska Natives and Native Americans. Based on what you have read, why do you think these are higher factors for Alaska Natives and Native Americans than for other ethnic groups?

Self-Check

Answer the following questions to the best of your ability.

1. Because they depend on others for their daily care, the very young and the very old lack what kind of status?
    a. economic
    b. political
    c. social
    d. familial

2. Injection drug users have the second highest rate of _____
    a. HIV/AIDS.
    b. suicide.
    c. infant mortality.
    d. homelessness.

3. Even well-educated immigrants to America experience a loss of social status due to what type of barriers?
    a. political
    b. economic
    c. physical
    d. language

Answer Key

1. c   2. a   3. d

3.5 Economic Conditions: Human Capital

An individual's human capital is measured by level of completed education, employment status and position, and living conditions. These factors are tied together because a person's ability to maintain a high-paying job increases relative to how much he or she has invested in his or her education. For example, consider the fact that a child's ability to learn during the school day is directly tied to both the condition of the school and the education offered, which are both tied to society's investment in the school by way of government funding. For both children and adults, public and private investment in the living conditions of neighborhoods and housing units deeply affects all aspects of life, from the ability to focus during the school day to the ability to maintain viable employment. Economic conditions directly affect human capital, and vice versa.

Vulnerable Mothers and Children

Human capital is directly linked to the timing and quality of prenatal care, the ability of the mother to recuperate after the birth, and the ability of the mother to care for the infant. Low-income regions have a lower rate of early and sufficient prenatal care than wealthier areas. Mothers living at or below the poverty line are significantly less likely to receive any prenatal care at all. A 1988 study found that only 53% of expectant mothers with less than a high school diploma sought early prenatal care, compared with 92% of expectant mothers with at least some college education (CDC, 2012c).

Abused Individuals

Though abused individuals exist at all socioeconomic levels, there is a direct causal relationship between poverty and lack of education and reported abuse. This is thought to be due to the additional stresses associated with inadequate housing and food, the perils of dangerous neighborhoods, and increased violence and drug abuse rates in low-income neighborhoods. The risk of abuse increases when the offender has more education and income than the victim, as the disparity in human capital causes a disparity in social status.

Chronically Ill and Disabled Persons

America's public school systems are intended to provide education for all children, regardless of aptitude. Most public schools offer specialized programs for children with disabilities. The focus of these programs is basic knowledge and daily living skills rather than the dissemination of advanced theories and thought processes. In this way, America invests in the education of disabled children. America also invests in disabled individuals through the Social Security system. The **Supplemental Security Income program (SSI)** provides financial support for disabled citizens. However, that program pays very little. Most people who depend on SSI also rely on government aid for housing and food. As poverty puts people more at risk for developing chronic illness and disabilities, conditions which in turn contribute to personal poverty, health vulnerability poses a particularly distressing situation for at-risk populations. More investment in human capital by way of neighborhood improvements and education funding for low-income neighborhoods is necessary to stop this cycle.

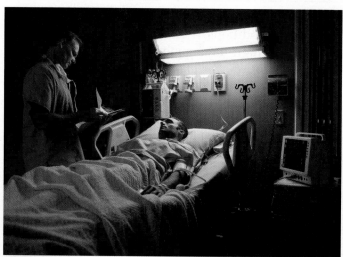

Courtesy of Thomas Norcut/Thinkstock

Federal funds and resources are available to help people living with HIV/AIDS.

Persons Diagnosed With HIV/AIDS

The financial cost of HIV/AIDS treatments is unmanageable for many patients, even those with health insurance coverage. However, treatments are more effective and less costly the earlier they are begun (U.S. Department of Health and Human Services, Agency for Health Care Research and Quality, 2011). Though the civil rights bill specifically forbids termination from a job based on HIV status, the effects of the disease can make it difficult to maintain employment. As many HIV/AIDS patients belong to low-income vulnerable groups, education and income levels were likely low before the onset of the disease. Low-paying jobs and loss of employment put people at risk for losing health insurance coverage and health care access.

The United States offers several federally funded resources to help those living with HIV/AIDS. Low-income HIV/AIDS patients are eligible for both housing assistance and disability-based income assistance through the federal government. The **Ryan White HIV/AIDS Program**, administered by the Health Resources and Services Administration, provides funding to states and community-based organizations to improve health care access and provide life-saving medications for HIV/AIDS patients in low-income areas.

A Closer Look: National HIV/AIDS Strategy

President Barack Obama implemented the National HIV/AIDS Strategy (NHAS) on July 13, 2010. NHAS was implemented to reduce the amount of new HIV infections annually, restrict the HIV transmittal rate, and improve health care access for those living with HIV/AIDS. For information on ways NHAS is addressing the HIV/AIDS epidemic, visit the White House Office of National AIDS Policy NHAS website at http://www.aids.gov.

Persons Diagnosed With Mental Conditions

Mental illness is more prevalent among low-income groups, but the causal relationship between poverty and mental illness is uncertain. The **social stress theory** posits that the stressors experienced by low socioeconomic groups—inadequate housing, drug abuse, neighborhood crime, lack of education, and unemployment and underemployment—cause mental health disorders. The opposing argument is the **social selection theory**, which argues that mental illness causes people to fall into low socioeconomic status.

Generally speaking, both theories are correct. The problems caused by poverty cause high stress levels, which can lead to adverse mental health outcomes. At the same time, the onset of mental illness can cause a person to withdraw from society and have difficulty maintaining gainful employment, causing the individual to lose socioeconomic status.

Suicide- and Homicide-Liable Persons

Low income and education levels can create competition for resources, including affordable housing and jobs. Many low-income neighborhoods lack the human capital necessary for improvement and, as such, experience a faster rate of deterioration than higher socioeconomic areas. As businesses vacate economically depressed regions, they take employment opportunities with them, further limiting investment in the community. This trend correlates to urban ghettoization, which in turn correlates to increased violence.

Suicide among males is nearly four times the rate of suicide among females (CDC, 2010). Native American and Alaska Native males have the highest suicide rate, which is attributed to social beliefs and low socioeconomic status within those cultures (CDC, 2012b). Caucasian males have the second highest suicide rate, which is attributed to internalized frustration and a perceived loss of power in response to changing social expectations.

In contrast, African American males of the same age group are more likely to externalize frustrations with the social deficits in education and employment opportunities plaguing this group. This externalization contributes to increased homicide rates among African American males. Rates of violent crime types differ between ethnic groups, partially due to the internalizing versus externalizing responses to social constraints and the issues facing different ethnic groups (see Figure 3.4).

Figure 3.4: Violent crime by ethnic group

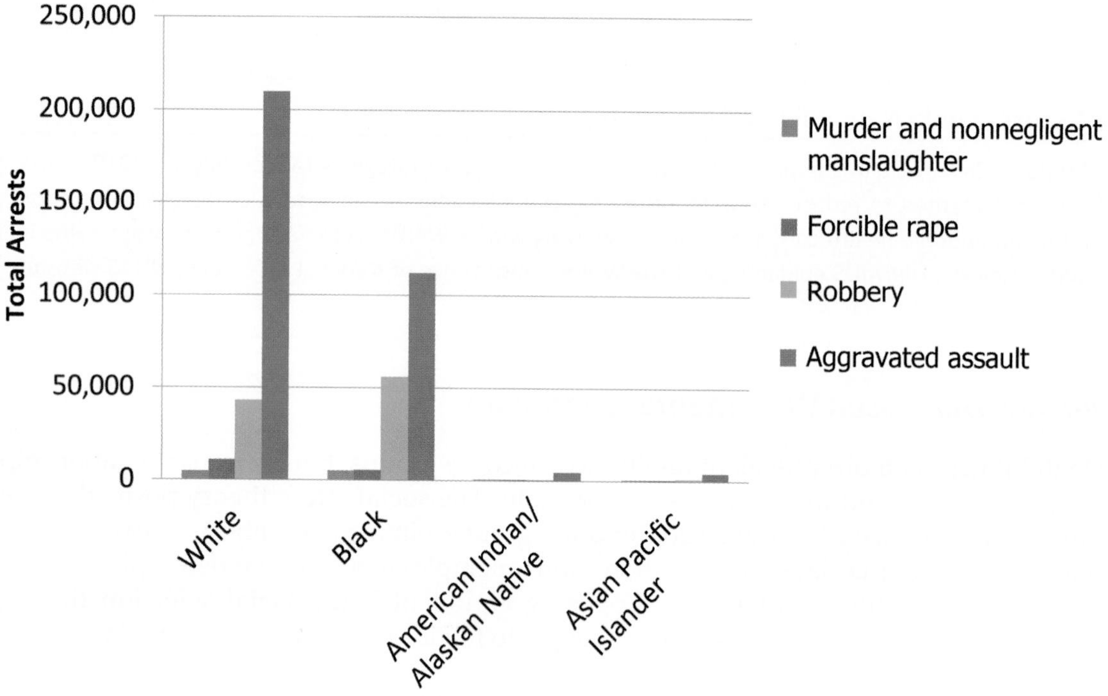

Aggravated assault is the most commonly committed violent crime across all ethnic groups.

U.S. Census. (2012). Retrieved from http://www.census.gov/compendia/statab/2012/tables/12s0325.pdf

Persons Affected by Alcohol and Substance Abuse

Varying levels of human capital contribute to differences in alcohol and drug abuse. Cigarette use is inversely related to education and income levels. The opposite is true with alcohol use, which increases with education and income levels (CDC, 2012c). Different illicit drugs are favored by members of different socioeconomic groups. In the 1980s, cocaine was associated with wealth, whereas crack continues to be more accessible to those of low socioeconomic standing. Methamphetamine is thought of as "a poor man's drug" because it is inexpensive to make. However, it is so highly addictive that methamphetamine use is growing among all socioeconomic groups.

Substance abuse is higher in economically depressed areas where underemployment and unemployment are rampant. The causal relationship between employment status and drug abuse is multidirectional. Substance abuse can create an environment where gainful employment cannot be maintained. It is also used by many as a coping mechanism for dealing with economic disparity and the loss of self-esteem associated with underemployment and unemployment.

A Closer Look: Monitoring Methamphetamine

The National Survey on Drug Use and Health began monitoring school-age children for methamphetamine use in 1999. As Figure 3.5 shows, reported methamphetamine use is declining among American children. This positive trend is attributable in part to preventive education programs that aim to keep children from trying methamphetamine even once. These programs are important because methamphetamine is highly addictive, and many addicted users claim to have become addicted after just one use (National Institute on Drug Abuse [NIDA], 2010).

Figure 3.5: Methamphetamine prevalence of abuse among 8th to 12th graders

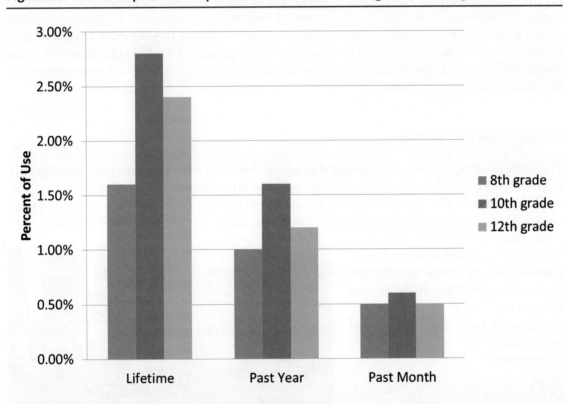

10th graders have a higher incidence of methamphetamine use than 8th or 12th graders across all three measured time periods.

National Institute on Drug Abuse [NIDA]. (2010). Retrieved from http://www.drugabuse.gov/publications/infofacts/methamphetamine

Indigent and Homeless Persons

A trend has been established that differentiates the current condition of homelessness from the homeless experience between 1950 and 1970. During that time, a majority of homeless people did have shelter, however inadequate it might have been. As the homeless rate increases and government spending on social welfare programs struggles to keep up, the current homelessness experience is significantly more likely to involve actually sleeping outdoors.

America's subsidized low-income housing has aged, and little has been done to remedy the inadequacies of faulty wiring, disintegrating roofs, and rusted plumbing. Instead of renovating crumbling structures, much of America's low-income housing has been demolished to make way for trendy, new urban homes for the upper-middle class. This is directly responsible for the diminished availability of affordable housing in socioeconomically depressed neighborhoods.

At the same time that America's low-income housing began being replaced by more expensive options, federal funding for social welfare programs and housing subsidies began a steady decline. Housing subsidies were cut 80% from 1980 to 1989. State and federal governments have continued to struggle with paying for housing subsidies and other social welfare programs, while tax income has decreased due to rampant unemployment and corporate tax incentives.

Immigrants and Refugees

There are essentially three immigrant statuses in America. **Overdocumented immigrants** have official refugee status. This term reflects the large amount of screening and paperwork required of this group to prove the health status and the ability to support themselves. **Undocumented immigrants** are often referred to as "illegal aliens" and have not completed the official immigration process. **Documented immigrants** have come to the United States through legal channels but have not had to undergo the rigorous level of screening experienced by refugees or overdocumented immigrants.

Of these three types, undocumented immigrants have the least amount of human capital. Many cross the border from Mexico to escape that country's violent drug war and seek employment. In response, the U.S. federal government seeks to control illegal immigration through the 1986 Immigration Reform and Control Act.

Courtesy of Richard Thronton/Shutterstock

Undocumented immigrants lack much of the human capital necessary to feel productive and included in society.

The flow of illegal immigration into the United States and frustration over current federal immigration laws have resulted in many states, including Arizona, enacting laws to address the increasing number of illegal immigrants in their states. In 2010, the Arizona legislature enacted stringent immigration laws. The Arizona law does not allow law enforcement officers to stop someone just to check on documentation papers, but officers may ask for documentation papers if someone is stopped for some other violation of the law. Suspected illegal immigrants are turned over to the Federal Immigration Services. In response to Arizona legislation, President Obama called on Congress to overhaul federal immigration laws that would clearly restrict state powers regarding illegal immigration.

Even as Americans argue over immigration law, undocumented immigrants continue to hold the country's lowest paying, least desirable jobs. Many work in hot, dusty fields as agricultural day laborers. They are paid in cash and are not provided with any stability, security, or benefits. Still, many seek the shelter of America's slums over the bloodshed and economic instability of their home countries.

Critical Thinking

Arizona's 2010 immigration law has become a hotly debated topic. Do you think states or the federal government should have authority over enforcing immigration violations?

Self-Check

Answer the following questions to the best of your ability.

1. Among young people aged 15–24, almost six times more males than females commit what act?
   a. murder
   b. rape
   c. suicide
   d. abandonment

2. What directly affects human capital?
   a. economic conditions
   b. political conditions
   c. weather conditions
   d. stock market conditions

3. Which group of immigrants has the least amount of human capital?
   a. overdocumented immigrants
   b. undocumented immigrants
   c. married immigrants
   d. female immigrants

Answer Key

1. c   2. a   3. b

Case Study: Food Deserts Put Children at Risk for Lifelong Health Problems

Courtesy of cheitt/fotolia

Neighborhoods without access to fresh fruits, vegetables, meat, and other healthy foods are known as food deserts.

It's 8:00 on a humid Saturday morning in August, and a group of volunteers is gathering with spades, shovels, buckets, and gardening gloves. Their mission: Build a community garden that will both provide a source of fresh produce in a low-income neighborhood and teach local residents how they can improve their health with a little effort and a lot of sunlight. As they work, children walk over to stare and wonder. The volunteers invite the kids over and begin explaining how to grow tomatoes. The children's mothers arrive, checking on their little ones, and the gardeners take advantage of the opportunity to engage the resident adults in the community garden. The volunteers explain that not only will the garden provide fresh, healthy food, but those who contribute to the work will also be engaging in pleasant exercise as they till and weed.

These volunteers are part of a nationwide movement to improve eating and exercise habits across the nation, and especially in underserved areas. Teaching healthy eating habits is fundamental to progress as America works to do away with food deserts and combat childhood obesity. Community programs, such as Food is Elementary, and urban gardens work to encourage children to make healthy eating choices and to help their families do the same. Simply building grocery stores in low-income neighborhoods is not enough. Healthy eating habits are much like the old adage, "You can lead a horse to water, but you can't make him drink." That is why First Lady Michelle Obama's Let's Move! campaign worked not only to encourage children and adults to adopt healthier lifestyles, but also funded public programs that gave people the skills to make healthy lifestyle choices and positively affected public policy that increased access to fresh fruits and vegetables to residents in low-income areas.

Most of America's food deserts are located in low-income areas. A study published in Rural Sociology in 2009 studied the body mass index (BMI) of students living in identified food deserts in rural Pennsylvania. Researchers found students who reside in identified food deserts have a higher rate of obesity than their peers who live in non food desert areas (Schafft, Jensen, & Hinrichs, 2009).

This research drives home the fact that food deserts do not completely lack access to food of any sort. Rather, food deserts are marked by a lack of fresh, healthy foods. Convenience stores that stock processed foods with long shelf lives do exist in food deserts. So, too, do fast-food restaurants that serve processed meals, which are high in fat, sugar, and cholesterol.

A diet that relies on high-fat, processed food is more likely to create obesity than a diet rich in fresh fruits, fresh vegetables, and lean meats. Obesity contributes to a range of health problems, including heart disease, diabetes, and arthritis. Childhood obesity predisposes America's youth to chronic diseases early in life. As eating habits are difficult to change, it is likely that the overweight children of today will grow into obese adults. Obesity, and the health risks associated with it, puts an increasing strain on America's health care delivery system.

Chapter Summary

Negative health outcomes are caused by factors on both micro and macro levels of society. Social capital refers to the social factors and resources that people rely on for emotional support and help through hard times. Close family ties can alleviate stress, lessening the risk of developing mental conditions. Strong social networks provide help with everything from child care to finding gainful employment. The political factors that affect health are based on the social status of the individual and the groups they are associated with. Women, children, and the elderly are particularly vulnerable regarding social status factors. Human capital is greatly enhanced by high levels of social status, as higher social-status groups generally have more education and income to invest in themselves and others. There is a defined spectrum of social, political, and economic factors and vulnerability that represents the haves and have-nots.

Critical Thinking

Community gardens have been one response to the food desert issue, but in most locations, gardens are not a year-round solution. Water availability can also be a major obstacle. If you had the power to make real and substantial changes to increase access to fresher and healthier foods in a food desert community, what would you do and why?

Self-Check

Answer the following questions to the best of your ability.

1. The average American life expectancy is expected to rise to 82.6 in 2050. True or false?
   a. True
   b. False

2. During the 1980s, HIV was stigmatized as what type of illness?
   a. "single man's" illness
   b. "old man's" illness
   c. "gay man's" illness
   d. "married man's" illness

3. Which two communities are associated with high suicide risk due to broken communities and the disintegration of their traditional cultures and family structures? (Select two.)
   a. Hispanic
   b. Alaska Native
   c. Native American
   d. Caucasian

4. Which social ideologies contribute to the power disparity that allows for abusive situations to occur? (Select three.)
    a. gun ownership as an exercise of the right to bear arms
    b. the woman's role in the household (tend the home and children, obedience to the man)
    c. the "right" way for men to act (strong, in control, and domineering)
    d. political beliefs (Republican or Democrat)

5. Tax income for housing subsidies and welfare programs has decreased due to what factor(s)?
    a. rampant unemployment
    b. corporate tax incentives
    c. understaffed government housing offices
    d. A and B only

6. First Lady Michelle Obama started the _____ campaign to encourage healthier lifestyles.
    a. Let's Move!
    b. Walk Your Dog!
    c. Smart Choices
    d. Chefs in Schools

Answer Key

1. **a**   2. **c**   3. **b** and **c**   4. **a**, **b**, and **c**   5. **d**   6. **a**

Additional Resources

Visit the following websites to learn more about the topics covered in this chapter:

Food is Elementary program

http://www.foodstudies.org/images/stories/hopkins%20article.pdf

First Lady Michelle Obama's Let's Move campaign

http://www.letsmove.gov/

USDA's interactive food desert map

http://www.ers.usda.gov/data-products/food-desert-locator/go-to-the-locator.aspx

Web Exercise

Using the three websites listed in this section, discuss the following in a two-page paper

- Define and identify a food desert and what criteria the USDA uses to determine where food deserts are located. (http://www.ers.usda.gov/data/fooddesert/documentation.html)
- What progress has been made regarding whether food deserts are problematic in the United States? (http://www.npc.umich.edu/news/events/food-access/final_bitler_haider.pdf)
- Discuss alternative solutions. (http://www.economist.com/node/18929190)

Key Terms

documented immigrant An immigrant who has come to the United States through legal channels but has not had to undergo the rigorous level of screening experienced by refugees or overdocumented immigrants.

food deserts Residential areas without readily available access to grocers who carry fresh fruits, vegetables, and meats.

gestational hypertension High blood pressure during pregnancy.

overdocumented immigrant A legal immigrant to the United States that has official refugee status.

real median income The middle average income level for the United States, adjusted for inflation.

Ryan White HIV/AIDS Program A federal program administered by the Health Resources and Services Administration that provides funding to states and community-based organizations to improve health care access and provide life-saving medications for HIV/AIDS patients in low-income areas.

social selection theory The argument that mental illness causes people to fall into low socioeconomic status.

social stress theory The argument that the stressors experienced by low socio-economic groups cause mental health conditions.

Supplemental Security Income program (SSI) A federal program administered by the Social Security administration that provides financial support for disabled citizens.

transient homelessness A state of homelessness wherein the affected individuals move from home to home, often staying with various family or friends for short periods of time before moving on.

undocumented immigrant Often referred to as "illegal aliens," immigrants from countries outside the United States or its territories who have not completed the official immigration process.

4

Seeking an Effective Care Continuum

Learning Objectives

After reading this chapter, you should be able to:

- Identify programs that address the health issues surrounding workplace accidents.

- Assess the need for a continuum of care that comprises a comprehensive approach to health care for vulnerable populations.

- Identify the preventive care services available to vulnerable populations.

- Examine the treatment services available to vulnerable populations.

- Explain the options that vulnerable populations have for accessing long-term care.

Introduction

Workplace injuries, deaths, and work-related illnesses cost the United States approximately $693.5 billion a year (National Safety Council, 2009). The **Occupational Safety and Health Administration (OSHA)**, established in 1970, ensures safe and healthy working conditions for men and women by setting standards and providing training, outreach, and education. In other words, OSHA focuses on the prevention of injuries by regulating the workplace.

In contrast, **workers' compensation** programs, which are administered through the Department of Labor, help workers who have already sustained a work-related injury or an occupational disease. These programs focus on wage replacement, medical treatment, and rehabilitation services coverage. Employers pay into the workers' compensation programs through companies that work to mitigate costs to insurance companies, called **insurance underwriters**, or government programs to help cover these expenses. Although paying into the national workers' compensation program represents a significant expense for employers, lost employee productivity is more costly. To minimize workers' compensation and lost productivity expenses, many employers have preventive workplace safety programs that include educational sessions on safety and even posters with images and safety messages to remind workers of best practices for safety. These preventive programs aim to minimize risks both to the workers and the employers. Some of these programs are available through OSHA, the national programs for workers' compensation, or their company insurance or liability underwriter.

Workplace safety programs and workers' compensation programs provide a continuum to address the health issues surrounding workplace accidents. From prevention to treatment to rehabilitation to return-to-work, workplace safety and workers' compensation programs address the specific health care needs of America's working population. This is one example of the way a continuum of care works and how programs can work together to create a continuum of care. Every population group can benefit from a strong continuum of care, but America's most vulnerable populations often have particular needs that are best met with a quality care continuum. This chapter discusses the need for an effective continuum of care and the existing programs that provide this type of continuum of care for America's vulnerable populations.

Critical Thinking

OSHA provides many programs to ensure workers' health and safety. Is there a similar program for health care elsewhere? If not, could OSHA be used as a model to create or redesign existing programs?

Self-Check

Answer the following questions to the best of your ability.

1. According to the 2009 National Safety Council, what cost the United States approximately $693.5 billion?
   a. DWI prosecution
   b. workplace injuries and illnesses
   c. health care fraud
   d. immigration services

2. Which types of programs help workers affected by workplace accidents?
   a. substance abuse counseling
   b. legal advice
   c. workers' compensation
   d. financial planning

3. Employers pay into workers' compensation programs through _____, which work to mitigate costs to insurance companies.
   a. insurance underwriters
   b. employees
   c. federal agencies
   d. undocumented immigrants

Answer Key

1. **b**   2. **c**   3. **a**

4.1 The Need for an Effective Continuum of Care

An effective **continuum of care** ensures access to preventive health services, treatment services, and long-term care services. These three types of health care do not function independently; rather, each is reinforced or weakened by the quality of the others, with treatment services in the central position. A solid continuum of care should be available throughout a person's life.

There is a push in the American health care system to increase access and use of **preventive care services**, which are medically related and medically based services that focus on maintaining health. These services range from patient education on healthy lifestyle choices, to medical and commonsense aids to help patients make healthy choices. For example, smoking cessation programs offer preventive care in the form of education on the risks of smoking while enabling patients to quit through support groups and pharmaceutical smoking cessation aids. Preventive care is vital for reducing the cost of health care in the nation, as it is less expensive than treatment and long-term care services. Maintaining physical health also improves quality of life and keeps people in the workforce.

Although physicians play an important role in prevention, preventive services in the United States more frequently come from community-based health services and resource development. **Treatment services** are delivered by physicians and the health care delivery system, which includes clinics, doctors' offices, hospitals, and long-term care facilities. The goal of treatment services is to restore health to ailing individuals. **Long-term care**, on the other hand, focuses on the constant, ongoing health care needs of individuals. It is delivered through both community-based programs, such as Hospice, and institutional settings, such as nursing facilities and assisted living facilities.

Courtesy of WavebreakMediaMicro/Fotolia

An effective continuum of care consists of three elements: access to preventive health services, treatment services, and long-term care services.

In an effective care continuum, each type of care works in tandem with the others to maximize patient physical and psychological functions. Unfortunately, these programs are often systemically divided in a sort of "left hand doesn't know what the right hand is doing" situation. For example, a woman might visit a gynecologist for annual preventive care but see a family practitioner when she gets sick. Unless they are located in the same office, the family practitioner does not have access to the patient's records from the gynecologist's office. In this way, the patient's preventive medicine and treatment services lack communication between the two, so each is ignorant of what the other is doing. For the care continuum to be truly effective, prevention, treatment, and long-term care must be integrated and accessible.

Access to preventive services is subject to the limiting factors associated with most community-based health resources, among which funding ranks highest. Many community-based health resources are only partially funded by the legislature and rely heavily on private donations. Both funding sources diminish during economic downturns, limiting what an agency is capable of providing. Similarly, financial constraints keep people from seeking medical attention when it is needed, and certainly there are many people with and without health insurance coverage who cannot afford to see a physician for preventive care. When community health resources cannot fill the gap, where are people to turn for health care?

A Closer Look: Community Health Departments

Community Health Departments exist to help fill the need for accessible, affordable health care. Unfortunately, many people are unaware of the wide array of services offered at public clinics. Still others avoid them for fear of costly services; however, Community Health Departments provide services at significantly lower rates than many other options.

An effective care continuum reduces medical costs, allowing community-based services to serve more people. It also reduces the need for treatment and long-term care services by maintaining health rather than treating illness. Building an effective, integrated care continuum that will reduce vulnerability for those most at risk means considering the strengths and shortcomings of existing programs.

Critical Thinking

There are many benefits associated with preventive care services. Can you think of a disadvantage?

Self-Check

Answer the following questions to the best of your ability.

1. Where do preventive services in the United States frequently come from?
   a. long-term care facilities
   b. hospitals
   c. physicians
   d. community-based health services

2. Which of the following is a typical challenge for preventive services?
   a. need
   b. access to population
   c. costs
   d. effectiveness

3. Which of the following is a main advantage to building an effective care continuum?
   a. reducing medical costs
   b. researching vaccination usefulness
   c. providing surgeries to newborns
   d. treating common illnesses

Answer Key

1. **d**   2. **c**   3. **a**

4.2 Health Maintenance Through Preventive Care Services

Vulnerability in the United States is rooted in poverty and social attitudes that determine how resources are distributed among the population. These attitudes have changed dramatically in the last six decades, from being a top concern among the people and government to being marginalized and defunding programs that address vulnerability. America's national poverty rate was 19% in 1964. President Lyndon B. Johnson created the War on Poverty in response to the nation's high poverty rate. The War on Poverty brought about the Economic Opportunity Act and the U.S. Office of Economic Opportunity, which served to address the reasons for poverty in the country at that time.

Courtesy of soupstock/Fotolia

As America shifted to a smaller federal role and decentralized government services in the 1970s, social attitudes about welfare programs began to change.

Social attitudes about welfare programs began to change in the 1970s. America began a shift to a smaller federal role and decentralized government services by giving the states more power to administer social welfare programs. America began to rely more heavily on an economy based on open competition among corporations with limited government regulation to address social needs. During the shift to an increasingly **free market economy**, the country experienced inflation and recession throughout the 1970s and 1980s. In doing so, programs such as the early childhood education program Head Start and Community/Migrant Health Centers, which provides health care access for low-income individuals, continue to lose funding, and, thereby, are increasingly limited in the services they can offer.

The economy and unemployment rate improved during the 1990s. However, there was a considerable increase in the number of low-wage jobs during that decade. During this time, income-assistance programs continued to lose government funding and were increasingly disadvantaged in the face of **inflation**, or the loss of currency value. The savings and loan, economic housing, and technology bubbles widened the gap between groups of different income levels, or **socioeconomic classes**, and the free market failed to provide adequately for the vulnerable. When those economic bubbles burst under the presidency of George W. Bush in the early 2000s, the American middle class slipped further down the socioeconomic ladder. The Great Recession of 2008 caused millions of Americans to lose their jobs and their homes—and increased the strain on underfunded social welfare programs.

Clear evidence exists that public health issues are rooted in politics and economics. However, social attitudes about health care and the free market encourage a primary focus on microlevel, or personal, behaviors and environments. Experts on health care delivery have suggested that focusing on the microlevel is not enough to mitigate the negative health outcomes that come from socioeconomic disadvantage, but that changes must be made at the sociopolitical macrolevel, in all society, in order to address the lack of organization, quality management, and funding that plagues public health organizations and initiatives.

Declining funding amounts for public prevention services and the sociopolitical attitudes that ignore the need for such services create additional strain on the private health care sector. The private sector historically focuses on treatment and often leaves health education and prevention to the public sector. In fact, a 2011 study published in the *Archives of Internal Medicine* found that many primary care physicians are reluctant to broach the subject of weight with patients, although patients are more likely to show motivation to lose weight when their doctors bring it up (Post et al., 2011). Additional problems with private sector, treatment-based health care include financial and organizational barriers that affect vulnerable groups in particular, leaving an unfulfilled need for preventive health education and services in the gap between the public and private sector access venues.

Vulnerable Mothers and Children

Preventive services are fundamental for the healthy development of children. Prenatal care focuses on prevention services to support healthy pregnancy and birth outcomes. Many government-funded programs support high-risk women and children through pregnancy and the early years of child-rearing (see Table 4.1).

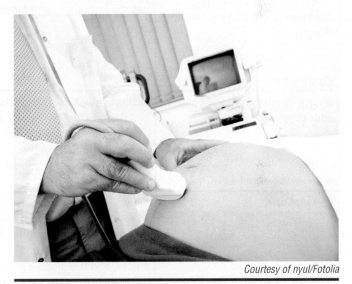

Courtesy of nyul/Fotolia

Title X of the Public Health Service Act focuses on providing health care and prevention services access to high-risk women and children.

Table 4.1: Preventive services available to high-risk mothers and children

Program	Pros	Cons
Maternal and Child Health (MCH) The Program for Children with Special Health Care Needs Title X of the Public Health Service Act	Focus on providing health care and prevention services access to high-risk women and children.	Federal funding continues to diminish by way of budget cuts and inflation.
Special Supplemental Food Program for Women, Infants, and Children (WIC) Food Stamp Program	Provide nutrition support services for qualifying families.	Federal funding is channeled through the states in block grants, which do not guarantee exact monies for specific programs. The Great Recession of 2008 increased dependence on these programs while funding from both the federal and state levels diminished.
Maternity and Infant Care Projects Community and Migrant Health Centers National Health Services Corp Planned Parenthood	Provide access to physicians and nurse practitioner clinics for low-income individuals and families.	Social attitudes about family planning and abortion services plague these groups, diminishing political support and funding.
School-based behavioral risk education programs	Encourage healthy lifestyle habits and risk prevention regarding smoking, sexual activity, and healthy eating within the structure of the educational system.	Many of the teachers are not qualified to teach some special topics. Many parents opt their children out of special topic education programs such as sex education.
Prenatal care	Allows for prevention services, screenings, and treatment services simultaneously. Prenatal care is provided in physicians' offices, and the mother often has control over her physician selection.	Though many women have health insurance to help offset the costs of prenatal care, it is expensive. Many high-risk mothers lack health care coverage and depend on public programs for prenatal care, which diminishes their autonomy.
The Early and Periodic Screening, Diagnosis, and Treatment (EPSDT) program	Covers early childhood physician services, including immunizations and screening services for Medicaid recipients.	Approximately half of eligible children receive these services. Program funding is endangered by budget cuts, inflation, and increased need.
Head Start	Provides health programs, preschool access, and social services to low-income preschool-age children.	Funding for this program is diminishing. Low enrollment numbers indicate a problem with accessibility.

Abused Individuals

Aggression is rooted in the human social structure, where power is gained by removing the competition and those with power are able to dominate those they view as inferior. Preventive services for abused individuals lie mainly in the realm of social programming. However, many health care providers work to prevent child abuse by providing support and information to new families (see Table 4.2).

Table 4.2: Preventive services available to abused individuals

Program	Pros	Cons
Public media campaigns	Use media, including television, billboards, and radio, to reach a great number of people with reminders about available support networks and warnings such as "Never shake a baby."	The programs they advertise are often viewed as inaccessible to low-income families. Social stigma and fear of child welfare services also compel parents to avoid seeking help for abusive habits.
Legal deterrence	Seeks to protect abuse victims and to punish and rehabilitate offenders. Mandatory reporting laws require teachers and other public servants to immediately report suspected abuse. Legislation seeks to inhibit abuse by restricting access to weapons and decreasing response times to abuse reports.	Legal deterrence is often a reaction to abuse, rather than a prevention.
Social services	Provide education and counseling on family planning, resource access, and abuse prevention. Home visits by social service professionals have been found to decrease the incidents of child and elder abuse both by being a deterrent and through supporting families.	Many people may see social services and home visits as an invasion of privacy. Funding continues to be an issue in the face of a growing workload.

Chronically Ill and Disabled Persons

Prevention of chronic illness and disability focuses on healthy lifestyle choices and safety (see Table 4.3). Educational programs like the Cooper Clayton method to stop smoking that is offered by many health departments throughout the United States teach people about the risks of smoking and provide support groups for those choosing to quit smoking (Cooper & Clayton, 2010). Prevention during prenatal care works to prevent complications like gestational diabetes in pregnant women and fetal alcohol syndrome in babies.

Preventive care is also critical for those who are elderly and who already have chronic illnesses. Educational preventive care for elderly patients often focuses on fall prevention to address mobility limitations that come with age. Many chronic illnesses, like diabetes, increase the risk of further problems. Preventive programs for people with chronic illness often seek to educate patients on their individual care needs to make patients active participants in their health. Teaching diabetes patients how to properly care for their feet and to cut toenails straight across reduces the risk of losing a foot due to diabetes complications.

Table 4.3: Preventive services available to the chronically ill and disabled

Program	Pros	Cons
Education services	Encourage healthy lifestyle habits and workplace safety through education and support services.	Because many education services are provided through physicians' offices and membership-based health clubs, these services have restricted access.
Prenatal care	Can detect health concerns early on. Prenatal care reduces the likelihood of negative pregnancy outcomes by helping to ensure healthy habits during pregnancy, thereby diminishing the chances of fetal alcohol syndrome, drug addiction, and physical disability.	Prenatal care educates the pregnant mother but often falls short of offering treatments for substance abuse, alcoholism, and cigarette use. Prenatal care is also expensive, and those who most need prenatal preventive services in order to grow healthy infants often do not receive early, regular prenatal care.
Health and injury prevention programs for the elderly	Focus on helping the elderly understand their changing health and safety needs.	Many elderly patients have little control over their environments. Unhealthy habits, such as cigarette use, are more difficult to change with age.

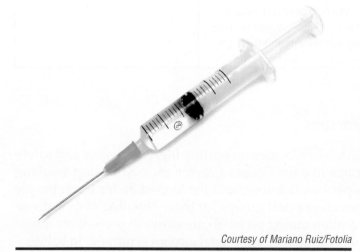

Courtesy of Mariano Ruiz/Fotolia

Needle exchanges reduce needle sharing among intravenous drug users, thereby reducing the transmission of HIV.

Persons Diagnosed With HIV/AIDS

Lifestyle choice education programs that focus on sexual behavior and drug abuse are common HIV/AIDS prevention programs (see Table 4.4). Some of this preventive education is done through public media campaigns that include television commercials, billboards, radio messages, and print advertisements that act as reminders to be selective about sexual partners and to use protection in the form of condoms when engaging in a sexual relationship. Some HIV/AIDS prevention programs are taught in schools in an attempt to provide HIV/AIDS prevention to entire generations.

It is important to note that HIV is not only spread through sexual contact. Needle sharing among intravenous drug users continues to spread HIV and other diseases throughout vulnerable populations. Needle exchange programs, like Clean Needles Now (n.d.) in Los Angeles, California, provide clean needles for drug users. Although such programs do not necessarily work to prevent intravenous drug use, they do work to prevent the spread of disease. Needle exchange programs were banned from receiving federal funds for 20 years because many in society worried that such programs contributed to drug abuse. The ban was lifted by Congress in 2009 (Sharon, 2009). By allowing needle exchange programs to receive federal funding, such programs can expand services to include drug abuse counseling and medical care.

Table 4.4: Preventive services available to people diagnosed with HIV/AIDS

Program	Pros	Cons
Public media campaigns	Transmit prevention education to a large audience through television, radio, and billboard advertising.	Public media campaigns are expensive, and many of the advertised programs are viewed as inaccessible by low-income individuals.
Community programs	The Centers for Disease Control and Prevention National Partnerships Program supports educational and HIV prevention programming through community-based organizations.	Community programs rely on community-based organizations such as schools and churches to educate the public, thereby creating issues of accessibility and programming differences.
Street outreach programs	Go directly to the communities that most need HIV prevention education and support.	Street outreach programs are costly to run and often rely on private donors and volunteers through community-based organizations. These programs are rare in most regions.
Needle exchanges	Reduce needle sharing among intravenous drug users, thereby reducing the transmission of HIV.	Social attitudes that view needle exchanges as enabling drug abuse restrict funding and access.

Persons Diagnosed With Mental Conditions

Preventive mental health services increased in popularity after the deinstitutionalization movement that began in the 1950s. The Community Mental Health Center Act of 1963 compelled states to fund community-based mental health programs. The act, combined with the development of more effective antipsychotic drugs, enabled patients to receive mental health care from early stages and to better manage symptoms like hallucinations experienced by people with schizophrenia, thus preventing the need for prolonged institutionalization (see Table 4.5).

Table 4.5: Preventive services available to people diagnosed with mental conditions

Type of Program	Pros	Cons
Universal	Targets the entire population. Includes programs such as prenatal and early childhood intervention programs and injury reduction programs.	These programs face funding challenges that restrict availability and accessibility.
Selective	Targets groups identified as having a higher risk of developing mental health disorders. Includes substance and alcohol abuse prevention and intervention programs.	Lack of funding for community-based programs targeting specific low-income, high-risk groups restricts delivery.
Indicated	Targets individuals identified as having a higher risk of developing mental health disorders. Includes evaluation, education, and therapeutic programming for individuals.	For an individual to be identified as having a higher risk of developing mental health disorders, that person must come in contact with the appropriate health care workers and community program organizers.

Suicide- and Homicide-Liable Persons

Violence is linked to systemic poverty. Low-income areas experience higher homicide rates than middle- and upper-class neighborhoods. The frustrations of poverty, including a limited ability to positively affect one's social status, poor educational opportunities, hunger, and inadequate living conditions all contribute to increased homicide and suicide rates, particularly among young adult males. Suicide and homicide prevention programs tend to focus on individuals rather than address the social issues that create an environment that exacerbates violence (see Table 4.6).

Courtesy of Loren Rodgers/Fotolia

Recent studies indicate low-income areas experience higher rates of homicide, partly due to inadequate living conditions and poor educational opportunities.

Table 4.6: Preventive services available to suicide- and homicide-liable persons

Program	Pros	Cons
Legal deterrence	Punishes offenders and attempts to limit violence with the threat of punishment.	Legal deterrence is more reactive than proactive; research indicates that legal deterrence is ineffective at limiting violence.
Family living education programs	Focus on education to support families, reduce unplanned pregnancies, and teach problem-solving skills.	Accessibility to these programs is limited, and willingness to participate is low.
Suicide prevention programs	Identify high-risk individuals and provide therapy and support for both the individuals and their families.	Functional screening tools and training for those in a position to recognize the warning signs (such as teachers, social service workers, and nursing home administrators) is fundamental for suicide prevention programs to work.

Persons Affected by Alcohol and Substance Abuse

Laws limiting access to drugs and alcohol often emerge from a moral stance that the use of drugs and alcohol is morally objectionable. However, access-limiting laws may reduce social risks by helping to limit the number of drug and alcohol users in the general population. Preventive services that focus on risky behaviors educate people on the risks of alcohol and drug abuse. Services that seek to reduce drug and alcohol use in individuals assume a disease-oriented attitude, that addiction is a treatable medical condition (see Table 4.7).

Table 4.7: Preventive services available to people affected by alcohol and substance abuse

Program	Pros	Cons
Legal deterrence	Limits access to illicit drugs and alcohol by intercepting disbursement and punishing offenders.	People who are addicted to drugs will find a way to get them; criminalizing drugs may cause increased antisocial behaviors. Studies have found that legal deterrence is ineffective as a means to stop drug and alcohol abuse.
Screening and counseling programs	Identify high-risk individuals and provide counseling and education of life skills and drug and alcohol avoidance.	For individuals to be identified for screening and counseling services, they must come in contact with workers who are trained to recognize risk factors.
Public education programs	Include media campaigns educating the public on substance abuse avoidance and available programs. These programs also include school-based curriculum and special programming to educate children early on about the risks of alcohol and drug use.	Funding can be difficult to maintain; the programs advertised by media campaigns may be viewed as inaccessible by some of the most at-risk groups.

Indigent and Homeless Persons

Preventing homelessness involves changing social attitudes about helping indigent people and providing affordable housing and other social welfare programs (see Table 4.8).

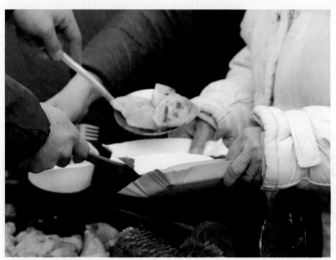

Courtesy of wjarek/Fotolia

Community-based programs provide meals and clothing for indigent people.

Support for government-funded housing has dwindled, leaving community-based programs to fill many needs. Although some community-based programs do provide housing, there are a great many that provide what they can in terms of food and clothing. Some even provide access to health care.

Preventive health care for homeless people focuses on providing preventive primary care, such as gynecological exams for women, as well as on health-related risk factors that homeless and indigent people are particularly susceptible to. Vaccination clinics for this vulnerable population work to prevent illness and the spread of disease by providing preventive care in the form of vaccines against common ailments such as flu and pneumonia.

Table 4.8: Preventive services available to indigent persons

Program	Pros	Cons
Government-funded housing	Provides three types of housing to fit individuals' needs: emergency housing, low-income housing, and supportive housing.	Negative social attitudes about welfare programs have allowed funding to diminish for government-supported housing programs.
Health care programs	Focus on health-related risk factors that indigent people are particularly vulnerable to, including gynecological care and family planning, substance abuse and mental health counseling, and HIV prevention.	These programs are more reactive to the needs of the homeless and only marginally useful for improving an individual's living situation.
Community-based programs	Provide meals and clothing for indigent people, help individuals find employment, and access programs to help them reclaim a reasonable standard of living.	There is little government funding support for many privately run community-based programs, so these programs are forced to rely on donors from surrounding areas.

Immigrants and Refugees

Many refugees have little or no health care in their native countries; thus, they are drawn to the United States for its robust health care system. Once here, many immigrants face the hard reality that America's health care system is inaccessible and unaffordable for many. Government health services are available to help meet the needs of immigrants, but many barriers exist to gaining access to such services, as we will see in later chapters. As a protective measure, the government does ensure that documented refugees undergo health screening before being approved to come into the country. However, undocumented migrants are not subject to these health screenings (see Table 4.9).

Table 4.9: Preventive services available to immigrants and refugees

Program	Pros	Cons
Public health services	Provide basic health care and health education services to low-income populations.	A myriad of unconnected agencies exist, including government-funded public health departments and private, nonprofit agencies like Planned Parenthood. This subset of the health care system is disjointed and can be difficult to navigate, especially for those who are not fluent in English. Undocumented immigrants often avoid these programs for fear of deportation.
Private health services	Include traditional health services from physicians, hospitals, and other "traditional" health care providers.	Private health services are expensive and inaccessibly so for people without health insurance.

Critical Thinking

"Social attitudes about health care and the free market encourage a primary focus on microlevel behaviors and environments." How does this statement relate to the American belief in "freedom of choice" and how it affects health care?

Self-Check

Answer the following questions to the best of your ability.

1. Prenatal care, which supports healthy pregnancy and birth outcomes, can be considered which type of service?
   a. educational
   b. preventive
   c. child placement
   d. nutritional

2. Suicide- and homicide-prevention programs tend to focus on individuals rather than address which types of issues?
    a. mental
    b. hunger
    c. social
    d. medical

3. What reality concerning the United States health care system do many immigrants face?
    a. Health care is expensive and inaccessible for many.
    b. Immigrants do not receive health care.
    c. Only immigrants from select areas receive health care.
    d. Only natural-born U.S. citizens receive advanced health care.

Answer Key

1. **b**   2. **c**   3. **a**

4.3 Reclaiming Health Through Treatment Services

The U.S. health care system is one of the most technology-oriented health care systems on the planet. This is partially driven by the free market mentality that rules America's economy, which encourages innovations in new technology. As such, the health care system is geared not toward preventive medicine but toward treating ailments. In doing so, health care providers are able to show results that can be billed for. The same advanced technologies that improve treatment also drive up the cost of care.

Problems arise when patients present with physical, social, and psychological symptoms that their treating physicians are not versed in. The American health care system is not well integrated between delivery channels and providers. A general practitioner might miss signs of psychological trouble due to lack of knowledge of that particular type of illness. Additionally, physicians often seek a quick fix (such as inexpensive antibiotics for a sinus infection) and fail to recognize the psychosocial elements of a patient's life that contribute to risk factors for the illness that occurs (such as a child living in a home with cigarette users). If that child is part of a vulnerable population, such as an abusive family, it is likely that the child will suffer recurrence of the presented illness until the root cause is addressed. If the physician only bothers writing a prescription and sends the family on their way, the child's health care needs are not appropriately met.

As such, a problem arises regarding patient wellness. For a low-income family, a child with recurring pneumonia might lead to lost income, making it increasingly difficult to afford the child's medical care. Preventive services mitigate this type of situation by reducing risky behaviors that contribute to illness. Much of America's health care system is based on the free market and run by privately held companies. These health care corporations focus on treatment because treatment uses more advanced technology and is therefore billed at higher rates than preventive care. The free market focus on treatment makes health care and wellness increasingly inaccessible to vulnerable people.

Vulnerable Mothers and Children

Treatment services for high-risk mothers and babies focus on prenatal care for the mother and postnatal care for the infant (see Table 4.10). Substance abuse cessation programs that help pregnant women to stop using drugs, alcohol, and tobacco help minimize risks to both mother and baby and limit the need for neonatal intensive care treatments. For those infants who are born with congenital heart or lung disorders, fetal alcohol syndrome, drug addiction, or other life-threatening complications, expensive treatments are available in neonatal intensive care units.

Courtesy of iStockphoto/Thinkstock

Substance abuse cessation programs can help pregnant women stop using harmful substances and also lessen the need for intensive care treatments.

Table 4.10: Treatment services available to high-risk mothers and children

Program	Pros	Cons
Substance abuse cessation programs	Help get pregnant women to stop using drugs, alcohol, and tobacco.	Accessibility to these programs is limited by access to prenatal care.
Neonatal intensive care units	Treat infants for a range of problems, including fetal alcohol syndrome and drug addiction.	Neonatal intensive care units are expensive to provide, and do not prevent poor outcomes, only address them.

Abused Individuals

Treatment services for abused individuals focus on emergency response, counseling, and legal ramifications for offenders (see Table 4.11). When injuries occur due to abuse, emergency medical services (EMS) and police are often called to the scene. Other times, the victims seek treatment at emergency rooms and outpatient medical clinics. It is common for victims of abuse to avoid medical services altogether for fear of legal intervention. When treatment is sought, it usually focuses on treating injuries and providing counseling services for both victims and offenders.

Table 4.11: Treatment services available to abused individuals

Program	Pros	Cons
Emergency and outpatient medical services	Treat injuries caused by abuse and screen for abusive situations.	Many abuse victims avoid medical services for fear of intervention.
Crisis response services and hotlines	Provide emergency counseling and physical protection in the form of police, EMS, and social service responders.	These services are nonexistent in many areas; training and maintaining personnel is costly.
Mental health services	Treat both the victims and offenders. These services focus on changing behaviors.	Victims and offenders must be active, willing participants.

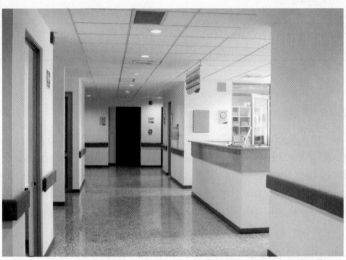

Courtesy of reflektastudios/Fotolia

Emergency rooms allow for fast medical intervention for injuries and can limit the likelihood of an injury causing long-term disability.

Chronically Ill and Disabled Persons

Treatment for chronic illness focuses on symptom relief and disease management. Disability treatment involves rehabilitation and educating patients on relevant life skills so they can live the fullest lives possible while dealing with their disabilities (see Table 4.12).

Table 4.12: Treatment services available to the chronically ill and disabled

Program	Pros	Cons
Care management services (managed care organizations [MCOs])	Coordinate medical care for chronically ill and disabled patients between the many facets of their health care needs, from pharmaceutical management, to treatments, to rehabilitation.	The absence of electronic health records makes it difficult for patients to manage and coordinate their own care between primary care physicians and any specialists the patient sees, so third-party care management services are often necessary.
Hospital care	Emergency rooms allow for fast medical intervention for injuries and can limit the likelihood of an injury causing long-term disability.	Emergency rooms are expensive and are short-term care.
Rehabilitation programs	Help patients learn to live with chronic illness and disability.	These programs can be expensive, which limits access.

Persons Diagnosed With HIV/AIDS

HIV symptoms can be reasonably well managed with antiretroviral drugs that suppress the human immunodeficiency virus (HIV). However, these life-prolonging therapies are expensive, partly due to the fact that the therapy usually necessitates the simultaneous use of multiple antiretroviral drugs taken multiple times per day. This makes these therapies somewhat inaccessible to America's most vulnerable populations (see Table 4.13).

Table 4.13: Treatment services available to people diagnosed with HIV/AIDS

Program	Pros	Cons
Counseling	Addresses the negative mental health effects of living with an HIV diagnosis and teaches skills for living with HIV/AIDS.	Accessibility is limited by insurance coverage, ability to pay, and geographical location of counseling centers. Also, the patient must be willing to participate.
Medical treatment	Life-prolonging antiretroviral drugs keep patients healthier, longer.	Medical treatment is expensive and difficult to access, especially for the most vulnerable populations. Medical intervention is most effective when begun early. Many patients do not take their medications regularly (often for financial reasons).

Persons Diagnosed With Mental Conditions

Since the deinstitutionalization movement that began in the 1950s, most treatment programs for mental health conditions are delivered on an outpatient basis (see Table 4.14). These services include pharmacological therapies to manage symptoms like feelings of sadness and confusion in people suffering from depression and hallucinations in people with schizophrenia. Outpatient therapy for people with mental illness also often includes regular counseling sessions and substance abuse cessation programs when needed. Crisis response services are available to fill in where outpatient mental health services are unavailable (such as after hours).

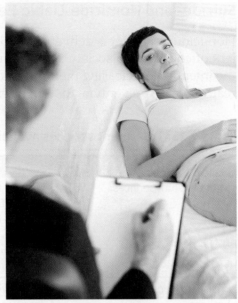

Courtesy of WavebreakmediaMicro /Fotolia

Outpatient mental health services include counseling and drug therapies and are available through a wide range of providers; many are relatively inexpensive, and some health insurance plans cover some outpatient mental health services.

Table 4.14: Treatment services available to people diagnosed with mental conditions

Program	Pros	Cons
Outpatient mental health services	Include counseling and drug therapies; are available through a wide range of providers; many are relatively inexpensive; and some health insurance plans cover some outpatient mental health services.	Patients with severe mental health disorders may be noncompliant with outpatient programs. Can be financially inaccessible for persons without health insurance coverage.
Crisis response services	Available on both an outpatient and inpatient basis; provide immediate help for patients suffering severe emotional traumas, such as psychotic episodes and nervous breakdowns.	Services can be expensive with limited accessibility to low-income individuals.
Substance abuse cessation programs	Available on both an outpatient and inpatient basis; focus on changing lifestyle habits that contribute to drug and alcohol abuse that then contribute to mental health disorders.	Inpatient programs are expensive; outpatient programs depend on the individual's level of compliance.

Suicide- and Homicide-Liable Persons

Homicide treatment is delivered via the criminal justice system, which both removes violent offenders from society and has programs in place to help rehabilitate offenders with the intention of releasing them to be contributing members of society. Suicide treatment is really suicide prevention, though often after failed suicide attempts (see Table 4.15).

Table 4.15: Treatment services available to suicide- and homicide-liable persons

Program	Pros	Cons
Mental health services	Address the mental health needs of suicide-prone patients; educate both suicide- and homicide-prone people about how to invoke positive coping mechanisms.	Patients must be compliant in attending counseling sessions and taking medications when necessary. Mental health services can be financially inaccessible.
Crisis intervention centers and hotlines	Are provided by many separate agencies, which increases accessibility; are vital resources for at-risk people and families.	Lack of coordination between agencies complicates quality assurance.

Persons Affected by Alcohol and Substance Abuse

Substance and alcohol abuse treatments vary from pharmacological therapies to counseling services. Many patients do best with a combination of therapies, but ongoing support is vital for prolonged recovery (see Table 4.16). Programs like Alcoholics Anonymous (AA) provide support groups and self-help methods to lead to recovery. Methadone clinics exist that allow people who are addicted to opiates, like heroin, to gain access to methadone in place of opiate drugs. Some such clinics also provide counseling and medical services to support treatment and improve outcomes.

Table 4.16: Treatment services available to people affected by alcohol and substance abuse

Program	Pros	Cons
Pharmacological therapies	May be used to replace a harmful, addictive drug; may be used to block the effects of a drug, which supports weaning from drug use; or may be used to relieve withdrawal symptoms.	Pharmacological therapies must be tailored to the individual patient and can be expensive; patients must be medication-compliant.
Behavioral therapies	Are available on both inpatient and prolonged outpatient basis, can be tailored to meet individual needs and evolve with patient needs.	Patients must be compliant with counseling session attendance, and counseling can be expensive; many patients lapse.

Indigent and Homeless Persons

Treatment services for home-less people focus on addressing health care needs and providing resources for preventive services (see Table 4.17).

Courtesy of Oleg Kozlov/Fotolia

The Health Resources and Services Administration Health Care for the Homeless program includes outreach programs to improve service accessibility, case management, and a multidisciplinary approach.

Table 4.17: Treatment services available to indigent persons

Program	Pros	Cons
The Robert Wood Johnson Foundation Health Care for the Homeless project (now The Health Resources and Services Administration Health Care for the Homeless program)	Directly addresses the needs of homeless people, including a holistic approach that considers social, economic, and health care needs; recognizes the relationship between wellness and the need for resources, including food and shelter. The program includes outreach programs to improve service accessibility, case management, and a multidisciplinary approach.	Funding is in danger; all involved personnel must be well trained on an ongoing basis.
Veterans Administration Homeless Chronically Mentally Ill and Health Care for Homeless Veterans programs; The National Institute of Mental Health Community Mental Health Services Demonstration Program; the Access to Community Care and Effective Services program	Address specific needs of specific homeless populations; many use the same holistic approach taken by the Robert Wood Johnson Foundation Health Care for the Homeless project; receive federal funding.	Social attitudes and constrained budgets cause federal funding for these programs to diminish.

Immigrants and Refugees

Documented immigrants and refugees to the United States experience the same hurdles attempting to access appropriate health care that the rest of the population faces. Undocumented immigrants have less access to health care for financial and legal reasons (see Table 4.18).

Table 4.18: Treatment services available to immigrants and refugees

Program	Pros	Cons
Emergency and inpatient medical services	An increasing number of hospitals and emergency clinics employ workers who speak languages other than English to better serve the immigrant population. Immigrants receive the same level of care as U.S. natives.	Accessibility is based on financial ability, and language barriers do still exist.
Outpatient medical and mental health services	Patients with health insurance or who can otherwise afford their care have the ability to select their health care providers. More affordable options include public health departments and privately run, not-for-profit clinics.	Financial accessibility and physical accessibility barriers can be prohibitive. Many undocumented immigrants avoid routine health care for fear of deportation.
Dental and vision services	Many refugees have never experienced specialized dental and vision care and the health benefits thereof.	Financial and physical accessibility are barriers; many immigrants do not use dental and vision services because they are not familiar with the practices.

Critical Thinking

The example was given earlier of a child who is prescribed antibiotics for a sinus infection. This may seem like a simple and obvious treatment for an infection, but one wonders if the doctor would have modified the treatment in any way if the doctor had known about the contributing factors to the child's illness, such as the fact that the child was consistently exposed to secondhand smoke in the home environment. Based on the information provided in this example, do you think that physicians have an obligation to investigate the environmental and socioeconomic risk factors that may play a part in their patients' illnesses?

Self-Check

Answer the following questions to the best of your ability.

1. Disability treatment involves rehabilitation and teaching which of the following skills to enable patients to live the fullest lives possible while dealing with their disabilities?
   a. life skills
   b. vocational skills
   c. social skills
   d. coping skills

2. HIV symptoms can be reasonably well managed with what type of drugs?
   a. antibiotics
   b. opiates
   c. antiretroviral drugs
   d. amphetamines

3. What is considered to be the most vital aspect in alcohol and substance abuse treatment?
   a. ongoing support
   b. pharmaceutical therapies
   c. faith-based support
   d. incarceration

Answer Key

1. **a**   2. **c**   3. **a**

4.4 Maintaining Quality of Life Through Long-Term Care

The Substance Abuse and Mental Health Services Administration (SAMHSA) estimates that one-quarter to one-half of all homeless people suffer from a mental disorder (National Coalition for the Homeless, 2009). In many cases, the disorder is the root cause of the homelessness, as some psychological illnesses can make it nearly impossible to maintain employment and close social connections. For this vulnerable subgroup, the long-lasting movement to deinstitutionalize people who need long-term care increases the risk for negative outcomes.

Long-term care facilities that specialize in rehabilitation, behavioral health, and nursing facilities for the elderly and infirm were once fairly common in the United States. Specialized facilities existed for patients with mental disorders and long-term illnesses. However, the deinstitutionalization movement had certain detrimental effects on the homeless population.

Although the move to deinstitutionalize patient care was born both out of concern about the effectiveness of long-term facilities and the economic costs of running them, mass deinstitutionalization did not see the majority of evicted patients placed into loving, capable homes. Even those who did return to family environments suffered from a lack of community resources to support the families caring for them at home.

As the baby boomer generation matures to old age, the number of institutionalized patients is increasing, and not just of the elderly. Skilled nursing facilities (SNFs), once associated only with caring for the elderly and a few seriously handicapped or activities of daily living (ADLs) aid-dependent patients, are now accepting an increasing number of vulnerable patients from many at-risk populations, including those affected by drug dependence and HIV. Nationwide programs through Leading Age and the American Health Care Association (AHCA) have been undertaken to improve the education of all SNF staff to enhance care and quality of life for those outside of the previous core constituency of long-term care providers. This education includes caring for the at-risk populations specific to needs and is focused on continuum of care and quality of life. Each new population introduced to the long-term care community has a unique plan of care, has a specific needs set, and demands their quality of life not diminish despite institutionalization. At the same time that more individuals are being institutionalized, adult caregivers of their own elderly parents are increasingly seeking support from community- or home-based resources. This is creating a refreshed focus on community-based programs and services that provide long-term care and support for patients and families across all populations.

Vulnerable Mothers and Children

Long-term care for high-risk mothers and babies is generally provided on an outpatient basis and focuses on parenting skills, social support, ongoing medical care, and case management to help them access the resources available to them (see Table 4.19). Home-visit programs through local health departments and social services provide long-term care for new mothers and babies by sending nurses or social workers to visit families with new babies in their

Courtesy of Dalia Drulia/Fotolia

Medical care addresses ongoing health and wellness of the healing mother and new infant.

own homes. A home visit allows the worker to build a relationship with the family while providing information on parenting skills and available resources.

Table 4.19: Long-term care services available for high-risk mothers and children

Program	Pros	Cons
Medical care	Addresses ongoing health and wellness of the healing mother and new infant. Medical care also provides immunizations and screenings for health issues and abuse risk.	Many high-risk mothers are unaware of the available resources and are unfamiliar with the fragmented delivery system.
Social services	Include home visits that provide social support, encouragement, and resources for high-risk mothers and babies.	Some mothers may decline help from social service workers for fear of unwanted intervention.

Abused Individuals

Long-term care for abused individuals includes counseling for victims and offenders, protection for victims, criminal punishment for offenders, and shelters for battered women and children (see Table 4.20).

Table 4.20: Long-term care services available to abused individuals

Program	Pros	Cons
Counseling services and peer support self-help groups	Support victims through the emotional ramifications of abuse; work with offenders to alter abusive behaviors.	These services and groups can have the negative effect of enabling a victim to prolong the relationship.
Protective services and welfare agency programming	Identify and intervene with abusive situations. Child protective services have the ability to immediately remove a child from a home if they believe the child is being harmed.	Funding and staffing are uneven and inadequate.
Shelters and safe houses	Provide safe housing for women and children escaping from abusive relationships. They also connect victims with other resources.	Most are privately funded and have small operating budgets.
Criminal justice system	Provides some protection of abuse victims and punishes repeat offenders.	Domestic disputes are handled differently by different responders and departments.

Courtesy of Lisa F. Young/Fotolia

Hospices allow terminally ill patients to remain at home with support from a medical team.

Chronically Ill and Disabled Persons

Long-term care of both chronically ill and disabled people involves managing different types of care and resources from many agencies. Care managers can be vital in helping both a patient and the family coordinate care (see Table 4.21). Long-term care facilities, including assisted living and nursing care facilities, are expensive. Many families choose to avoid that expense and to keep their loved ones nearby or care for them in their own homes. In-home care can also be very expensive and can put a lot of stress on care providers. Services exist to help with in-home nursing and to give caregivers breaks so they can run errands or even have a night off without worrying about the loved one left at home.

Table 4.21: Long-term care services available to the chronically ill and disabled

Program	Pros	Cons
Nursing homes and independent living communities	Provide varying levels of care to meet the differing needs of patients in different stages of life.	These communities are costly; furthermore, much of the expense of these homes is not covered by Medicare.
Hospices and in-home care	Allow terminally ill patients to remain at home with support from a medical team.	Hospice receives some government funding but mostly relies on insurance payments and private donations. Other in-home options are paid for by insurance or out of pocket.
Social health maintenance organizations (S/HMOs) and the Program of All-Inclusive Care for the Elderly (PACE)	These consolidated health care models deliver long-term, primary, and preventive services through comprehensive delivery systems. S/HMOs are designed to keep people out of medical institutions.	S/HMOs are a form of private health insurance; PACE is dependent on federal funding.
U.S. Department of Education, Office of Special Education and Rehabilitative Services	Funds state programs for special education of disabled children to age 21.	Resources stop at age 21; federal funding is always in danger.
The Basic Vocational Rehabilitation Service Program	Funds state programs to help disabled individuals find gainful employment. There is no age limit.	Federal funding is always in danger.

Persons Diagnosed With HIV/AIDS

Most nursing homes are not prepared to care for dying HIV/AIDS patients. Therefore, specialized AIDS hospices and community-based programs exist to help ailing HIV/AIDS patients (see Table 4.22). Some palliative, or end-of-life, care facilities do not accept HIV/AIDS patients because the palliative period is difficult to predict. Specialized hospices, like Project Transitions (n.d.) in central Texas, go beyond palliative care and include housing, counseling, and support groups for HIV/AIDS patients nearing the end of their lives.

Courtesy of mangostock/Fotolia

Volunteers provide meals, transportation, housekeeping, and other services free of charge or at very low rates to HIV/AIDS patients.

Table 4.22: Long-term care services available to people diagnosed with HIV/AIDS

Program	Pros	Cons
AIDS hospices	Provide specialize palliative care for people dying of AIDS.	AIDS hospices depend largely on volunteers and private donors.
Home health care services	Provide licensed home-based health care for AIDS patients.	Home health care services are very expensive; access depends on private health insurance coverage and the individual's ability to pay.
Volunteer services	Include community-based services that depend on volunteers to provide meals, transportation, housekeeping, and other services free of charge or at very low rates to HIV/AIDS patients.	These services depend on private donors and volunteers to function.

Persons Diagnosed With Mental Conditions

Although private psychiatric hospitals still exist, many emotionally disturbed patients are cared for at home with the help of outside resources (see Table 4.23). Partial-care centers act as daytime care for adults with mental illnesses who cannot be left alone while family members go to work. Unfortunately, partial-care centers are not available in all regions. Community-based programs are available from a wide range of organizations, including the National Institute of Mental Health (NIMH). Such programs provide access to services, including education and counseling, for both the patient and the caregivers. Case managers are useful in helping families find the right combination of resources to best meet their needs.

Table 4.23: Long-term care services available to people diagnosed with mental conditions

Program	Pros	Cons
Institutionalization	Few government-run psychiatric institutions still exist, but private institutions do still fill the need for full-time care. Nursing homes care for a large number of elderly patients with dementia and other mental conditions. Jails and prisons act as de facto institutions for people with mental disturbance when they are arrested for breaking laws. Satellite housing, halfway houses, and other board and care homes also exist as institutionalization options.	All these resources together are not enough to provide safe, secure housing for people with severe mental conditions in this country.
Home care	A resource that provides for mentally ill patients to remain home with family.	The caregivers need a lot of resources and support.
Partial-care centers	A resource for families caring for a mentally disturbed loved one who cannot be left alone during the day when the caregivers must go to work.	Affordability can be a barrier to access.
Community-based care including:		
The National Institute of Mental Health Community Support Program, the Child and Adolescent Service System Program, and the Program of Assertive Community Treatment	Various resources for educating, housing, and supporting mentally ill people. These resources focus on coordinated, comprehensive care continuums for those with mental disorders.	A case manager is often needed to help families and individuals with mental conditions access the many disjointed resources.

Courtesy of Alexander Edmonds/Fotolia

Prisons are violent environments, and studies indicate that they are not effective rehabilitation centers.

Suicide- and Homicide-Liable Persons

Long-term "care" of violent offenders focuses on removing them from society rather than on rehabilitation. Reports on the effectiveness of programs designed to alter violent behaviors indicate that the social situations that propagate violence must be addressed to reduce the risk level for homicide-prone individuals. Inpatient mental health services and vocational rehabilitation programs exist to help suicide- and homicide-liable persons (see Table 4.24).

Table 4.24: Long-term care services available to suicide- and homicide-liable persons

Program	Pros	Cons
Criminal justice system	Removes violent offenders from society.	Prisons are violent environments, and studies indicate that they are not effective rehabilitation centers.
Residential treatment centers	Treat violent and suicidal youth.	Treatment and funding are uneven.
Community-based programs	Include social services and private and volunteer programs that provide counseling and support services for violent offenders, suicide-prone individuals, and their families.	Most community-based programs do not interface with other programs to create a continuum of care.

Persons Affected by Alcohol and Substance Abuse

Long-term care and treatment services for alcoholism and substance abusers go hand in hand (see Table 4.25). While detoxification helps remove substances from the body, ongoing counseling and support is usually necessary for ongoing rehabilitation.

Table 4.25: Long-term care services available to people affected by alcohol and substance abuse

Program	Pros	Cons
Medical detoxification	Uses pharmaceuticals given in a hospital or other type of inpatient medical facility to remove the drug from the patient's body.	Medical detoxification needs to be followed with long-term counseling to be effective.
Social detoxification	Allows the body to clean out the drug naturally while the patient is in a specialized facility under the watch of trained personnel.	Social detoxification is not covered by all insurance plans; physicians may be called in but are not always on the premises.
Rehabilitation and recovery	Includes programs that enable the patient to recover from a drug addiction and restore functioning needed for a healthy lifestyle.	These programs are not covered by all insurance plans; patient must be compliant for the program to work.
Custodial programs	Provide shelter, food, and support on an ongoing basis, but the patients may come and go at will (usually within set hours).	Many of these programs are supported through donor funding and nonprofit organizations.
Nonresidential programs	Include therapy sessions, both in groups and on an individual basis, that provide treatment and recovery services to patients.	Patients must be compliant with session attendance.

Indigent and Homeless Persons

Long-term care of homeless people involves getting them off the streets and treating the factors that contributed to their homelessness (see Table 4.26).

Courtesy of elavuk81/Fotolia

It is estimated that 50% of homeless people in the United States have some type of significant mental condition.

Table 4.26: Long-term care services available to indigent persons

Program	Pros	Cons
Inpatient mental health programs	It is estimated that 50% of homeless people in the United States have some type of significant mental condition. Inpatient mental health programs offer a way to get these patients off the streets and address the mental disorders that may have led to their homelessness.	Some inpatient institutions will reject patients perceived to be problematic; all inpatient programs must be paid for somehow.
Housing placement	Outreach programs are key components to placing homeless people in long-term housing. Some programs, like the Veterans Administration, have developed creative programs to place individual patients in board and care homes. Some private agencies and local governments support free and low-income housing for which many homeless people are eligible.	Case management services offer a more effective method of placing homeless families and individuals in the right type of home. Funding for all of these programs is dependent on government budget decisions and individual donors.

Immigrants and Refugees

Long-term care for immigrants and refugees focuses on community-based support to help them access resources (see Table 4.27).

Table 4.27: Long-term care services available to immigrants and refugees

Program	Pros	Cons
English as a Second Language (ESL) courses	Help immigrants by teaching them to speak, read, and write English. The programs are often available free of charge.	Program funding can be difficult to maintain.
Social assistance programs	Aid with housing, transportation, securing employment, and connecting refugees with available resources.	Many of the programs are disconnected from the others, making the system difficult to manage.
Voluntary refugee assistance programs	Provide sponsorship and support for refugee families through networks of volunteers. Many are supported by churches.	Some groups may engage in illegal activity by acting as an underground railroad for undocumented immigrants.

Critical Thinking

Many discussions about the future of health care address the importance of long-term care. Given the fact that the population of the United States is aging, why is this such an important issue?

Self-Check

Answer the following questions to the best of your ability.

1. Which of the following do shelters and safe houses provide to victims of abuse?
    a. housing and connections to support
    b. counseling
    c. legal advice
    d. a contact point for police investigations

2. It is estimated that _____ of homeless people in the United States have some type of significant mental condition.
    a. 30%
    b. 42%
    c. 50%
    d. 67%

3. Which of the following groups provide sponsorship and support for refugee families through networks of volunteers?
    a. churches
    b. state government
    c. local businesses
    d. professional organizations

Answer Key

1. **a**   2. **c**   3. **a**

Case Study: Health Insurers Support Preventive Services

Humana, one of the nation's largest health insurance companies, launched HumanaVitality© in 2012. The program is available to Humana members at no additional charge. HumanaVitality rewards members who log exercise, weight loss, and other healthy lifestyle habits with points that can be redeemed for merchandise from various partner retailers. The program is similar to credit card rewards, but in addition to points to spend, members gain a healthier lifestyle and Humana saves money on medical treatments and long-term care (HumanaVitality, 2012).

Many athletic clubs and gyms offer similar rewards systems. Some YMCAs throughout the country have instituted FitLinxx programs that allow members to log workouts and earn points. Rewards range from YMCA water bottles and T-shirts to gift cards for local restaurants. The more workout points a member earns, the better the rewards become. Using rewards systems to encourage healthier lifestyles is fairly new because society's focus on health care has changed from treating illness to preventing it.

Only in the last few decades have preventive services become popular in health care settings. Due to the skyrocketing cost of health care in the United States, patients, the government, and health insurance companies all have a vested interest in the propagation of preventive services. Insurers, including Medicare and Medicaid, are increasingly covering preventive health care services with no patient co-pays. The Patient Protection and Affordable Care Act of 2010 mandates that insurers cover many preventive services at no co-pay charge to the patients. This was a move by the federal government to mitigate the costs of America's obesity epidemic and other chronic diseases in the face of rising health care costs.

Many health insurance companies support the mandate as a way to encourage customers to use less expensive preventive services instead of waiting and costing the insurers more money on treatments and long-term care. In addition to dropping patient co-pays for preventive care services, many insurers created programs that encourage their clients to make healthy lifestyle choices and use the covered preventive services.

Chapter Summary

An effective continuum of care sees a patient through all phases of life. Prevention services begun when young lessen a person's risk of developing a need for treatment and long-term care services later in life. Even when preventive services are accessed in later life stages, programs that help people quit smoking, lose weight, and maintain a healthy diet lower their risk of negative health outcomes. Even so, everybody gets sick at some point, and treatment services are necessary to restore health and functioning. When health cannot be fully restored, long-term care services must be accessible to help patients and families with health and mental care needs. Accessibility to prevention, treatment, and long-term care services is limited for America's most vulnerable.

Critical Thinking

Discuss with supporting examples the need for a continuum of care that comprises a comprehensive approach to health care for vulnerable populations.

Self-Check

Answer the following questions to the best of your ability.

1. A solid continuum of care should be available throughout a person's life.
   a. True
   b. False

2. Which of the following caused millions of Americans to lose their jobs and their homes—and increased the strain on underfunded social welfare programs?
   a. the War on Terror
   b. the Y2K Glitch
   c. the Great Recession of 2008
   d. the Swine Flu Epidemic

3. The American health care system is not well integrated between which of the following groups? (Select two.)
   a. older generations
   b. delivery channels
   c. providers
   d. corporations

4. Problems arise when patients present with which of the following symptoms that their treating physicians are not versed in? (Select three.)
   a. orthopedic
   b. physical
   c. social
   d. oncological
   e. psychological

5. Mass _____ did not see the majority of evicted patients placed into loving, capable homes.
   a. deinstitutionalization
   b. decentralization
   c. immigration
   d. inflation

Answer Key

1. a   2. c   3. b and c   4. b, c, and e   5. a

Additional Resources

Visit the following websites to learn more about the topics covered in this chapter:

Patient Centered Medical Home

http://www.gilbertcenter.net/home.html

The American Health Care Association

http://www.ahcancal.org/Pages/Default.aspx

The website for the National Association of Community Health Centers and their mission to fill the gaps in health care services

http://www.nachc.com/

Web Exercise

Watch the following videos and script your own video (you do not have to produce the video, just write a script) about preventive health care. You may use other video sources but remember they must be reliable and valid (YouTube and Wikipedia do not count as valid), and you must cite your source(s).

- Andrew Weil discusses preventive medicine in a short on Discovery.com:
  http://dsc.discovery.com/videos/curiosity-is-preventative-medicine-becoming-more-important-in-healthcare.html
- First Lady Michelle Obama and others discuss preventive health care in the health care reform act:
  http://www.whitehouse.gov/photos-and-video/video/preventive-health-care-coverage-under-health-reform
- An example of how Medicare covers preventive health care:
  http://www.dailymotion.com/video/xkebvp_medicare-made-clear-preventive-health-care-services_people

Key Terms

continuum of care The combination of preventive health services, treatment services, and long-term care services that spans a patient's lifetime and provides for the best health outcomes.

free market economy An economy based on open competition among corporations with a lack of government regulation.

inflation Loss of currency value.

insurance underwriters Companies that evaluate the risk and exposure of potential clients, decide how much coverage the client should receive, and determine how much the client should pay for it.

long-term care Care that focuses on constant, ongoing health care needs.

Occupational Safety and Health Administration (OSHA) Established by the Occupational Safety and Health Act of 1970, this group was created to ensure safe and healthful working conditions for working men and women by setting and enforcing standards and providing training, outreach, education, and assistance.

preventive care services Medically related and medically based services that focus on maintaining health.

socioeconomic classes A combined economic and social measure of a person's work experience and family economic position in relation to others.

treatment services Services intended to restore health to ailing individuals.

workers' compensation A form of insurance that provides wage replacement, medical treatment, and rehabilitation services to employees injured in the course of employment.

5

Paying for Health Care

Learning Objectives

After reading this chapter, you should be able to:

- Distinguish the benefits and shortcomings of private sources of payment for the care of vulnerable persons.

- Identify the benefits and shortcomings of public sources of payment for the care of vulnerable persons.

- Recognize the most common public payer options, and understand their eligibility requirements.

- Understand how health care is financed for people with no health insurance coverage.

Introduction

The cost of health care is rising, in part because of expensive new technologies and procedures, and in part because of the market failure of the health care industry. It has been argued that deregulation of health insurers, combined with a free market health care industry, has changed health care from a service-based structure to a **commodity**, or a product available for purchase. America's health care delivery system is geared toward the multibillion dollar health insurance industry rather than individual payers, many of whom lack the financial ability to cover health care expenses out of pocket, from general emergency room care to a

Costly new technologies and the free-market nature of the health care industry have raised the cost of health care.

life-threatening illness. After all, few people have $10,000 in their budgets to cover the cost of an emergency room visit for a broken arm.

Americans purchase health insurance to cover medical bills, but health insurance is too expensive for many families to afford. In 2010, 64% of the American population had private health insurance for all or part of the year. That isn't a very large majority, considering that everybody needs medical attention at some point. In that same year, 31% of the population had government-run public health insurance, and 16.3% had no health insurance at all for all or part of the year (DeNavas-Walt, Proctor, & Smith, 2011). The question across America, from Congress to kitchen tables, is how to insure all, how to tackle rising health care costs, and how to decipher a fair and equitable payee process.

Critical Thinking

What do you think will be the impact if health care costs are not addressed? What future problems do you predict?

Self-Check

Answer the following questions to the best of your ability.

1. According to a study in 2011 by DeNavas-Walt, Proctor, & Smith, what percentage of Americans had no health insurance?
    a. 17%
    b. 36%
    c. 42%
    d. 16.3%

2. What has changed health care from a service-based structure to a commodity?
    a. deregulation
    b. lack of government intervention
    c. high consumer demand
    d. high employer demand

3. America's health care delivery system is geared toward what part of the health insurance industry?
    a. individual payers
    b. employer benefits
    c. the multibillion dollar segment
    d. children and infants

Answer Key

1. **d**   2. **a**   3. **c**

5.1 Private Payers

The **private payer sector** comprises programs that provide financial access to health care, which includes insurance companies, employer-run health coverage programs, and individuals who pay for health care out of pocket. Individuals who pay for all of their health care out of pocket are rare, as the cost of health care is prohibitive. Employer-run health coverage programs are types of insurance wherein the employer company manages the plan. Most Americans with private health care coverage have insurance plans that are sold and managed by insurance companies. These plans are available for purchase individually, though 60% of employers offer health insurance as an employee incentive (The Kaiser Family Foundation [KFF] & Health Research and Educational Trust, 2011).

Private payer coverage is unattainable for many of America's most vulnerable. This is primarily due to low income. Additionally, many of America's middle class are losing private payer health insurance due to rising premium prices and employers' inability or unwillingness to continue offering health insurance as an employee benefit. Many employers who continue to offer health insurance benefits have had to either lower the amount of coverage available or raise the out-of-pocket amount paid by the patient, called the **deductible**, due to rising premiums. This section discusses private payer coverage in terms of how it is able to meet the particular problems of each vulnerable population, whether or not the coverage is adequate, and the unique issues faced by each population when trying to navigate the private payer system.

Vulnerable Mothers and Children

Many people cite health insurance as a strong incentive to work, but as employers omit or limit insurance coverage as a benefit, private payer insurance becomes increasingly

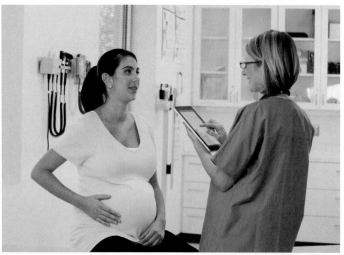

Courtesy of Blend_Images/iStockphoto

Though insurance coverage for young children has improved, prior to giving birth mothers are becoming responsible for covering the cost of an increasing portion of their medical care.

difficult to obtain for America's most vulnerable. According to the Forum on Child and Family Statistics (2011), 60% of America's children had private health insurance in 2009. Private health insurers have improved preventive care coverage for children, often covering well-child visits and immunizations at no **co-pay**, or the portion of the bill that the patient is responsible for. However, coverage for care of the mother and baby during pregnancy, called **prenatal care**, has diminished, leaving the patient responsible for an increasing amount of the associated medical bills. Prenatal care is increasingly expensive as malpractice insurance premiums continue to rise, causing many obstetricians to increase their rates or drop out of the practice altogether. As the cost of prenatal care rises in response to these conditions, private health insurers are increasing patient co-pays in order to meet the higher costs.

Abused Individuals

Injuries that occur as a result of physical abuse are often treated in hospitals and urgent care centers. Many abuse victims avoid seeing their designated general practitioners and pediatricians for fear of detection. These injury treatments, and the mental health services that many victims access to recover from abusive relationships, are covered by private payers at varying levels depending on the specifics of their individual insurance plans.

Chronically Ill and Disabled Persons

Private insurance coverage for chronic illnesses and disabilities varies depending on the individual insurance plan. Many insurance companies have preexisting condition clauses that make it difficult to obtain insurance coverage or that reduce coverage for specified chronic illnesses. As the cost of delivered health care rises, many insurance companies are increasing individuals' financial responsibilities in the form of co-pays or rejecting payment of **insurance claims**. Although it is difficult for insurance companies to deny claims for many procedures associated with chronic illness and disability, many have reduced coverage for mobility and motility aids that help with activities of daily living (ADLs).

Courtesy of Lisa Eastman/fotolia

Insurance companies have increased co-pays and decreased the amount and types of procedures they will pay for in order to offset the rising costs of delivered health care.

Persons Diagnosed With HIV/AIDS

Antiretroviral drug therapy is expensive, and HIV/AIDS patients with compromised immune systems often need costly inpatient hospital treatment. Private health insurers have discriminated against people diagnosed with HIV/AIDS by charging them higher premiums, limiting coverage, and screening for preexisting conditions. HIV/AIDS patients benefit from managed care, as managed care plans can lower medical costs through planning, organization, and deal brokering and can help HIV/AIDS patients maximize their health insurance benefits.

Recent legislation works to increase access to health care coverage for people with disabilities, chronic illness, HIV/AIDS, and mental conditions. The Patient Protection and Affordable Care Act (2010) created a Pre-Existing Condition Insurance Plan (PCIP) to provide affordable health insurance coverage to all people living with medical conditions, including those with HIV/AIDS. The act also prohibits insurers from declining coverage based on preexisting conditions, beginning in 2014.

Persons Diagnosed With Mental Conditions

Plan coverage for mental health services has increased in recent decades. Many private insurance plans offer some level of coverage for outpatient therapy sessions and allow intense nonresidential therapies. Mental health benefits often have higher co-pays than general practitioner benefits.

On the insurer side, managed behavioral health care programs (MBHCPs) have become a common method of managing mental health costs. MBHCPs come in two basic formats:

- Administrative services-only payments, which are flat monthly fees that are paid in advance, usually based on the number of **enrollees**, or insurance plan participants
- Monthly **per capita** payments made by the insurer to a managed behavioral health care organization (MBHCO) that make the MBHCO liable for services costs and administration costs

The monthly per capita pay structure involves contracting a network of providers to perform the services. In this form of plan, mental health services have different coverage from other medical services covered under the plan. Per capita payment plans face challenges in minimizing the tendency for high-risk patients to be excluded from coverage and for providers to unnecessarily perform covered services to increase their ability to bill.

Suicide- and Homicide-Liable Persons

Caucasian males have the highest suicide rates and also have the highest incidence of subscribing to private health insurance plans. Suicide ideation and planning is an aspect of major depression, which is considered a mental condition eligible for insurance coverage. As discussed, many plans do offer mental health services benefits, which may be helpful in stopping a person from committing suicide but are not useful after the fact.

Persons Affected by Alcohol and Substance Abuse

Most private insurance plans offer some amount of coverage for alcohol and substance abuse services. In the private payer sector, these services are usually administered by providers that focus on patients with private insurance or the financial ability to pay out of pocket. Private sector alcohol and substance abuse programs boast nearly double the revenue per admission that public sector providers charge. Private payer programs usually limit alcohol and substance abuse program spending by capping the amount of benefit available in dollars and by limiting the number of program inpatient days and outpatient visits per enrollee, per year. State law varies on the subject, so some insurance plans offer more coverage than others.

Courtesy of Hemera/Thinkstock

Not all homeless people are without health coverage; 4% reported having private insurance, and another 10% claimed coverage by other means.

Indigent and Homeless Persons

Not all homeless people are without jobs or family ties, which might account for the 4% of homeless people who reported having private health insurance in the 1996 National Survey of Homeless Assistance Providers and Clients published by the U.S. Census Bureau (U.S. Census Bureau, 1996). Another 10% reported having health coverage by means other than private and public payer organizations. Unsurprisingly, those who reported some form of private or "other" health insurance coverage (as opposed to public payer), were significantly more likely to belong to homeless families, rather than being on their own.

Immigrants and Refugees

Immigrants in the United States are less likely than native-born citizens to have any type of health care coverage. In the private payer sector, this is attributable to the fact that immigrants hold fewer white-collar jobs, which are more likely to offer health care coverage benefits. Language barriers may also contribute to a lack of private insurance access because a language barrier makes it more difficult for a person to negotiate benefits with employers and insurers. Language barriers and lower incomes also make it difficult for immigrants to purchase health insurance individually. Immigrants with jobs that do offer private insurance have access equal to their native-born colleagues.

Critical Thinking

Many of America's middle class are losing private payer health insurance due to rising premium prices and employers' inability or unwillingness to continue offering health insurance as an employee benefit. How do you think this will affect the health care system? Do you think it will change demand and costs?

Self-Check

Answer the following questions to the best of your ability.

1. According to the 2009 Federal Interagency Forum on Child and Family Statistics, what percentage of America's children had private health insurance?
   a. 60%
   b. 80%
   c. 40%
   d. 50%

2. Beginning in 2014, what federal act will prohibit insurers from declining coverage based on preexisting conditions?
   a. Medicare Part D Act
   b. Welfare Reform Act
   c Patient Protection and Affordable Care Act
   d. Housing and Insurance Act

3. Which of the following factors makes it difficult for immigrants to purchase health insurance individually?
   a. nationality
   b. language barriers
   c. citizenship
   d. physical handicaps

Answer Key

1. **a**   2. **c**   3. **b**

5.2 Public Payers

The **public payer sector** comprises government-funded programs that provide financial access to health care. These programs include Medicaid, Medicare, health care available to military veterans through the Veterans' Administration, the Federal Employees' Health Benefits Program, states' employees' health benefits programs, and the states' Children's Health Insurance Program (CHIP). These programs all differ in coverage and accessibility.

Medicaid provides health insurance to qualifying adults, primarily those with limited income and resources. It is funded through a federal program but is administered by the states; they provide 20% to 50% of each state's own Medicaid funding through state budgets. Approximately half of the people who receive Supplemental Security Income (SSI) also receive Medicaid benefits based on eligibility due to physical and mental disabilities and disorders. The Patient Protection and Affordable Care Act (PPACA) worked to

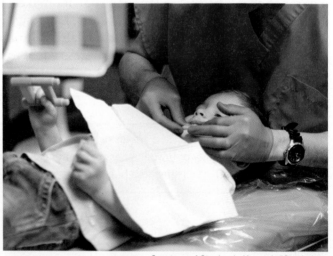

Courtesy of Stephanie Kennedy/iStockphoto

Dental care for children provided by Medicaid is funded with a combination of state and federal monies.

increase access to public payer programs by changing eligibility requirements, among other program changes. In March 2012, the U.S. Centers for Medicare and Medicaid Services (CMS) announced a "final rule" on the PPACA that increases coverage and accessibility to government-funded health care plans. The final rule outlined that Medicaid eligibility would expand in 2014 to include childless adults without disabilities. It also increased the income eligibility requirements to 133% of the federal poverty level (U.S. Centers for Medicare and Medicaid Services [CMS], 2012a), which translates to $14,856 for an individual and $30,656 for a family of four (U.S. CMS, 2012a).

Legislation on both federal and state levels has worked to increase Medicaid access, particularly for vulnerable women and babies. The **Children's Health Insurance Program (CHIP)** is part of the Medicaid collaboration between the federal government and the states, though it is not part of the Medicaid program. CHIP provides extended eligibility and coverage for qualifying children up to age 19. CHIP coverage differs by state, but in all cases provides preventive care, hospital care, and dental care (U.S. CMS, 2012b). As of February 2011, a record 90% of children in the United States had health insurance coverage, either through private payers, Medicaid, or CHIP. However, 8 million children continue to be uninsured. Of these, 5 million are eligible for Medicaid and CHIP but are not enrolled (The Kaiser Family Foundation (KFF), 2012d).

Children and the elderly are the most vulnerable subgroups in any at-risk population. Whereas children are eligible for CHIP, many elderly people are eligible for **Medicare**, a federally run health insurance program. Medicare also covers adults who are unable to work due to permanent disabilities. Medicare can be combined with private payer coverage, though private coverage is the consumer's responsibility.

Medicare provided health insurance coverage for 47,672,971 people in 2011 (KFF, 2012c). Medicare eligibility is based on a few factors:

- You or your spouse must have worked for a minimum of 10 years in Medicare-covered employment, and
- you must be age 65 or older, and
- you must be a citizen or legal permanent resident of the United States.

People with end-stage renal failure or disabilities may be eligible for Medicare even if they are under age 65. Some people are eligible for both Medicare and Medicaid based on income and illness or disability. These individuals are called "dual-eligibles."

Medicare offers a variety of coverage levels, referred to as "Parts." Medicare Part A has no premium for people over age 65 and covers specified inpatient medical treatments in hospitals, skilled nursing facilities, long-term care facilities, hospice care, and other inpatient settings. Medicare Part B costs the insured person a monthly premium ($99.00 in 2012) and covers preventive care and medically necessary services. This includes some coverage for mental health therapies. People who wish to enroll in a Medicare private fee-for-service plan or a Medicare managed care plan must be enrolled in both Medicare Parts A and B. It is important to note that Medicare Parts A and B do not cover long-term residential care, dental care, and eye care. Prescription drug coverage is available through Medicare Part D. This section discusses how vulnerable populations access public payer coverage like Medicaid and Medicare (Medicare.gov, 2012).

Courtesy of Rosemarie Gearhart/iStockphoto

Public health care coverage resources make it possible for high-risk mothers and their children to receive basic health care.

Vulnerable Mothers and Children

Generally speaking, women are paid less than men, and women represent a higher percentage of the low-income population. Women also report more cost barriers to accessing health care for themselves and their children than are reported by men (DeNavas-Walt, Proctor, & Smith, 2011). This is one of the reasons that public health care programs benefit high-risk mothers and children so significantly. Medicaid and the Children's Health Insurance Program (CHIP) are the traditional public health care coverage resources for high-risk mothers and children. These programs are state-run, so benefits coverage is vastly different depending on location. Since the Omnibus Budget Reconciliation Act of 1981 (OBRA), these programs have lost funding and eligibility requirements have tightened repeatedly. OBRA restricted tax deductions for child care expenses, work-related expenses, and earned-income credits. In doing so, many working poor who did not have health insurance through their employers were, in effect, pushed above the income threshold eligibility requirement for public payer health coverage, though their incomes did not increase.

This had negative consequences on child and maternal health outcomes. The legislature responded with the PPACA in 2010, by extending the income eligibility threshold to 185% of the poverty level for families and 133% for individuals. The application process was also sped up with shortened application forms, and the programs were made more accessible by placing Medicaid administrators in locations other than just welfare offices.

The Welfare Reform Act of 1996 (WRA) created the Temporary Assistance for Needy Families (TANF) program, thus limiting coeligibility between welfare and Medicaid. TANF decreased accessibility to high-risk mothers and children by demanding that mothers who could work, must work to be eligible for TANF benefits. Many women who got jobs or continued in their current employment made too much to be eligible for Medicaid, even though they were the working poor and lacked access to private health insurance.

The Patient Protection and Affordable Care Act of 2010 (PPACA) expands access to coverage for all people, but high-risk mothers and babies may stand to gain the most from the expanded access (see Figure 5.1). The PPACA mandates expand private health insurance access through many qualifying employers. It also increases the income threshold eligibility requirement for Medicaid, allowing access for more of America's working poor.

Figure 5.1: Improved access to health insurance under the Patient Protection and Affordable Care Act

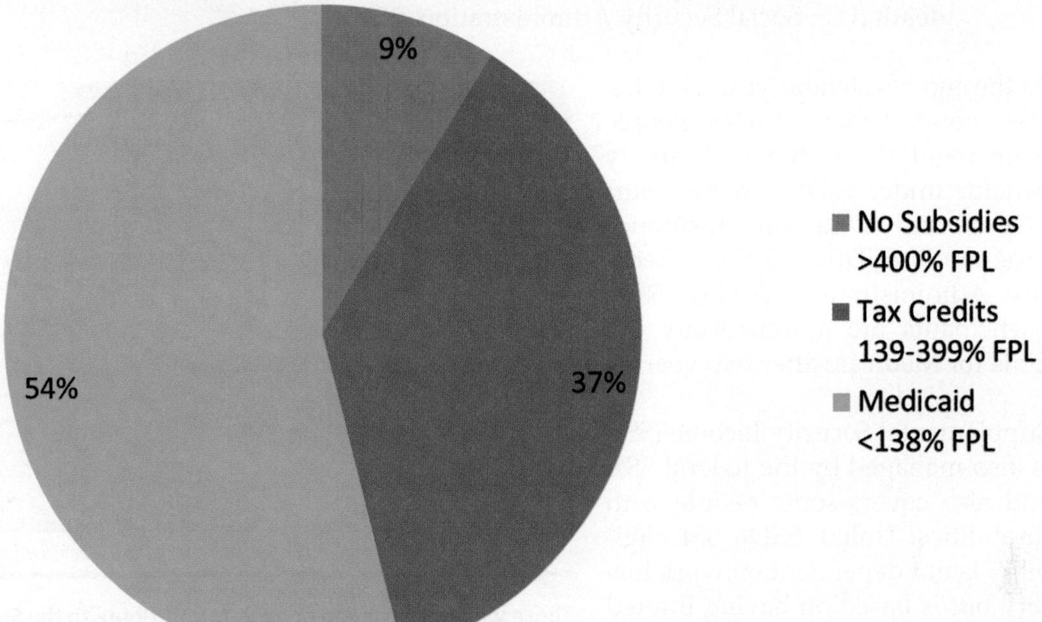

- No Subsidies >400% FPL
- Tax Credits 139-399% FPL
- Medicaid <138% FPL

More than half of high-risk mothers are eligible to receive coverage through Medicaid.

The Henry J. Kaiser Family Foundation (KFF). (2010a). Retrieved from http://www.kff.org/womenshealth/upload/7987.pdf

Abused Individuals

Estimates of treatment for bone injuries, brain injuries, internal injuries, burns, poisoning, and other abuse-related ailments put the total inpatient annual cost in the United States around $20 million. Child abuse is more prevalent among low-income households (U.S. Department of Health and Human Services, Administration for Children and Families, Administration on Children, Youth and Families, Children's Bureau, 2011). As such, most of the cost of treating patients for injuries from abuse is paid for by public payer programs, namely Medicaid. Similarly, Medicare bears the brunt of the cost of treating injuries resulting from elder abuse.

Chronically Ill and Disabled Persons

Under the **Social Security and Disability Insurance (SSDI) program**, the federal government provides a financial safety net for people who become disabled. SSDI pays monthly income to eligible people who have worked enough to contribute to the SSDI program before becoming disabled. The Social Security Administration (SSA) determines eligibility by using the following criteria:

- The applicant cannot do the same type of work that was done before incurring his or her disability or medical condition;

- The applicant has been unable to adjust to other work because of the disability or medical condition(s); and
- The disability has lasted or is expected to last for at least one year or to result in death (U.S. Social Security Administration, 2011).

At the end of calendar year 2011, the SSA reported that 8,576,000 people were regularly receiving disability benefits under SSDI: Old-Age, Survivors, and Disability Insurance program (OASDI) (U.S. Social Security Administration, 2012a). SSDI participants are automatically eligible for Medicare after two years.

Supplemental Security Income (SSI) is also managed by the federal SSA and also covers some people with disabilities. Unlike SSDI, SSI eligibility is not dependent on work history but is based on having limited means to support oneself. SSI participants immediately gain access to Medicaid in most states. Some states supplement SSI payments, increasing the benefit.

Courtesy of Dean Mitchell/iStockphoto

Those who have worked enough to contribute to the Social Security and Disability Insurance (SSDI) program before becoming disabled are eligible to collect monthly SSDI benefits if they also satisfy other criteria.

Those receiving disability benefits under SSDI and SSI may benefit from the Ticket to Work and Self-Sufficiency program (Ticket). Ticket helps place SSI and SSDI participants in jobs, while allowing them to continue to receive benefits. Ticket participants can receive rehabilitation services without endangering their disability benefit eligibility as well. Under the Ticket program, working beneficiaries are not audited for disability qualification by the Administration; benefits can only be diminished or lost based on income eligibility requirements as workers advance their careers and if deemed no longer disabled. Ticket also allows many workers who lose income benefits from SSI and SSDI to continue Medicaid and Medicare coverage (U.S. Social Security Administration, 2012b).

Many SSI and SSDI participants are covered by either or both Medicare and Medicaid. Adults over age 65 who have Medicare may also qualify for Medicaid. Medicare and private insurance plans offer limited coverage for institutionalized care, including nursing homes, and the costs associated with long-term care often drain patients' financial resources. This has created a system in which Medicaid is the single largest payer for long-term care services.

Persons Diagnosed With HIV/AIDS

Public payer programs bear the brunt of medical costs for HIV/AIDS. This is partially because HIV is more prevalent among low-income populations, which utilize Medicare and Medicaid programs. Though public payer programs do limit benefits for antiretroviral drug therapies, treatments for illnesses that result from having a compromised immune system due to HIV/AIDS, such as viral infections and pneumonia, are covered. Grant-funded Ryan White clinics (see Chapter 3) are located in many public health departments to meet the specific needs of HIV/AIDS patients. Additionally, federal and state governments offer preventive programs and nonmedical support to HIV/AIDS patients, which add to the total cost of HIV/AIDS to the government.

As many as 50% of people diagnosed with HIV/AIDS are estimated to receive Medicaid benefits. The number of children living with HIV/AIDS receiving public payer health coverage is estimated to be as high as 90%. In 2011, the United States federal government spent an estimated $27.2 billion in domestic and international HIV/AIDS programs and research (KFF, 2010b). Figure 5.2 shows a detailed breakdown of how the money was spent.

Figure 5.2: Federal spending on HIV/AIDS programs in 2011

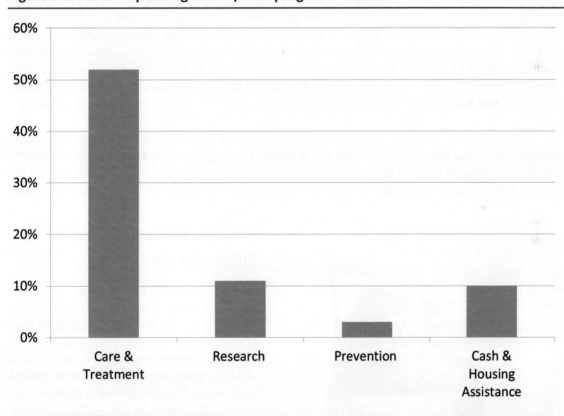

Expenses for care and treatment make up more than half of the spending on HIV/AIDS programs.

The Henry J. Kaiser Family Foundation (KFF). (2010b). Retrieved from http://www.kff.org/hivaids/upload/7029-06.pdf

Persons Diagnosed With Mental Conditions

According to the Substance Abuse and Mental Health Services Administration (SAMHSA), Americans spent $135 billion on mental health and substance abuse services in 2005, which accounted for 6.1% of all health care spending. Public payer programs covered the majority of mental health costs, accounting for 58% of the total spent on mental health care. Medicaid alone covered 28% of the total spent on mental health during that year (Substance Abuse and Mental Health Services Administration [SAMHSA], 2010).

SAMHSA estimates that spending on mental health and substance abuse treatments will continue to increase but will do so at a slower pace than spending on other medical care, as there is less need for mental health and substance abuse treatments than for all other medical care combined. It is projected that overall spending on mental health and substance abuse will be $239 billion in 2014 (Levit et al., 2008). Forecasting predicts that 2014 mental health and substance abuse spending will continue to be covered by public payers at the current rate of 58% of the country's total.

Suicide- and Homicide-Liable Persons

Low-income minority males have the highest homicide rate (Xu, & Kochanek, & Murphy, & Tejada-Vera, 2010). This group also represents a significant number of people who have no health care coverage or use public payer programs. As such, public programs like Medicaid are responsible for much of the cost of violent deaths. Medicaid offers limited coverage for emergency care of gunshot wounds. Many social programs that work to prevent suicide and homicide focus on children. These include Head Start, Child Abuse and Neglect Program, Foster Care programs, and Child Welfare Services. Programs that focus on adults and the elderly include block grants, social services, and community services.

The criminal justice system is responsible for the vast majority of costs associated with violent crime and death. These costs are accrued through investigation of violent deaths and prosecution of offenders. Once offenders are successfully prosecuted, they enter the penitentiary system, where the government pays their room, board, and health care costs.

Courtesy of Big City Lights/Fotolia

More than one third of the United States' substance abuse spending in 2005 was covered by public payers, excluding Medicaid.

Persons Affected by Alcohol and Substance Abuse

SAMHSA (2010) reports that spending on substance abuse treatments comprised 1.2% of the nation's health care spending in 2005. Of the portion spent on substance abuse, 52% was spent at centers that specialize in mental health and alcohol and substance abuse. State and local public payers, excluding Medicaid, paid for 36% of the nation's substance abuse spending in 2005. Medicaid paid 21% of the cost, and private insurance paid 12%. Overall, public payers were responsible for 80% of the nation's substance abuse medical spending. Most of this spending went to publicly owned and not-for-profit programs that mostly serve indigent people.

There has been a shift in substance abuse treatment therapies from the 1980s to 2005. Inpatient treatments represented 56% of substance abuse treatment spending in 1986. A shift to outpatient therapies due to improved pharmaceuticals and deinstitutionalization is evident in the decrease in inpatient spending to 17% in 2005. Outpatient spending rose from 23% in 1986 to 48% in 2005 (SAMHSA, 2010).

Indigent and Homeless Persons

The Homeless Eligibility Clarification Act of 1986 (HECA) improved Medicaid access for indigent people. HECA mandated that a person without a mailing address or income may be denied Medicaid eligibility. Two programs that focus on connecting indigent people with available resources, such as food stamps, Medicaid, and job training, include the Health Resources and Services Administration Health Care for the Homeless department and the Department of Veterans Affairs Health Care for Homeless Veterans program.

Immigrants and Refugees

Access to public payer programs is restricted for immigrants for various reasons. Language barriers make it difficult for immigrants to access and apply for government programs. Some cultures prohibit the use of these programs, regardless of need. American attitudes toward immigrants, and undocumented immigrants in particular, have encouraged legislation that limits public program eligibility for many foreign-born people.

The Welfare Reform Act of 1996 (WRA) stripped many immigrants of their SSI and Medicaid eligibility by declaring that noncitizen immigrants are not eligible for the programs. It went on to make all immigrants ineligible for public means-tested programs for their first five documented years in America, after which point they must declare their sponsors' incomes on means-tested applications. State and local laws often go further, making undocumented immigrants entirely ineligible for public benefit programs.

The Patient Protection and Affordable Care Act of 2010 (PPACA) improves immigrant access to health coverage only slightly. Undocumented immigrants remain ineligible for Medicaid and many other public assistance programs and are also ineligible to purchase health insurance through the insurance marketplace created by the PPACA. Under PPACA, states may waive the five-year waiting period for Medicaid and CHIP program eligibility for documented immigrants. Documented immigrants are also granted access to the health insurance marketplace, and marketplace tax benefits are not subject to the five-year waiting period for Medicaid. The PPACA grants naturalized citizens full access to Medicaid and insurance marketplace benefits that all U.S. citizens have (KFF, 2012c).

Critical Thinking

According to the reading, 90% of children in the United States are eligible to receive some type of health insurance, either through private payers, Medicaid, or CHIP. Do you think it is possible to provide health insurance to 90% of adults? What obstacles stand in the way? What possible solutions would you recommend?

Self-Check

Answer the following questions to the best of your ability.

1. According to the U.S. Substance Abuse and Mental Health Services Administration (SAMHSA), Americans spent how much on mental health and substance abuse services in 2005?
   a. $135 billion
   b. $17 trillion
   c. $13 million
   d. $20 trillion

2. Which of the following social programs works to prevent suicide and homicide and focuses on children?
   a. Health in the Community
   b. KinderCare
   c. Head Start
   d. Montessori

3. Which group of immigrants is granted access to the health insurance marketplace and may not have to wait for five years?
   a. undocumented immigrants
   b. those from Cuba
   c. those from Canada
   d. documented immigrants

Answer Key
1. a   2. c   3. d

5.3 Uninsured People

Approximately 16.3% of the United States population has no health insurance coverage. Children under age 18 lack health insurance at a rate of 9.3% overall and at a rate of 15.4% for those living in poverty (DeNavas-Walt et al., 2011). Uninsured people are more likely to avoid or delay seeking health care. Although there is little evidence to suggest that this lack of preventive care increases emergency room (ER) visits for the uninsured, those living below the poverty line have a significantly higher incidence of ER visits, as shown in Figure 5.3 (Garcia, Bernstein, & Bush, 2010). When uninsured people do seek medical care, they are often stuck with the entire bill. In some cases, they may be eligible for financial assistance through the health care organization where they were treated and other charities that exist to help people pay for medical treatments.

Many hospitals offer financial aid programs for patients who cannot afford medical treatment. These programs are eligibility-based. When a patient cannot pay his or her medical bills and does not qualify for financial aid, the hospital absorbs some of the cost. But how? The answer here is both simple and complex. The simple answer is that the hospital absorbs the loss and passes it to others through cost-of-service increases. The complex answer is that the high rates everyone pays through the system are charged at such a high rate to pay for the service *and* all those services the hospital will never get paid for. The insurance companies absorb the cost of this and pass the rest to the populace through the use of insurance premiums. So those with insurance pay for that service in a snowball chain and thereby end up paying for it twice. Large insurance pools spread this out a little further, where it is shared more equally.

Figure 5.3: Prevalence of emergency room visits by poverty level

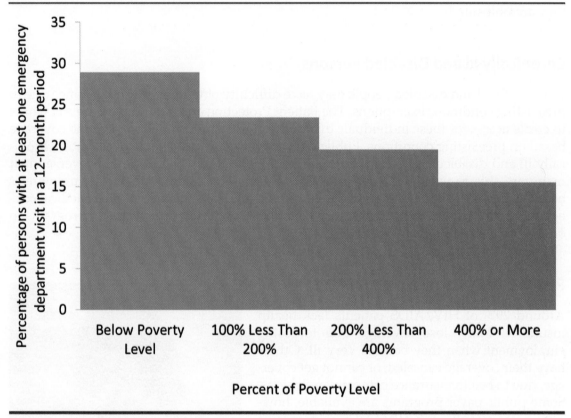

Emergency room visits per year decrease the farther a person moves above the poverty level.

CDC/NCHS, National Health Interview Survey. (2010). Retrieved from http://www.cdc.gov/nchs/data/databriefs/db38.pdf

Vulnerable Mothers and Children

Women of childbearing age have a particularly high incidence of having no health care payer coverage. Only 64% of America's pregnant women are estimated to have any amount of coverage for pregnancy and childbirth expenses, whether they have insurance or not. This is partially due to health insurance plans that do not cover pregnancy expenses, and partially due to the fact that one-quarter of pregnant mothers lack health insurance of any type when they become pregnant. These women are often low income, of minority ethnicity, young mothers, and unwed. Obstetricians and other women's health service providers can provide these women with information and access to resources, including the Program for Children with Special Health Care Needs, which supports providers who care for these high-risk mothers. Through programs like this, the uninsured rate decreases to 15% by the time of delivery.

Abused Individuals

As abusive offenders are often under- or unemployed, it stands to reason that many offenders and victims of abuse have no health insurance coverage at all. It is thought that abused individuals may also avoid seeking public payer coverage for fear of being found out. No data is available on the number of uninsured abused individuals or the reasons they are uninsured.

Chronically Ill and Disabled Persons

Chronically ill and disabled people may have difficulty obtaining health insurance due to preexisting conditions exemptions. The Patient Protection and Affordable Care Act works to create access for these individuals by diminishing insurers' ability to decline coverage based on preexisting conditions. Public payer programs are available to the most chronically ill and disabled, who are unable to work due to their conditions. However, a great many are able to work but unable to work full time or maintain gainful employment because they have limited functioning. Low wages and jobs that do not offer medical coverage benefits make it difficult for those who do not qualify for public payer programs to obtain private health insurance.

Persons Diagnosed With HIV/AIDS

Around 29% of HIV/AIDS patients lack health insurance. Many lose coverage due to losing employment when they become very ill. Others have their coverage canceled, or cannot get coverage, due to health insurance company exclusions. Some public payer programs are available, however, some people with HIV/AIDS who receive Social Security and Disability Income benefits may not be eligible for government health care programs because their incomes are too high.

Courtesy of kmiragaya/fotolia

Persons Diagnosed With Mental Conditions

Lack of health insurance is particularly problematic for those with severe, chronic mental conditions. According to the National Alliance on Mental Illness (NAMI) and SAMHSA, one-fifth of all patients with serious mental illness are uninsured (National Alliance on Mental Illness [NAMI], 2007). The truth is that these patients need a great amount of inpatient and outpatient therapies. Many are prescribed costly pharmaceuticals to help stabilize their conditions. Drug compliance can be difficult to maintain in this

According to the National Institute for Mental Health and the National Center for Health Statistics, psychiatric patients have a 2% higher incidence rate of being uninsured than other medical patients.

vulnerable group, and lack of health insurance to offset the price of mental health drugs exacerbates the compliance problem when uninsured patients cannot afford to have their prescriptions filled.

Suicide- and Homicide-Liable Persons

Mental health therapy is often cost prohibitive for uninsured suicide-prone people and homicide-prone people, both victims and offenders, pose a particular strain on the public health system. Young African American and Hispanic males are both homicide-prone and have high uninsured rates. Emergency room visits for gunshot wounds are expensive. Many hospitals offer financial aid for patients who qualify. For those who don't, the bills for treatment can lead to financial ruin.

Persons Affected by Alcohol and Substance Abuse

Most Medicaid and private insurance plans limit coverage of substance abuse treatments. State Medicaid coverage of substance abuse therapies differs on scope and price coverage. An estimated 13% of the total cost for treatment is paid directly by patients in the private sector. Because low-income, vulnerable populations have a higher incidence of substance abuse, it follows that the majority of patients treated for substance abuse either are on public health plans or have no insurance at all.

Indigent and Homeless Persons

The majority of homeless people and many indigent people lack health insurance of any kind. However, many are eligible for Social Security and Disability Insurance (SSDI) and Medicaid. Although the Welfare Reform Act of 1996 tightened eligibility requirements, making it more difficult for many people to qualify for SSDI, Medicare, and Medicaid, the Patient Protection and Affordable Care Act worked to widen eligibility requirements to cover more people. Even with increased eligibility, the safety net of services for the homeless has large gaps in access and coverage. Connecting the homeless with medical coverage services continues to be extremely difficult.

Immigrants and Refugees

Many immigrants and refugees hold low-paying jobs that do not offer health insurance as a benefit of employment. The language barriers and low incomes make it difficult for them to find private health insurance on their own. Many make too much to qualify for public payer coverage but cannot access private payer coverage through work. Undocumented immigrants cannot get health insurance because they lack the necessary documentation, such as a Social Security card. The U.S. Department of Health and Human Services data shown in Figure 5.4 illustrates that Hispanics are disproportionately represented among the uninsured, as they compose 14% of the American population but represent 30% of the total number of uninsured in America (U.S. Department of Health and Human Services, Office of the Assistant Secretary for Planning and Evaluation, 2005).

Figure 5.4: Portion of uninsured as compared with portion of the total population

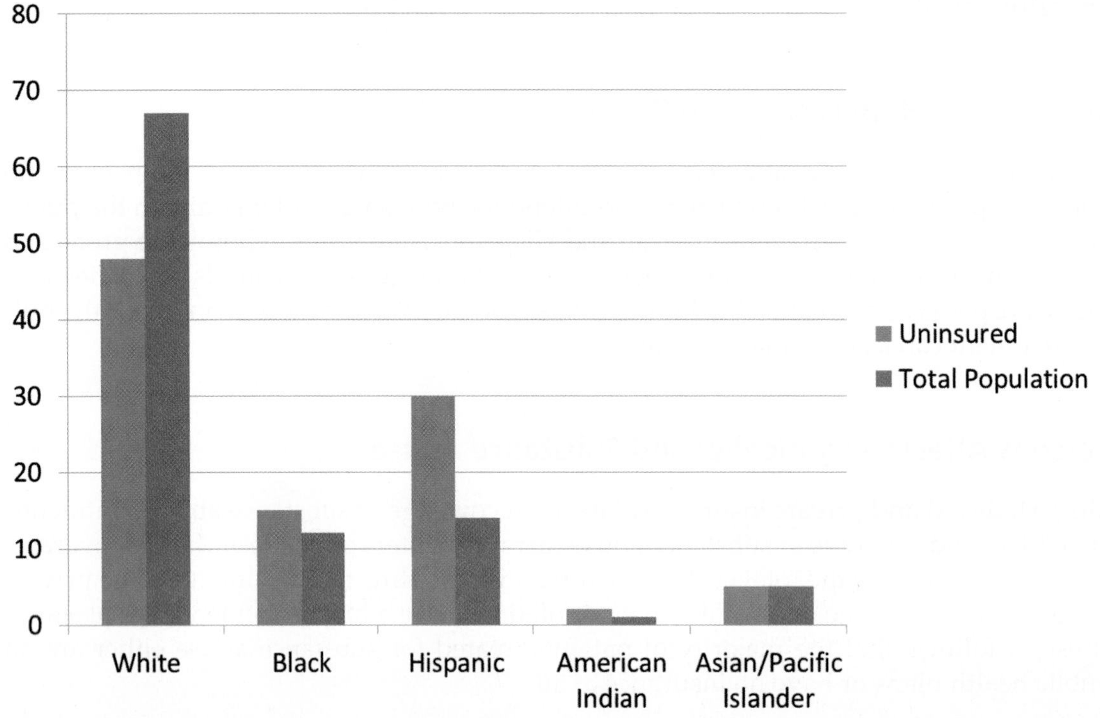

Blacks and Hispanics are uninsured disproportionately to the percentage of the American population they represent.

Department of Health and Human Services. (2005). Distribution of the uninsured and total U.S. population by race/ethnicity in 2004. Retrieved from http://aspe.hhs.gov/health/reports/05/uninsured-cps/ib.pdf

Critical Thinking

Many hospitals and insurance agencies pass on the cost of caring for uninsured patients. How effective is this policy, and what changes might be made to improve it?

Self-Check

Answer the following questions to the best of your ability.

1. What proportion of pregnant mothers lack health insurance of any type when they become pregnant?
   a. 64%
   b. 50%
   c. 25%
   d. 15%

2. What percentage of HIV/AIDS patients lack health insurance?
   a. 17%
   b. 20%
   c. 29%
   d. 42%

3. An estimated 13% of the total cost for treatment is paid directly by patients in the private sector who suffer from what condition?
   a. HIV/AIDS
   b. at-risk pregnancies
   c. PTSD
   d. substance and alcohol abuse

Answer Key

1. **a**   2. **c**   3. **d**

Case Study: Thinking Outside the Cash Box at St. Jude Children's Research Hospital

For America's uninsured, and even those with public or private health insurance, catastrophic medical events can create financial hardship. Many hospitals offer financial aid services for families that cannot afford to pay for treatments. Some have hospital foundations that are used to cover these expenses. Of these, St. Jude Children's Research Hospital is a shining example.

St. Jude treats approximately 7,800 pediatric patients per year. The 78-bed research hospital sees critically ill children, mostly on a recurring, outpatient basis. Among its many accomplishments is the creation of treatment protocols that improved the survival rate for acute lymphoblastic leukemia, the most common cancer type among children, from 4% in 1962 to the current 94% survival rate (St. Jude Children's Research Hospital, n.d.).

St. Jude's daily operating cost is $1.7 million for research and patient treatments (St. Jude Children's Research Hospital, n.d.). Absolutely none of that money comes from the patients' families' pocketbooks. St. Jude is bankrolled by the hospital foundation, which exists almost entirely thanks to public donations. Through fund-raising efforts, St. Jude's foundation is able to continue to treat patients without billing directly to families, and further research lifesaving cures for catastrophically ill children.

Chapter Summary

The United States spends more per capita, meaning for each person, on health care than any other nation at $8,086 per person (Centers for Disease Control and Prevention [CDC], 2011). For the sake of comparison, the United States spent $7,538 per capita on health care in 2007, Norway spent $5,003 per capita in that same year, and the United Kingdom (which has a single-payer health care system) spent $3,129 per capita on health care in 2007 (KFF, 2011b). In 2009, spending on health care accounted for 18% of the gross domestic product (GDP) in the United States. As health care costs continue to increase, America struggles to find a way to mitigate the problem of growing costs while creating affordable coverage for everybody.

A small majority of Americans have private payer health insurance, usually provided through employers. For those who do not have affordable access through employer benefits plans, health care costs limit access to providers. Public payer programs like Medicare and Medicaid exist to provide affordable coverage to many Americans. However, many argue that these programs are a burden on the country's budget. Private plans and public programs still do not cover all Americans, and the working poor and immigrants often fall through the cracks in America's health care delivery system.

Critical Thinking

Considering the amount the United States spends on health care each year, what changes could be made to increase access to health insurance for the working poor and immigrants? Would increased spending be an effective way to address this deficit? Can you think of other possible solutions to this problem?

Self-Check

Answer the following questions to the best of your ability.

1. In 2010, 64% of the American population had private health insurance.
   a. True
   b. False

2. The Patient Protection and Affordable Care Act created a Pre-Existing Condition Insurance Plan (PCIP) that will begin in what year?
   a. 2016
   b. 2015
   c. 2014
   d. 2018

3. To be eligible for SSDI, the Social Security Administration requires that
   a. the applicant's medical condition or disability is very severe.
   b. the applicant is unable to perform the same type of work that he or she did before incurring the medical condition.
   c. the applicant's medical condition has lasted for at least six months.
   d. the applicant's income is at or below the poverty line.

4. What available resources exist for homeless people through the two federal programs Health Resources and Services Administration Health Care for the Homeless department and the Department of Veterans Affairs Health Care for Homeless Veterans?
   a. community outreach
   b. service animals
   c. Medicaid
   d. faith-based programs

5. What makes it difficult for those who do not quality for public payer programs to obtain private health insurance?
    a. low wages
    b. jobs that do offer insurance
    c. understaffed government housing offices
    d. preexisting conditions

6. _____ and low incomes make it difficult for foreign-born people to find private health insurance on their own.
    a. Language barriers
    b. Immigration regulations
    c. The Welfare Reform Act
    d. The Patient Protection and Affordable Care Act of 2010

Answer Key

1. **a**   2. **c**   3. **b**   4. **c**   5. **a**   6. **a**

Additional Resources

Visit the following websites to learn more about the topics covered in this chapter:

The SSA's website explains disability benefits.

http://www.ssa.gov/dibplan/index.htm

St. Jude's website

http://www.stjude.org/stjude/v/index.jsp?vgnextoid=f87d4c2a71fca210VgnVCM1000001e0215acRCRD

Shriner's Hospital for Children

http://www.shrinershospitalsforchildren.org/

Web Exercise

Using the Internet, locate three *local* health care foundations that benefit patients. Create a 10-slide PowerPoint presentation that covers your findings. Be sure to include the following:

*   contextual information (who, what, where)
*   history of foundation
*   mission or belief of service

- population served
- funding sources/types
- any affiliations (corporate, such as McDonald's or Wendy's, or noncorporate, such as Shriner's, Knights of Columbus, Masons, Rotary, etc.)

As always, spelling, grammar, and readability are important.

Key Terms

Children's Health Insurance Program (CHIP) Administered under the Medicaid services umbrella, CHIP provides extended eligibility and coverage for qualifying children up to age 19.

commodity A product available for purchase.

co-pay The portion of a patient's bill for which he or she is responsible at the time a medical service is provided.

deductible The portion of expenses a person must pay out of pocket before an insurer pays any expenses.

enrollees Insurance plan participants.

insurance claims Bills sent to the insurance company to pay for a covered patient's health care services rendered.

Medicaid A health insurance program funded with state monies, which provides health insurance to qualifying low-income adults.

Medicare A federally run health insurance program for people age 65 and over, and those unable to work due to permanent disabilities.

per capita For each person.

prenatal care Care of the mother and baby during pregnancy, including ultrasounds, gestational diabetes screening, and obstetric and gynecological care.

private payer sector Programs that provide financial access to health care, which includes insurance companies, employer-run health coverage programs, and patients who pay for health care out of pocket.

public payer sector Government-funded programs that provide financial access to health care.

Social Security and Disability Insurance (SSDI) program A federal government that provides a financial safety net, in the form of monthly income checks, for people who become disabled and who have worked enough to contribute to the SSDI program before becoming disabled.

6

Accessing Health Care

Learning Objectives

After reading this chapter, you should be able to:

- Identify where access barriers originate.

- Examine the organizational barriers to accessing health services as experienced by vulnerable populations.

- Explain the financial barriers to accessing health services as experienced by vulnerable populations.

- Consider ways to improve access to health care.

- Explain the politico-social forces affecting access to health care.

Introduction

Though institutionalized racial segregation ended decades ago, many would argue that Americans continue to be segregated by socioeconomic class. Economic status determines where people live and attend school, and even where they go to the doctor. Vulnerable populations face access barriers to health care in both financial and organizational forms. For example, many physicians do not accept patients on Medicaid, and many who do limit the number to a certain percentage of their practices or a certain number of appointments per week. This creates an *organizational barrier* to health care access for Medicaid recipients. At the same time, many low-income people struggle to find the money to pay for services that aren't covered by Medicaid or the co-pays on the services covered by their employers' insurance, thereby creating a *financial barrier* to access. As more physicians abandon small private practices in favor of joining large health care conglomerates where they can improve reimbursement rates and lower malpractice insurance rates, and more people receive Medicaid or Medicare, reliable access for the vulnerable becomes increasingly tenuous.

Courtesy of Sheri Armstrong/Fotolia

Though a patient may be covered by Medicaid, many are unable to take full advantage of that coverage because of physician-imposed limits and restrictions.

Critical Thinking

The text states, "More physicians abandon small private practices in favor of joining large health care conglomerates." Do you think that these larger corporations would be more willing to accept Medicaid patients and thus increase accessibility?

Self-Check

Answer the following questions to the best of your ability.

1. Which populations face access barriers to health care in both financial and organizational forms?
   a. vulnerable
   b. naturalized citizens
   c. employed
   d. school-age children

2. Many physicians limit the number of what types of patients to a certain percentage of their practices or to a certain number of appointments per week?
   a. HIV/AIDS
   b. elderly
   c. those on Medicaid
   d. charitable cases

3. Many low-income people struggle to find the money to pay for what services covered by their employers' insurance?
   a. enrollment fees
   b. wage taxes
   c. political contributions
   d. co-pays at medical facilities

Answer Key

1. **a**   2. **c**   3. **d**

6.1 Organizational Barriers

Organizational barriers to health care access for America's most vulnerable include health care deserts with a limited number of health care locations in poor, urban areas; understaffed health care offices in vulnerable areas that are unable to meet the needs of the number of patients in the area; cultural gaps between providers and patients in low-income regions; and fear. Fear, in fact, creates a two-sided access barrier. On the provider side, many practitioners choose not to locate their practices in poor regions for fear for the safety of the staff, fear of lawsuits from socioeconomically disadvantaged individuals seeking to take advantage of physicians' malpractice insurance, and fear of financial hardship caused by too many patients who cannot pay their medical bills. On the patient side, fear creates an access barrier due to fear of an inability to pay for services, fear of intrusion into their lives, and fear of a health care delivery system that is populated by practitioners who cannot relate to vulnerable patients' struggles. Each vulnerable population experiences organizational barriers to access differently; these varied experiences will be explored in greater detail in the next few sections.

Vulnerable Mothers and Children

The effects of organizational barriers for high-risk mothers and babies begin before conception. Many women do not receive **gynecological care**—medical care specializing in the female reproductive system—from their family doctors. This means that many women, regardless of socioeconomic class, must act as an informational go-between among their multiple medical providers, carrying test results between doctors' offices and remembering to provide complete medical histories from memory. Without **electronic health records**, which store a patient's health data in a digital database that is accessible by all of a patient's authorized providers, the delivery system for women's health care remains disjointed and difficult to maneuver. Vulnerable mothers often lack access to appropriate gynecological care and reproductive health counseling, which increases the risk of unplanned pregnancies. They often seek prenatal care later in their pregnancies than those with stronger support systems. Many women with incomes below 200% of the federal poverty level report not seeking health care due to an inability to take off work during clinic hours. Others report that physical access to health care is restricted because they lack transportation to get to doctors' offices (Ranji & Salganicoff, 2011).

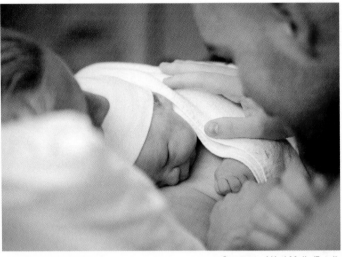

Courtesy of Kati Molin/Fotolia

Many women with incomes below the poverty level are not able to seek health care because of an inability to leave work during regular clinic hours.

Many of the organizational barriers to accessing health care faced by women can be mitigated by extending clinic hours and locating services along public transportation routes and in low-income urban and rural areas. Unfortunately, national trends have been in the opposite direction. Instead of locating their offices in low-income areas, many physicians are moving out of them (U.S. Health Resources and Services Administration, 2012).

The number of doctors who treat pregnant women for pregnancy, called **obstetricians**, is also diminishing. Those who remain increasingly give up small, independent practices in favor of joining large for-profit health care conglomerates. By doing so, they are able to minimize malpractice insurance premiums and their individual liability (U.S. Health Resources and Services Administration, 2012). Many of the large hospitals that do provide obstetric care are located in more affluent areas, where private payers and patients are better able to pay higher fees for medical care. This, of course, creates an organizational barrier for vulnerable mothers, who must find appropriate transportation to access these areas.

Abused Individuals

Organizational barriers to health care for abused individuals reside in a fragmented treatment system that includes a menagerie of medical and mental therapies, as well as intervention from social services and the criminal justice system. Law enforcement, educators, and doctors are often the first reporters of domestic abuse of women and children (Child Welfare Information Gateway, 2012). Their reports of suspected abuse are made to government social services agencies including Child Protective Services (CPS). Once a report is made, social workers investigate, and if severe abuse or neglect is present, the process of removing the victims from the home and the rehabilitation of families begins. A breakdown in the reporting process occurs when school and medical center staff are poorly trained in recognizing the symptoms of abuse and have reservations about the ramifications of reporting suspected abuse.

Adult victims of domestic violence can be more difficult to remove from an abusive situation than are children. Legally, CPS social workers can remove a child from an abusive situation if they deem it to be necessary. However, social workers from agencies like Adult Protective Services (APS) cannot forcibly remove an adult who does not want to leave or declines to leave for fear of retribution from the abuser. The criminal justice system gets involved in punishing offenders of child, intimate partner, and elder abuse and is often the only line of defense for an adult victim of domestic violence. This does not necessarily mean that reported offenders are arrested or jailed. The criminal justice system also facilitates restraining orders and orders of protection.

Among the community organizations and government departments that address domestic violence, there is little overlap and partnership in programming, as independently involved organizations often focus on different aspects of the abuse. For example, many programs that exist for treating child victims of abuse do not address the needs of the adults in the relationship. Most battered women shelters will accept children, although having children may alter a woman's ability to remain at the shelter due to shelter rules about the length of time a child may be housed or individual childcare issues such as keeping the children in their enrolled schools. More cooperation is needed between the disassociated agencies that are in place to address the needs of abused individuals.

Chronically Ill and Disabled Persons

Organizational barriers for chronically ill and disabled individuals revolve around physical access to programs and providers, as well as program eligibility requirements and an uncoordinated selection of programs.

People with mobility problems may have difficulty simply getting to treatment centers. This is particularly true for low-income disabled and chronically ill patients who statistically lack social capital, which can be thought of as the number of relationships a person has and/or the number of social networks a person belongs to, all of which provide resources and support. For example, a person in an advanced stage of multiple sclerosis (MS) may have difficulty walking without the use of a cane. This may mean that he or she can only access doctor's offices that have parking structures within reasonable walking distances. Additionally, without

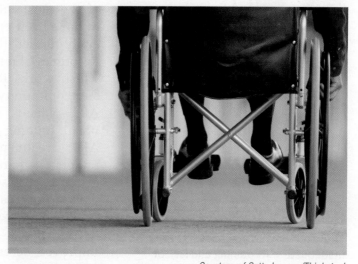

Courtesy of Getty Images/Thinkstock

Often, treatment is hindered for people with mobility problems due to an inability or difficulty in getting to treatment centers.

a friend or relative who can help navigate the walk from the parking structure to the office, he or she may find the trip too arduous to complete on his or her own.

Even when an individual is eligible for particular programs—whether that be caretaker respite programs, meal delivery programs, home visits, and transportation services—these programs may not be available in his or her area. Often, coordination is lacking when services are available, which creates a barrier to access. Individual community programs and government programs operate independently, and each often has its own focus. For example, a meal delivery program may not offer caretaker respite. In these situations, it is up to the individual person to find available resources and enroll in needed programs.

Persons Diagnosed With HIV/AIDS

HIV/AIDS patients face organizational barriers to health care access in many different forms. Limited space is designated in long-term centers specifically for HIV/AIDS patients; staff is sometimes undertrained in HIV/AIDS care; some medical staff may purposefully limit their contact with HIV/AIDS patients for fear of contracting the disease or for other personal reasons; and the sparse number of community support services is often underfunded and has long waiting lists. Ways of counteracting these barriers include improved staff training on the history, or **pathology**, of HIV/AIDS; its **epidemiology**, which refers to the distribution and prevalence of disease in a population; and best practices for HIV/AIDS–related patient care.

Courtesy of Minerva Studio/Fotolia

Inadequate staff training and lack of funds can prevent HIV/AIDS patients from receiving proper care.

Improved financial access to antiretroviral drugs would continue to lower the number of HIV/AIDS patients in need of long-term care, and improved funding for community-based resources would help shorten waiting lists. One of the most important public health initiatives to have been enacted in recent years is the federally funded Ryan White Comprehensive AIDS Resources Emergency (CARE) Act program, which works to improve access to health care and community resources for low-income HIV/AIDS patients. The act provides grants and additional funding to secure the success of HIV/AIDS treatment and prevention programs in underserved areas. (For more information on the community-based and health care organization–based resources supported by the CARE Act, visit http://hab.hrsa.gov/.)

Improved access to general care providers and preventive counseling among those most at risk for contracting HIV would work to lower the number of new infections. Among homeless intravenous drug abusers, access to preventive care and treatments is severely limited. Without functional inpatient care, homeless and intravenous drug abusers who have HIV/AIDS find it difficult to maintain treatment compliance, as physical and financial access barriers make it difficult to obtain medication and maintain treatments plans.

Persons Diagnosed With Mental Conditions

Before the first antipsychotic drug, Thorazine, was used to treat mentally ill patients, America's most severely mentally ill were regularly housed in government-run institutions (Torrey, 1997). Ten years after Thorazine became common in psychological therapy, Medicaid was created to improve health care access for low-income individuals. The combination of these two events, in tandem with a shift in social ideology regarding forced institutionalization and involuntary care, created an atmosphere wherein physicians were encouraged to deinstitutionalize mental health care for the most severely affected. By the 1990s, most of America's long-term care facilities for the severely mentally ill were no longer in service. Now, the onus of inpatient care of severely mentally ill patients rests on nursing care facilities, the criminal justice system, and the diminished number of specialized long-term inpatient care centers that treat mental illness.

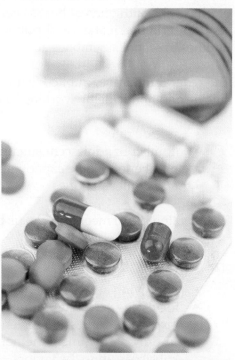

Courtesy of WavebreakmediaMicro /Fotolia

Thorazine was used to treat mentally ill patients before antipsychotic drugs were available.

Housing is perhaps the most pressing health care access problem for individuals with severe mental conditions. Without proper housing, they are liable to suffer the myriad negative health outcomes of homelessness. Some of these patients also end up in the criminal justice system, where their health care access is limited by the institution (U.S. Bureau of Justice Statistics, 2006). Outcomes are improved for those patients who live with their families, but access is often limited to community resources for the caregivers of mentally ill patients. If there is a lack of community resources, the strain on caregivers may be overwhelming; as a result, patients may end up having to leave their homes. More funding for community support programs and resource organizations like the National Alliance for the Mentally Ill (NAMI) may lead to increased access and improved outcomes. Many of these same support programs can also help create positive outcomes for people with mental conditions who live independently, in board and care homes, group homes, and veterans' housing.

The Surgeon General's 1999 report on mental health in the United States reflected that social attitudes that encourage a microlevel personal view of mental health that put all the responsibility of care on the individual negatively affect funding proposals that would support mental health services (National Institute of Health, 1999). Legislation increasing financial support of mental health programs, and increasing coverage for mental health therapies, could change social opinions and raise awareness of the existence of a vulnerable population living with mental conditions. Resourcing staff who once worked in long-term care institutions for the mentally disturbed to train new staff in community-based programs would increase those programs' ability to effectively help psychiatric patients (Koyanagi & Bazelon, 2007).

Suicide- and Homicide-Liable Persons

Suicidal and homicidal behaviors stem from a mix of mental health problems and socioeconomic inequality. As such, the programs in place that work to lower suicide and homicide rates are uncoordinated. Programs on violence prevention exist in the fields of physical health, mental health, community-based support programs, education, social services, criminal justice, and public health and wellness. Initiatives range from suicide hotlines to school assemblies about violence prevention to support group therapies.

The federal initiative, Public Health Objectives for the Nation, 2020 (PHON), addresses suicide and homicide by working to reduce the following (U.S. Healthy People, 2012):

- suicide rate
- number of adolescent suicide attempts
- number of people experiencing major depressive episodes in both adolescent and adult categories

PHON attempts to meet these goals by doing the following:

- increasing the number of primary care facilities offering mental health treatment services
- improving access to mental health services for children
- increasing screening for mental health problems in juvenile residential facilities
- increasing depression screening in primary care settings
- improving treatment methods for people with both mental health disorders and substance abuse behaviors

Although clinical interventions are important for treating individual patients, community interventions have a greater effect on homicide and suicide rates on a macro level. One of PHON's community intervention plans is an initiative to improve programs and access to those programs for treating patients who have suffered traumatic events. Improved training for hospital social workers, emergency room staff, physicians, and educators will increase the recognition of adults and youth who are prone to violence or are subjected to violence, and get them into prevention programs faster. Improving local economies and living conditions in low-income areas may also reduce the overall number of attempted homicides and suicides by reducing stress on the people who populate those areas.

Persons Affected by Alcohol and Substance Abuse

Alcohol and substance dependence has both **physiological** and **psychological** components. Physiological dependence on a substance is evidenced primarily by the development of physical symptoms (withdrawal symptoms) when the substance is no longer consumed. Psychological dependence, on the other hand, manifests as a desire, or "craving," for a substance. Although effective treatment for alcohol and substance abuse must address both the physiological and psychological aspects of a person's addiction, some treatment programs address only one or the other. This means that patients are sometimes forced to coordinate two kinds of care in order to address their chemical dependencies. In some circumstances, both physiological and psychological therapies are offered in tandem

Courtesy of Jochen Sands/Thinkstock

Many alcohol and substance abuse programs do not holistically treat the patient, instead addressing either only the psychological symptoms or only the physical symptoms.

under the umbrella of one provider organization. Many patients are under treatment as mandated by social services or the criminal justice system. These patients often lack the means to seek out the best possible treatment options for their particular circumstances, and instead receive the minimum mandated care.

Alcohol and substance abuse programs are improved by increasing awareness of the socioeconomic struggles that lead to higher drug abuse rates in some communities. Culturally sensitive treatments use cultural components, like religion and cultural-based social norms, to encourage and empower the patient to continue treatment and make the necessary physical and emotional changes that can keep them from relapsing. Treatment centers can also reduce organizational barriers by hiring bilingual staff and locating in underserved areas.

Indigent and Homeless Persons

Homeless individuals are far more likely to lack a regular family doctor. Many avoid seeking care unless absolutely necessary. When medical care does become an immediate need, homeless persons without a regular physician often end up at urgent care centers and hospital emergency rooms. Social attitudes about homeless people often lead to their being met with negativity and hostility. Many homeless people report being sent away from some medical care clinics to seek treatment elsewhere. Transportation difficulties make it difficult for this vulnerable population to move from clinic to clinic seeking medical treatment.

Courtesy of Brand X Pictures/Thinkstock

Between 2009 to 2010, a lack of health care and increasing rates of reckless behavior have raised demand for emergency food assistance by nearly 24%.

Financial barriers, social stigmas, and physical access barriers like limited transportation lead to an exacerbated health deficit for America's homeless. Increased rates of unprotected sex, drug abuse, and HIV, combined with a lack of regular health care, have caused America's homeless numbers to strain the support system that is in place to address their needs. The U. S. Conference of Mayors' 2010 Hunger and Homelessness Survey reported that demand for emergency food assistance increased almost 24% from 2009 to 2010. Mayors reported that increasing the availability of affordable housing topped their initiatives lists as a means to mitigate a growing homeless population. Unemployment was the most cited cause of homelessness for family units. Together, increasing employment opportunities and affordable housing offer a macrolevel solution to reducing the number of America's homeless and to reducing the need for medical care among this population. Fewer homeless puts less strain on the health care delivery system and may increase access to those still homeless by having a smaller pool of people who rely on the already small pool of funds for emergency care of the homeless.

Immigrants and Refugees

Naturalized citizens face fewer organizational access barriers than undocumented immigrants and refugees. Many refugees live in government-subsidized housing. Others may live in areas that are more densely populated with other immigrants. Physicians' offices and other medical clinics are often sparse in these areas. In some cases, medical providers have the legal right to request proof of legal immigration before seeing patients. Many undocumented immigrants avoid seeking medical care for fear of deportation.

Immigrants and refugees also face language barriers and cultural barriers to accessing health care. Medical providers can limit these barriers by hiring bilingual staff and training staff to understand and meet the needs of their patients based on cultural ideals and norms. For example, a physician's office that treats a significant number of Muslim families should be familiar with acceptable behaviors related to the body, such as rules concerning clothing and disrobing in front of a person of the opposite gender, as dictated by the religion of Islam. Other cultural barriers involve differences in how health and well-being are defined. Cultural acceptance is fundamental to providing quality care to immigrant populations.

Critical Thinking

Many vulnerable patients have a "fear of a health care delivery system that is populated by practitioners who cannot relate to vulnerable patients' struggles." How do you interpret this statement? How might a practitioner overcome this fear?

Self-Check

Answer the following questions to the best of your ability.

1. Authorized providers can access a patient's health data _____.
   a. on the Internet
   b. in electronic health records

c. in a centrally located records department
d. in a warehouse in Washington, DC

2. Many of the support services available to disabled people are delivered through what type of programs?
   a. Veteran's Affairs
   b. Medicaid
   c. community
   d. state department

3. Currently, which entities are responsible for inpatient care of severely mentally ill patients?
   a. nursing care facilities
   b. private homes
   c. local businesses
   d. professional organizations

Answer Key

1. **b**   2. **c**   3. **a**

6.2 Financial Barriers

The United States spends more on health care per capita than any other nation, and health care costs are still rising across the globe. This is partially due to America's free market economy, which avoids regulating industry as much as possible. It is also because America is a forerunner in the development and adoption of new medical technologies and pharmaceuticals. New technologies and drugs cost more than older ones because the manufacturers price them high to help recoup the costs associated with research, development, and federal safety approval.

Courtesy of George Doyle/Thinkstock

Deregulation of the industry and the rapid development of new medical technologies and pharmaceuticals have resulted in the United States spending more on health care per capita than any other nation.

Most insurance plans include co-pays, deductibles, and cost sharing. These patient charges result in decreased financial accessibility to medical care, even for patients with private payer insurance. As it is difficult for patients to know what their out-of-pocket expenses will be for many tests and procedures done in physician offices, many people avoid health care treatments as much as possible. In some circumstances, patients are subject to blood tests and other procedures without an opportunity to consider the costs before they are administered. Imagine the shock of one patient who received a bill for $7,000 for a DNA test that was not covered by insurance and was done at the same time that blood was drawn for routine annual blood work.

Both public and private payers limit the amount of coverage per patient. Medicaid negotiates lower reimbursement rates for physicians. Because of this, many physicians maximize the percentage of clientele with private payer insurance because private payers have higher reimbursement rates. This practice, based on financial decisions, leads to organizational barriers to care when Medicaid and uninsured patients cannot find doctors and medical clinics that will treat them.

Vulnerable Mothers and Children

Prenatal care is expensive, partially due to the cost of treatment, and partially due to high liability insurance premiums that obstetricians must pay to avoid financial ruin from malpractice lawsuits. When doctors pay high insurance premiums, that cost is reflected in what they charge patients for care.

Courtesy of Carlos Santa Maria/Fotolia

In 2009, 22.3% of women of **childbearing age** (women in the age range of highest fertility, which is 15 to 44) had no insurance coverage of any type. This was an 11% increase from that of 2008 (March of Dimes Foundation, 2010). Uninsured women are significantly less likely to seek early prenatal care because the cost of prenatal care is so high. Medicaid patients are a bit more likely to seek care earlier in their pregnancies; however, many women eligible for Medicaid during pregnancy do not get through the application process until later in the gestational period (March of Dimes Foundation, 2010).

In 2009, almost 25% of women of childbearing age were without insurance coverage.

For those who do have Medicaid coverage, finding an obstetrician who accepts Medicaid patients is increasingly difficult. Progress has been made to reach out to obstetricians by increasing Medicaid reimbursements to incentivize them to accept Medicaid patients. With a dwindling number of practicing obstetricians, many uninsured and Medicaid-covered pregnant women seek prenatal care at local health departments, where their care is often uncoordinated.

Abused Individuals

It is argued that the social services departments that handle domestic abuse are underfunded and understaffed. Community programs that help abused women escape bad situations often rely on grants and individual donations. These programs are nearly nonexistent for male victims of domestic abuse. Males do not report the abuse for a number of reasons; hence, a program for males will not be fruitful until reducing the stigma of male reporting becomes a public health goal. Individual financial barriers exist in many abusive relationships where the victim is dependent on the offender for financial security, housing, and insurance coverage. This dependence makes it difficult for a victim to leave or improve an abusive situation. Shelters and other programs do exist to help battered women with housing and with finding work at little or no charge.

Chronically Ill and Disabled Persons

Chronically ill and disabled people have expensive, ongoing health care needs. Lifetime caps on insurance benefits, cost sharing between insurance companies and patients, and patient co-pays can all add up to large out-of-pocket costs for this vulnerable population.

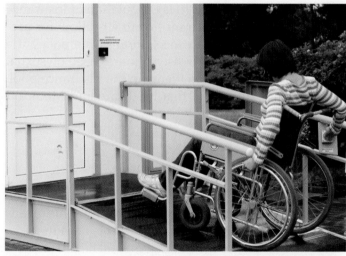

Courtesy of Tatiana Belova/Fotolia

The cost of treating a long-term illness is often highest in the first two years, during which time disabled people who are unable to work must wait before receiving Medicare SSDI benefits.

The Medicare SSDI program for disabled people who are unable to work has a two-year waiting period, though eligible people can apply for welfare and Medicaid in the meantime (U.S. Social Security Administration, 2012c). The first few years of a chronic condition or disability are often the most expensive in terms of health care needs. For the uninsured, this two-year waiting period can lead to two years' worth of unpaid medical bills. Those with private payer insurance may reach their lifetime coverage limits and essentially lose their private payer coverage while they apply for Medicaid and wait for Medicare SSDI eligibility. Preexisting condition clauses in health insurance policies enable insurance companies to refuse coverage for many of America's chronically ill and disabled people, but SSDI does not have preexisting condition clauses as it is designed to help these very people.

Medicare and Medicaid do cover some long-term treatments, such as nursing home care and physical rehabilitation services. However, coverage is restrictive and based on a myriad of factors, including the chances of positive outcomes from the treatments and patient ability to cover some or all of the costs. Medicare will only cover long-term care for a maximum of 120 days, if the patient is making marked recovery or rehabilitative strides toward some end goal. At that point, Medicaid may pick up caring for the patient if they have less than $2,000 in total assets and make less than 133% of the poverty amount for an individual. Managed care plans and health care coordinators help limit costs by coordinating care across multiple disciplines (physical therapy, home visits by nurses, and so on) and negotiating better fees for both payers and patients alike.

Persons Diagnosed With HIV/AIDS

Financial barriers to health care access for HIV/AIDS patients are rooted in cost of care and social stigma. As HIV/AIDS drug therapies continue to improve, patients are living longer, which increases their lifetime cost of care for HIV/AIDS treatments. New improvements in treatment therapies are expensive because pharmaceutical companies price new drugs high to recoup research and development expenses. High prices and increased longevity lead to increased out-of-pocket expenses for HIV/AIDS patients. Early detection is essential, as many patients die within two years of the onset of AIDS without antiretroviral therapy. Early treatment can also help reduce the cost of medical care by slowing the progression of the symptoms of both the primary and related illnesses.

Social stigma surrounding the HIV/AIDS epidemic has led to lax regulation of insurance coverage for HIV/AIDS patients. Many private payer insurance contracts allow for pre-approval testing for HIV. Still others allow for immediate cancellation of the policy if a patient becomes HIV positive. Many states allow insurers to discriminate based on sexual orientation, and thereby limit the number of HIV positive patients in the insurance pool. HIV/AIDS patients with public payer coverage often find that Medicare and Medicaid coverage for HIV/AIDS–related treatments is minimal.

Persons Diagnosed With Mental Conditions

Though federal health care laws do address the problem, there is still a **parity** gap between mental health treatment coverage and treatment coverage for physical health. This means that mental health services are not as available as physical health services, both in terms of geographic proximity to patients and in the ability of the existing mental health services delivery system to meet demand. Similarly, an **equity** gap also exists between mental and physical health services. This essentially means that patients who can afford better insurance coverage and higher out-of-pocket expenses have better access to mental health services than do those who cannot afford them. Medicaid does provide mental health benefits for qualifying patients, under which they can sometimes get more services, longer treatment duration, and good treatment from masters-level professionals—which is usually the requirement. The Patient Protection and Affordability Act of 2010 (PPACA) addresses mental health parity by expanding the applicability of federal mental health parity laws and mandating coverage for specified mental health and substance abuse recovery treatments (National Conference of State Legislatures [NCSL], 2011).

Both public and private payer coverage is usually less for mental health services than for other services. Many plans include annual maximums in number of treatments and covered treatment costs with some federal- and state-mandated exceptions. Many also have higher out-of-pocket expenses for patients, which means that the insurer pays less of the total cost for mental health services than most do for physical health services. Medicaid in most states pays providers significantly less for mental health services than it does to physical health service providers. This has led to mental health professionals limiting the number of Medicaid patients they will accept.

Suicide- and Homicide-Liable Persons

Violence prevention programs are historically underfunded and plagued by delivery problems. These programs work to prevent violence through social and economic investments in underserved, low-income communities and in individuals. A significant number of these programs are community-based and are financially dependent on private donations and grants. Many health care trauma centers that once attempted to serve low-income areas were put out of business in part by the increasing costs of treating victims of violence who were unable to pay for their care. As Chapter 7 illustrates, studies have found that violence prevention programs cost hospitals and trauma centers significantly less than does treating victims of violence.

Courtesy of powerofforever/iStockphoto

Violence prevention programs work to prevent violence through social and economic investments in underserved, low-income communities and in individuals.

Persons Affected by Alcohol and Substance Abuse

A significant disparity exists between alcohol and substance abuse treatments available to patients with private payer insurance and those with public payer insurance. Providers in the private sector earn more revenue while treating fewer patients. Though private payers limit the amount of coverage for substance abuse therapies, particularly inpatient treatments, patients with private payer coverage are better able to afford the out-of-pocket costs and, as such, demand higher-quality treatments.

A benefit of these upscale treatment facilities is that many offer coordinated treatments, including both physical and mental health services, all under one roof. While private payer patients "recuperate" in these facilities, they often enjoy more comfortable accommodations than are available in institutions that serve public payer patients. In fact, many public payer substance abuse patients receive treatment under **compulsory** terms, meaning they are forced into treatment by social services or the court. While courts and social services are forcing people into substance abuse programs, welfare reformers have been cutting funding and eligibility for substance abuse coverage under Medicaid. The results of these cuts are that felons who are convicted of drug charges are not eligible for substance abuse program coverage in many states (when living outside of jails and prisons). This has particularly affected pregnant women who are addicted to alcohol and other drugs. However, some amount of treatment is available to jailed offenders. The Federal Bureau of Prisons has strengthened its substance abuse treatment programs in an effort to reduce relapse, improve convicts' abilities to rejoin society, and improve the safety and social atmosphere inside penitentiaries (U.S. Department of Justice, Federal Bureau of Prisons, 2012).

Indigent and Homeless Persons

Most homeless people do not have any type of health insurance, and even those with insurance often cannot afford to pay their share of the cost of health services. Many different state and federal agencies (for example, Department of Health and Human Services and Department of Veterans' Affairs) have programs in place to address the problem of homelessness and the needs of homeless people. Some of these departments offer grants to community-based services and health care clinics and professionals who are willing to treat indigent people as a significant portion of their client base.

Many of these funding opportunities are administered under the Stewart B. McKinney Homeless Assistance Act of 1987, which specifically recognized the need for federal monies to address homelessness and the needs of this population. Since 1987, many agencies have had the designated funding for homeless programming cut, and recipient programs often lament the fact that the grant approval processes are unduly long and difficult to navigate.

Immigrants and Refugees

Financial access to health care for immigrants is similar to that of other groups in the United States. However, some immigrant and refugee members of the population encounter barriers to accessing public payer insurance because legislation like the Welfare Reform Act of 1996 decreased eligibility for nonnaturalized citizens. Undocumented immigrants have no access to public payer health care insurance in most states. Naturalized immigrants and those who qualify for public payer and private payer insurance generally have the same financial benefits and restrictions as other subscribers.

Critical Thinking

Health care tests and procedures are often performed without consulting patients on the costs and financial liabilities until after they have been rendered. Do you think it would be better if patients understood costs before services are rendered, or do you think discussing costs should be of secondary importance to the patients' health? What do you think would be the result if health care providers were suddenly required to have patients sign off on the cost of each individual procedure before being rendered?

Self-Check

Answer the following questions to the best of your ability.

1. What programs are nearly nonexistent for male victims of domestic abuse?
    a. community support
    b. federal programs
    c. faith-based services
    d. public transportation to and from work

2. Many states allow insurers to discriminate against individuals on the basis of
    _____.
    a. a preexisting condition
    b. pregnancy
    c. sexual orientation
    d. immigration status

3. The Federal Bureau of Prisons has strengthened its substance abuse treatment programs in an effort to reduce what?
    a. occupancy
    b. in-prison drug use
    c. fetal alcohol syndrome births
    d. relapse

Answer Key

1. **a**   2. **c**   3. **d**

Case Study: Patient Profiling and Inequalities in Care as Organizational Barriers

Susan was a 22-year-old Caucasian female who worked at a coffee shop. She did not have health insurance through work and had never considered checking for Medicaid eligibility. Susan and her boyfriend regularly used illicit substances, including crack, cocaine, and marijuana.

When Susan became pregnant, she sought prenatal care at a local health department. Health department staff helped Susan sign up for Medicaid, and she continued with regular prenatal care at that facility. During one appointment in the third trimester, Susan's doctor asked her if she ever had or currently used illicit drugs. Susan replied honestly and told her doctor that she had stopped using most drugs when she learned she was pregnant, though she continued to smoke marijuana and cigarettes on a regular basis. Susan later reported that the doctor nodded, took notes, and never counseled Susan on the negative effects of the use of those substances during pregnancy or offered cessation help.

*Courtesy of Stockphoto4u/
iStockphoto*

Susan abused drugs before and during her pregnancy and was threatened with the possibility of giving up her baby to social services.

Weeks later, Susan gave birth to a full-term baby girl. The next morning, a physician she had never met before entered her hospital room with a social services worker. They told Susan that the doctor who had treated her at the health department throughout her pregnancy had reported Susan's drug use to social services. They had already drawn blood from the baby to test for drug dependence, and Susan would be hearing from social services with the test results. They warned that if the baby tested positive, they were prepared to remove the infant from her mother's care. Either way, Susan and the baby would be working with social services for the next year, or until their assigned social worker determined that there was no danger to either the mother or child.

After two worry-filled days, the social worker arrived unannounced at Susan's door. The baby had tested negative for everything and was deemed to be in good health. After six months working with her social worker, Susan was removed from the social services program after many follow-up visits and multiple negative drug tests.

Susan reported feeling singled out by the doctors and social services and felt that she was punished for her honesty. Her basis for feeling singled out was that a friend of hers was simultaneously pregnant and had private payer health insurance. The friend reported never having been asked about cigarette, alcohol, or substance use or abuse history by any of her physicians or hospital staff.

Part of the difference in their experiences was simply that they had different doctors. But the friend had a physician in an office that specializes in obstetric care for women with private payer insurance. It may be that Susan was profiled because she received her prenatal care at the public health department.

Chapter Summary

Organizational and financial barriers to health care are intertwined. These barriers range from the physical location of health care providers to providers' reluctance to treat patients who have difficulty paying for treatment. Legislation that limits coverage eligibility and increases the ability of insurance companies and medical providers to deny coverage and care creates organizational barriers for both private payer and public payer patients. Some organizational barriers are created by the insurance companies' and medical providers' need to maximize profits. Many barriers can be overcome with legislation that improves eligibility and coverage. Still others can be overcome by targeting the social and economic problems that plague America's most vulnerable populations.

Critical Thinking

This chapter discusses several issues related to the barriers faced by America's vulnerable populations to accessing health care. Now that you have read this chapter, what do you think is the root of the problem? What short-term changes would you recommend to improve access? What long-term changes would you recommend to improve access?

Self-Check

Answer the following questions to the best of your ability.

1. Among PHON's community interventions plan is an initiative to eliminate programs and access to those programs for treating patients who have suffered traumatic events.
   a. True
   b. False

2. The U.S. Conference of Mayors' 2010 Hunger and Homelessness Survey reported that demand for emergency food assistance increased how much from 2009 to 2010?
   a. 4%
   b. 13%
   c. 24%
   d. 42%

3. Cultural acceptance is fundamental to providing quality care to which populations?
   a. religious
   b. immigrant
   c. minority
   d. pregnant female

4. In 2009, what percentage of women of childbearing age had no insurance cover-
    age of any type?
    a. 8.2%
    b. 15.6%
    c. 22.3%
    d. 48.6%

5. How long is the waiting period for the Medicare SSDI program for disabled
    people who are unable to work?
    a. 2 years
    b. 7 years
    c. 12 years
    d. 15 years

6. Many health care _____ that once attempted to serve low-income areas
    were put out of business by the increasing costs of treating victims of violence
    who were unable to pay for their care.
    a. substance abuse centers
    b. criminal justice courts
    c. domestic abuse victim services
    d. trauma centers

Answer Key

1. **b**   2. **c**   3. **b**   4. **c**   5. **a**   6. **d**

Additional Resources

Visit the following websites to learn more about the topics covered in this chapter:

Information on the community-based and health care organization–based resources supported by the CARE Act

http://hab.hrsa.gov/

Healthy People, which discusses the goals of HHS for the next 10 years

http://www.healthypeople.gov/2020/default.aspx

The American Foundation for Suicide Prevention

http://www.afsp.org/

Web Exercise

Research at least five (5) credible websites regarding patient profiling as described in the case study toward the end of the chapter. Write a five-page paper that does the following:

- defines and describes patient profiling
- describes two specific cases of patient profiling (one positive and one negative)
- identifies three positive issues and three negative issues of patient profiling
- identifies your personal stand on this issue and why you took that position

Remember: All papers must meet APA format. YouTube and Wikipedia are not considered creditable sources. Citations must be included.

Key Terms

childbearing age The age range of highest fertility, which is 15 to 44.

compulsory Forced by legal or physical means.

electronic health records Digital databases that store patient health information, making it accessible to all of a patient's approved providers.

epidemiology The study of how a disease moves through populations.

equity Access and coverage being the same for all people.

gynecological care Medical care specializing in the female reproductive system.

obstetricians Doctors who treat pregnant women for pregnancy.

parity Access and coverage being the same across health service types.

pathology The history of a disease.

physiological Having to do with the physical body.

psychological Having to do with the mind.

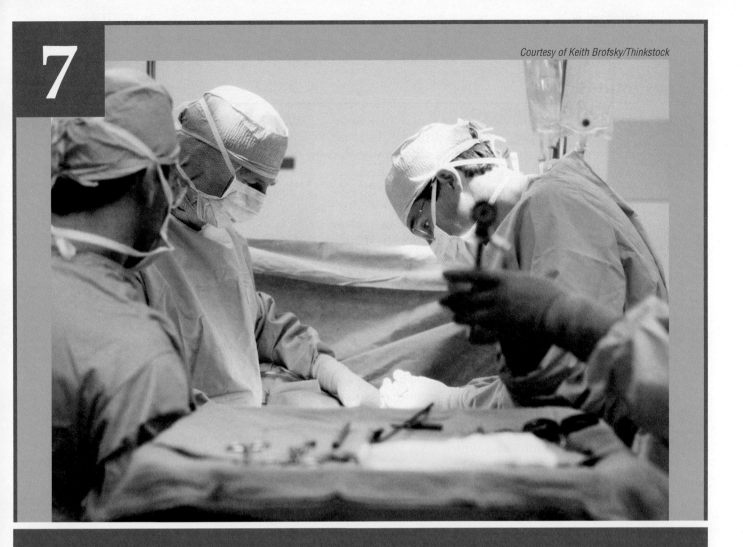

7

Evaluating the Cost of Care

Learning Objectives

After reading this chapter, you should be able to:

- Identify the factors that determine the true cost of care.

- Identify the direct and indirect costs of health care.

- Examine the concept of cost-benefit analysis related to the evaluation of a health care program.

- Examine the concept of cost-effectiveness analysis related to the evaluation of a health care program.

- Recognize programs that pass and fail cost-benefit and cost-effectiveness analysis.

- Apply cost-benefit and cost-effectiveness analysis to health care programs.

Introduction

Comparing data across studies and across organizations and programs is difficult because each one measures information differently. For example, one medical provider might measure services by the number of patients seen, whereas another might measure each billable procedure regardless of the number of patients seen. How do we determine which organization best uses its resources?

First, we must determine what the true cost of care is. For this, we need information on the cost of supplies per service, the cost of physicians and staff needed for a procedure, and the facility's cost per procedure. Once this data is tallied to find a total cost of care, the data must be analyzed to determine whether the money and resources were well spent. By doing so, decision makers can make informed selections regarding which services to continue and which ones to revise or discontinue.

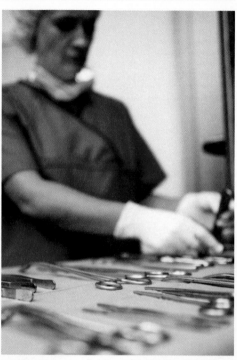

Courtesy of Jochen Sand/Thinkstock

The expenses of several resources, including health care personnel, supplies, and facility, must be taken into consideration when calculating the true cost of a medical procedure.

Critical Thinking

Throughout this text, various statistics have been presented and discussed. For example, in Chapter 6, you read that "Many women with incomes below 200% of the federal poverty level report not seeking health care due to an inability to take off work during clinic hours." Statistical data is gathered through various resources, one of which might be the electronic health records mentioned in previous chapters. Do you think that true costs can be better evaluated with this tool?

Self-Check

Answer the following questions to the best of your ability.

1. How might one organization measure costs?
    a. by the number of patients seen
    b. by counting every penny in the facility
    c. by estimating the reimbursement amount from Medicare/Medicaid
    d. by adding up the cost of every piece of medical equipment

2. Which of the following should be assessed to determine the true cost of care?
    a. the cost of the valet service
    b. the cost of paving the parking lot
    c. the cost of physicians and staff for a single procedure
    d. the cost of medical lobbyists

3. Why is it difficult to compare data across studies and across organizations and programs?
    a. Each measures information differently.
    b. Different researchers look at different issues.
    c. Employee satisfaction varies widely.
    d. Medical certifications are not the same everywhere.

Answer Key

1. **a**   2. **c**   3. **a**

7.1 Totaling the Cost of Care

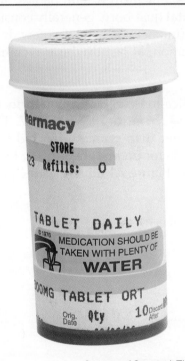

Courtesy of Comstock/Thinkstock

The cost of caring for a medical condition includes the expense of tangible materials as well as more abstract expenses caused by diminished productivity at work, taking sick days, and so forth.

There are both measurable and abstract costs associated with any medical condition. Measurable costs are the **direct costs** of treatment, including the price of pharmaceuticals and materials, such as bandages and sutures, as well as the salaries of nurses, physicians, and pharmacists. Direct costs can be measured by totaling the financial prices of all of the resources used to treat a patient. To a provider of a service, these include costs related to property, plant, and equipment. These costs are typically called "overhead costs," and the cost of direct care is typically inflated to include these costs. If it is tangible, it is a direct cost.

Indirect costs are more abstract. The indirect costs of an illness, for example, include lost work hours, reduced productivity, and reduced family involvement and civil involvement. For a patient with a mental condition, fees paid to a psychiatrist are a direct cost; reduced work productivity due to taking time off to see the psychiatrist is an indirect cost. Both direct and indirect costs must be weighed when determining resource allocation to care for vulnerable populations.

Vulnerable Mothers and Children

The United States experienced a record-breaking birthrate in 2007 of 4,316,233 total births. The slight economic surge in 2006 and 2007, which preceded the Great Recession of 2008 and allayed fears over an impending recession, is a contributing factor to 2007's elevated birthrate, as people are more comfortable growing their families during times of economic surplus. The U.S. population also reached an all-time high of 300 million people in late 2006, and the enlarged population added to the following inflated birthrate. The 2007 baby boom was followed by a steady decline in 2008 and 2009, partially due to the Great Recession that began in late 2008. The birthrate declined 4% from 2007 to 4,131,019 total births in 2009 (Sutton, Hamilton, & Mathews, 2011). The live birthrate further declined 3% from 2009 to 4,000,279 in 2010 (Hamilton, Martin, & Ventura, 2011).

The good news is that the numbers of births to teen mothers and preterm births also declined between 2007 and 2010. The birthrate to females ages 15–19 fell from 42.5 births per 1,000 women in that age group in 2007 to 39.1 births per 1,000 women in that age group in 2009 (Sutton et al., 2011). While the preterm birthrate rose 20% from 1990 to 2006, this upward trend reversed in 2007. The preterm birthrate for 2006 was 12.8% of all live births; the rate fell to 12.7% in 2007, and again to 12.3% in 2008 (Martin, Osterman, & Sutton, 2010). This decline is important, as preterm babies, low birth weight babies, and babies born to teen mothers incur higher maternity, **neonatal** (just-born, generally considered to be the first day or two after birth), and **postnatal** (infancy after the first few days postdelivery) medical costs than babies born at full gestation, at healthy birth weights, and to more mature mothers.

In terms of direct costs, newborns with no medical complications such as prematurity or low birth weight have an average postnatal care cost of $4,551 as of the year 2007. The average cost of care for newborns with complications other than prematurity and low birth weight is $10,273. The cost rises significantly to $49,033 for premature and low birth weight babies. Of these costs, health insurers pay the bulk. Figure 7.1 illustrates the payment breakdown of expenses (March of Dimes, 2008).

Figure 7.1: Cost for maternal and infant care

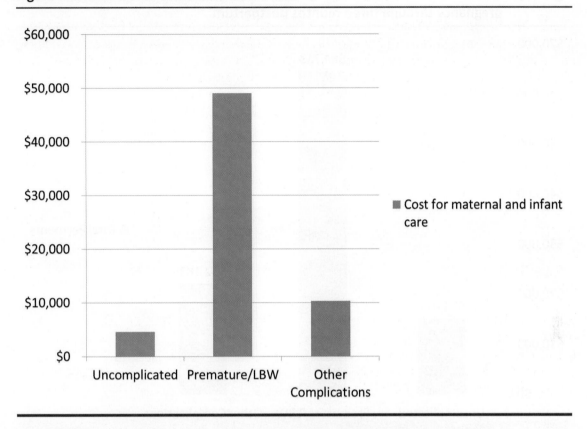

The cost of care for babies born premature or underweight is five times more than for other complications and ten times more than for babies born with no complications.

March of Dimes. (2008). Retrieved from http://www.marchofdimes.com/peristats/pdfdocs/cts/ThomsonAnalysis2008_
SummaryDocument_final121208.pdf

As for maternal care, uncomplicated cesarean deliveries cost significantly more than uncomplicated vaginal deliveries, at averages of $13,329 and $9,415, respectively. The total average for all complicated deliveries, both vaginal and cesarean, is $14,667. Maternal care costs include prenatal care and care for three months postpartum (March of Dimes, 2008).

The costs for maternal and infant care should also be considered together to get a clear view of the total cost of having a baby. The average total cost of care for both mother and child is estimated at $21,328. Uncomplicated pregnancies and deliveries average a mother and infant total of $15,047, significantly lower than the overall average. The overall average is driven up by the total for premature and low birth weight cases, which average $64,713 for both mother and child. Other complications are only slightly more expensive than the overall average, at an average cost of $22,183. Figure 7.2 illustrates the breakdown of the total average costs for mother and infant care (March of Dimes, 2008).

Figure 7.2: Breakdown of the total average costs of maternal and infant care, pregnancy through three months postpartum

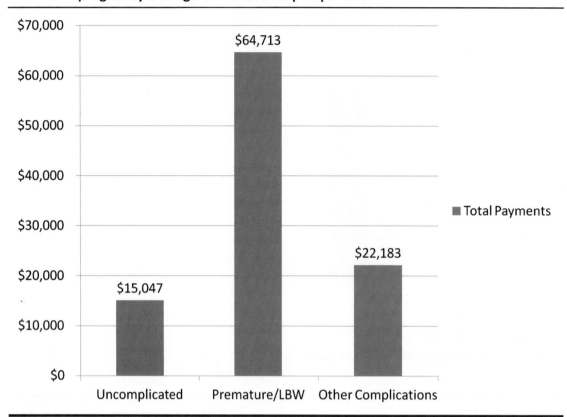

Three months postpartum, the gap in expenses closes marginally for complicated, premature, and uncomplicated births.

Source: March of Dimes

The indirect costs associated with birth include nonmaterial costs like time off work. The average maternity leave from work in the United States is six weeks. Many working mothers are not able to take more recovery time even for complicated pregnancies and deliveries. When complications like preterm delivery and low birth weight arise, other household members, such as grandparents and fathers, may need to take additional time off work to help the mother. Time off work, whether paid or unpaid, means a loss in productivity to employers. Exact numbers are difficult to estimate because productivity loss is an indirect cost, but the total productivity cost loss to U.S. employers is estimated to be around $260 billion per year due to all health-related work losses (Mitchell & Bates, 2011).

Abused Individuals

Nonfatal child abuse is estimated to cost the United States a total lifetime economic burden of $124 billion, based on 2008 figures (Fang, Brown, Florence, & Mercy, 2012). The lifetime cost estimate for each victim of nonfatal child abuse and neglect is $210,010. The direct costs associated with this number include the following:

- $7,999 for special education costs
- $7,728 in child welfare costs for programs such as Child Protective Services (CPS)
- $6,747 in costs related to criminal justice
- $10,530 in abuse-related adulthood medical costs per victim
- $32,648 in abuse-related childhood medical costs per victim

The per-victim total also includes indirect costs associated with productivity loss of $144,360 (Fang et al., 2012). Additional indirect costs associated with the effects of child abuse on the adult victim's ability to grow social capital in the form of strong relationships are difficult to measure.

However, measuring the indirect cost of adult domestic partner abuse is easier. In 1995, the Centers for Disease Control and Prevention (CDC) estimated the annual indirect cost of domestic partner abuse, including productivity loss, at nearly $1.8 billion. The direct costs of domestic partner abuse are related to medical treatment for injuries, mental health treatment, and criminal justice. The annual direct cost was estimated at nearly $4.1 billion. Accounting for inflation, the 1995 total estimated annual cost of $5.8 billion becomes $8.3 billion in 2003 (Futures without Violence, 2010; National Center for Injury Prevention and Control, 2003). This increase only reflects the loss in the value of U.S. currency, called **monetary inflation**, and does not account for any changes in amount or severity of domestic partner abuse. A lack of research on the direct and indirect costs of domestic partner abuse makes it more difficult to know which programs are most effective and to allocate resources accordingly.

According to Brown (2011), the National Center on Elder Abuse and the Administration on Aging report spending at least $206.2 million in Social Services Block Grants funds and $42.3 million in Medicaid funds that were allocated to Adult Protective Services (APS) programs in fiscal year 2009. These funds, set up to assist the elderly with their medical care, were spent on protecting them from their abusers instead (Brown, 2011).

Chronically Ill and Disabled Persons

The direct and indirect costs of chronic illnesses have a significant effect on the United States' economy and workforce. Focusing on the seven most common chronic ailments offers a clear view of the problem without over or under inflating the numbers. In a study by the Milken Institute (2007), the following are the seven most common and expensive chronic ailments in the United States and their total annual treatment expenditures in order of cost:

- stroke: $13.6 billion
- diabetes: $27.1 billion
- hypertension: $32.5 billion
- pulmonary disease: $45.2 billion
- mental disorders: $45.8 billion
- cancer: $48.1 billion
- heart disease: $64.7 billion

The direct cost of treating these seven ailments for noninstitutionalized patients (those who do not reside in prisons, long-term care facilities, specialized homes for mentally unstable patients, and the like) is around $277 billion annually. (The costs of treating secondary conditions related to the seven conditions listed are not included in this figure.) Furthermore, the direct and indirect costs associated with chronic disease are expected to skyrocket in the coming decades. Figure 7.3 illustrates the estimated costs for 2023.

Figure 7.3: Forecast of direct and indirect costs associated with chronic disease

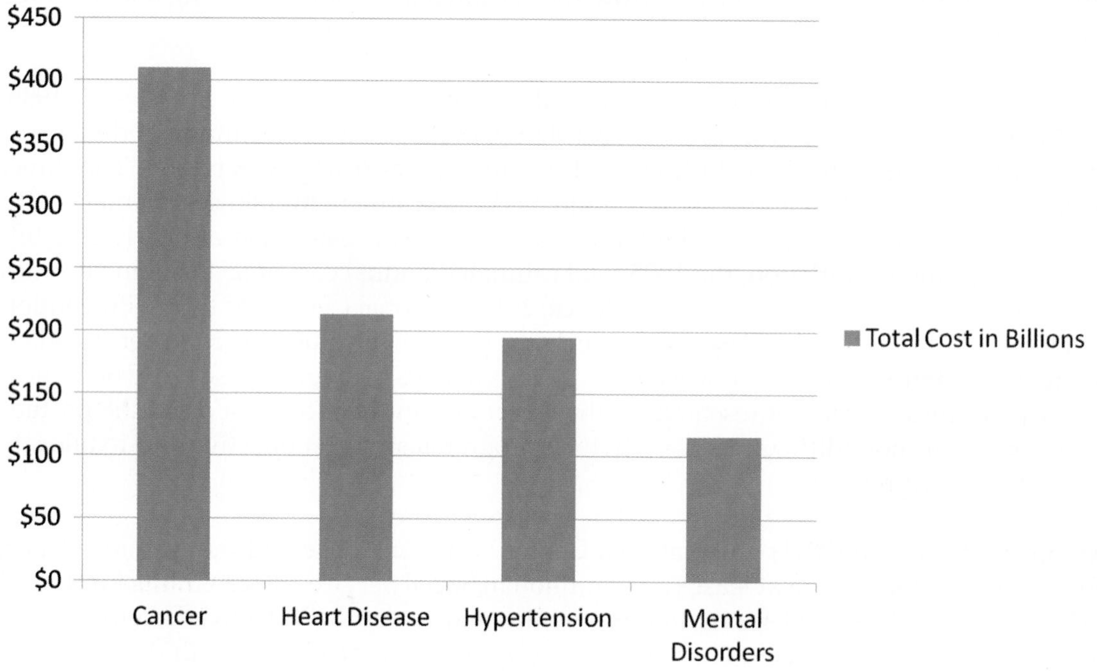

By 2023, it is expected to cost the nation more than twice as much to treat cancer compared to other leading chronic diseases.

Milken Institute. (2007). Retrieved from http://www.milkeninstitute.org/healthreform/pdf/AnUnhealthyAmericaExecSumm.pdf

The indirect costs associated with lost productivity for individuals with chronic conditions can be staggering. **Absenteeism** is the missing of days of work by employees. Workers with chronic conditions also often experience **presenteeism**, where they show up for work but have severely lowered productivity over a length of time. For example, a worker with hypertension might arrive on time every day but feel sluggish and tired and so not accomplish his or her best possible work output. The Milken Institute study indicates that presenteeism creates significantly more output loss than absenteeism. Output loss is not limited to chronic disease sufferers. Caregivers like spouses and adult children caring for elderly parents also experience output loss due to the strains of caring for somebody with a chronic disease. Overall, output loss due to chronic disease is estimated to cost the country over $1 trillion annually (Milken Institute, 2007).

It is important to remember that although chronic diseases are among the most expensive health issues the country faces, the problem of chronic disease is potentially the area with the most possibility of cost savings. Preventive medicine in terms of obesity control, nutrition, immunizations, and smoking cessation creates an opportunity for a healthier populace with fewer chronic conditions. It is estimated that improving lifestyle habits now could save the country $1.1 trillion annually by 2023 (Milken Institute, 2007). Public programs, like First Lady Michelle Obama's "Let's Move" campaign, work toward this savings goal by educating and encouraging the public at large to improve our health by improving our lifestyles.

Persons Diagnosed With HIV/AIDS

The Centers for Disease Control and Prevention (CDC) estimate that new cases of HIV cost the United States and its territories a total of nearly $16.5 billion per year and that the cost for a lifetime of HIV treatment is $379,668 per person (Centers for Disease Control and Prevention, 2012d). Preventing new cases of HIV is an important part of the nation's health objectives, and the CDC is tasked with monitoring HIV prevention. Reducing the number of people with HIV/AIDS not only creates a healthier citizenry but it also saves the nation a lot of money. To that end, the CDC earmarked $359 million annually for the years 2012–2016 to help fund HIV care and prevention programs in state-run health departments throughout the nation. That number is significantly increased from the $111 million total that the CDC used from 2007 to 2010 to fund

Courtesy of jcarillet/iStockphoto

When citizens are healthy, the nation saves a lot of money that would have otherwise been used to fund the treatment of acute and chronic illnesses, such as HIV/AIDS.

HIV testing, which was estimated to have created a savings of $1.2 billion in medical costs during that same time (CDC, 2011b). The CDC estimates that every HIV infection that is prevented saves the country $355,000 in lifetime medical costs per patient (CDC, 2010b).

Persons Diagnosed With Mental Conditions

Mental conditions impose a heavy financial burden on patients and the country in terms of both direct and indirect costs. Mental health care costs are estimated to be as much as 6% of the nation's total annual health care costs—an expenditure of about $57.5 billion per year. Spending on mental health in America is tied with spending on cancer (National Institute of Mental Health [NIMH], 2011). The CDC estimates that the direct cost of treating mental illness is closer to $100 billion annually (Reeves et al., 2011).

The indirect costs associated with mental illness are much higher than the direct costs. In addition to the $100 billion annual cost of care estimated by the CDC, mental illness is estimated to cost the country $193 billion in lost wages and earnings due to absenteeism and presenteeism. Add another $24 billion annually in disability benefits, and the indirect costs are close to two and half times the annual direct cost (Reeves et al., 2011).

Suicide- and Homicide-Liable Persons

The indirect costs of suicide are estimated to be much higher than the direct costs associated with suicide. This is partially because most of the direct cost of suicide is actually a direct cost of mental illness, like severe depression, and so is measured as mental illness, not as suicide. The most recent estimates on the annual cost to the country of suicide puts the direct cost around $1 billion and the indirect costs of lost productivity and wages, as well as indirect costs to the remaining family, close to $32 billion (Crosby, Ortega, & Stevens, 2011).

Homicides are quite a bit costlier. A study conducted at Iowa State University found that the total for both direct and indirect costs of a single murder is $17.25 million. The study estimates that every murderer costs the country $24 million (DeLisi et al., 2010). The direct costs included in these figures include costs associated with the criminal justice system, whereas the indirect costs include lost productivity of the criminal, the victim, and the victim's friends and relatives.

Persons Affected by Alcohol and Substance Abuse

The costs associated with alcohol and substance abuse are both health and socially oriented. The overconsumption of alcohol alone is estimated to cost the country over $223.5 billion per year, a rate of nearly $1.90 for every alcoholic drink consumed. The majority of the estimated cost, 72.2%, is from indirect costs associated with lost productivity. Only 11% of the annual cost goes to health care, and criminal justice costs are a close third, at 9.4% of the total. The government picks up around 42.1% of the tab at $94.2 billion annually (Bouchery, Harwood, Sacks, Simon, & Brewer, 2011). Tobacco usage is another costly health issue. According to the CDC, tobacco use costs the country $96 billion in tobacco-related health care costs and $97 billion in lost productivity every year (CDC, 2012e). Drug abuse costs the United States $193 billion annually. This number includes both direct costs of

Courtesy of iStockphoto/Thinkstock

The nation loses almost $100 million every year because of diminished productivity due to tobacco use.

health care and criminal justice as well as indirect costs associated with productivity loss and indirect costs of crime, such as emotional distress to the victims. Health costs contribute the smallest portion of the annual bill with productivity loss and crime costs accounting for the bulk (U.S. Department of Justice, National Drug Intelligence Center, 2011). The scope of the economic effects of drug abuse is difficult to measure, and the health care cost to individuals is significant. The cost for residential drug abuse treatment is approximately $29,240. Outpatient therapy is significantly less expensive, costing around $4,318 (U.S. Department of Justice, National Drug Intelligence Center, 2011).

Indigent and Homeless Persons

Tracking the cost of health care for America's homeless is as difficult as tracking the individuals themselves. Health care and homelessness are tightly interwoven issues. On the one hand, many homeless people do not have health insurance and regular access to health care. On the other hand, inflated health care costs can lead to bankruptcy and other financial problems that can lead to homelessness.

Homeless and indigent people have a high incidence of emergency room visits, largely due to a lack of access to other health care providers. Although they may qualify for Medicaid, a great number of qualifying individuals do not have Medicaid coverage, due in part to difficulties in applying for it, such as physical access to Medicaid offices, lack of photo ID, and lack of a street address, to name a few. To address the health care needs of America's transient homeless population, the federal government funds programs through the Department of Veterans Affairs (VA) and the Health Care for the Homeless (HCH) program. The VA provides medical care and other services for all veterans of the United States military and funds special initiatives to address the medical needs of homeless veterans. The HCH provides primary and emergency health care as well as mental health and substance abuse ser-

Courtesy of Monkey Business/Fotolia

Because the homeless lack access to many health care providers, they visit emergency rooms much more frequently.

vices for America's homeless. These and other government-funded programs, in addition to private organizations and agencies, health insurers, and out-of-pocket payments, cover the cost of health care for the nation's homeless. Though the total health care cost of America's homeless is difficult to ascertain, a study by the Lewin Group found that the cost per homeless person per day in a hospital ranges from $1,200 to around $2,000 (Lewin Group, 2004).

Immigrants and Refugees

Overall, immigrants to the United States use fewer health care resources than native-born citizens. This is due to a combination of access barriers, affordability, and cultural differences. Even when comparing insured immigrants with insured natives, native-born Americans use more—and more expensive—health care resources. The same is true when comparing uninsured immigrants and refugees with uninsured natives. Uninsured immigrants use about 61% less health care than uninsured native-born citizens. Native-born citizens of the United States use significantly more in quantity and more in quality health care resources (Udall Center for Studies in Public Policy, 2006).

Overall, immigrants and refugees use health care at a rate of only 55% of that used by native-born citizens. Sadly, the largest gap in health care use is among native and non-native children. Native U.S. citizen children use upwards of 74% *more* health care resources than do their immigrant peers (Mohanty et al., 2004). These gaps in health care use span populations with public payer insurance, private payer insurance, and the uninsured. More than the dollar amounts, the size of the usage gaps is important, as they inform public policy regarding health care access in the United States. The usage gaps debunk the argument that immigrants, both documented and undocumented, unduly drive up the cost of health care in America.

Critical Thinking

Consider the statement, "The usage gaps debunk the argument that immigrants, both documented and undocumented, unduly drive up the cost of health care in America." Think about immigration and its relationship to health care costs. Do you agree with this statement? Why or why not?

Self-Check

Answer the following questions to the best of your ability.

1. The total cost of health-related productivity loss to U.S. employers is estimated at
   _____ per year.
   a. $260 billion
   b. $290 billion
   c. $320 billion
   d. $370 billion

2. According to the text, who else suffers from job output loss but is not a chronic disease sufferer?
   a. employers
   b. insurance providers
   c. non-professional caregivers
   d. health providers

3. The indirect costs of what special population are close to two and half times the annual direct cost?
    a. people diagnosed with mental conditions
    b. the elderly
    c. nonviolent abuse victims
    d. HIV/AIDS patients

Answer Key

1. **a**   2. **c**   3. **a**

7.2 Analyzing the Cost of Care

Decision makers use economic tools to analyze the financial and social costs associated with caring for the vulnerable. A **cost-benefit analysis (CBA)** assigns **monetary value**, or dollar total, to both direct and indirect costs, then compares the costs and benefits of a project to determine the likelihood of the project producing a positive outcome and a good return on the financial investments of the project. The difficult part of cost-benefit analysis is assigning monetary value to abstract social costs. Here is a simplified example of a cost-benefit analysis for a program that would provide free immunizations to schoolchildren:

Step 1: Assign monetary value to both direct and indirect costs.

Direct costs:

> Trained staff ($1,000 for one day)
>
> Syringes ($0.50 per child × 300 children = $150)
>
> Vaccinations ($5 per child × 300 children = $1,500)
>
> Alcohol pads ($0.10 per child × 300 children = $30)
>
> Bandages ($0.10 per child × 300 children = $30)

Total direct costs: $2,710

Indirect costs:

> Missed classroom time (cost to run the school for one day = $5,000)

Total indirect costs: $5,000

Step 2: Determine the expected benefit of the program.

> Children who have received the vaccine are less likely to miss school due to illness (this reduces the resources needed to catch children up on missed schoolwork).
>
> Teachers are less likely to catch illness from the vaccinated children and so are less likely to miss work (cost per missed day of work = $200 per teacher, per missed

day). If the program lowers the average number of missed days from three to two, the financial benefit of fewer missed work days is $12,000:

3 missed days × $200 per day × 60 teachers in the school = $36,000

2 missed days × $200 per day × 60 teachers in the school = $24,000

Step 3: Compare the costs and benefits.

Total of direct and indirect costs = $7,710

Monetary value assigned to anticipated benefit = $12,000

Total savings caused by the immunization program = $4,290

Step 4: Make a decision.

The program provides a positive return on investment, both in financial terms and in terms of the school population's health.

Cost-benefit analysis focuses on the value of one program. Conversely, **cost-effectiveness analysis (CEA)** is a method of comparing two or more programs. Unlike cost-benefit analysis, cost-effectiveness analysis, when used correctly, assigns both monetary value and social value to program outcomes. With CEA, finances are not the only determinant of a program's value. For example:

Smoking prevention program for teenagers:

- cost to run program: $5,000
- anticipated percentage of students who will not smoke (based on available research of this program or similar ones): 75%

Smoking cessation program for adults:

- cost to run program: $2,000
- anticipated percentage of program participants who remain nonsmokers after leaving the program (based on available research of this program or similar ones): 20%

Now consider the cost of caring for a long-term smoker who may present with emphysema, heart disease, or cancer. Although the smoking prevention program may initially cost more, CEA indicates that it offers better return on the financial and social investment.

Cost-effectiveness can also be expressed using a mathematical formula:

$$\text{CE ratio} = \frac{\text{Cost}^{\text{new program}} - \text{Cost}^{\text{current program}}}{\text{Oucome}^{\text{new program}} - \text{Outcome}^{\text{current program}}}$$

The mathematical formula does not put as much weight on social value as does the listing method.

Even with cost-benefit analysis and cost-effectiveness analysis to normalize data across programs and organizations, it is still challenging to make comparisons necessary to determine resource allocation. This is partly due to the lack of standardized data reporting techniques and a general lack of research on the cost analysis of many programs. This is especially true of programs that care for certain vulnerable populations, as we will discuss in the next few sections.

Vulnerable Mothers and Children

Family planning services offer a cost-effective way to reduce health care costs associated with vulnerable mothers and children. In 2008, an estimated 36 million women needed family

Courtesy of Katie Little/Fotolia

The public expenditures for family planning materials pale in comparison to the cost of pre- and postnatal care for America's youngest and poorest mothers.

planning services. Of those, 17.4 million were in need of publicly funded access to contraceptives and family planning–related services, including prevention-oriented education. In 2010, public expenditures for family planning materials and services were $2.37 billion, of which 75% came from Medicaid (Guttmacher Institute, 2012).

That might sound like a lot to spend on contraceptives and counseling, but the estimated savings generated by the expenditures on family planning services are significantly higher. For the $2.37 billion spent on family planning, it is estimated that federal and state governments together save $5.1 billion per year. Broken down, that amounts to $3.74 in Medicaid savings for every $1 spent on family planning (Guttmacher Institute, 2012). These savings are based on the cost of prenatal and postnatal care for mothers and infants. Considering the incidence rate of babies with low birth weight and other health issues among America's youngest and poorest mothers, preventing a pregnancy at the cost of contraception and counseling given at annual doctor appointments is significantly less than the cost of neonatal care for an infant in distress.

Abused Individuals

Cost analysis of abuse prevention is complicated by the difficulty in reaching victims and potential victims and by the challenge of estimating the indirect costs associated with abuse. Additionally, it is difficult to estimate the economic benefits of abuse prevention, particularly educationally based prevention programs. Consider a prevention program for teenage girls. A school may spend $500 on educating young women as to how to avoid abusive relationships, but tracking those students 10 years later and verifying whether or not they ever found themselves in a situation to avoid an abusive relationship presents a significant challenge. Then there is the human aspect to consider—if just one of those girls uses what she was taught in the prevention program to avoid an abusive relationship, is it worth the full cost of the program?

Violence prevention programs struggle to convince decision makers (particularly those holding the purse strings) that violence prevention programs are cost effective (Browne-Miller, 2008). When studying abuse prevention programs for cost-efficacy, the programs tend to be separated into three separate categories:

- primary prevention programs that focus on public education and awareness
- secondary prevention programs that focus specifically on identified high-risk groups, such as teen mothers and families affected by drug or alcohol abuse
- tertiary prevention programs that focus efforts on families that have already experienced abuse

Of these, primary prevention is often considered to be most effective due to the human cost savings of avoiding abuse altogether.

Cost-benefit analysis of different primary prevention programs produces varying results. Overall, home-visiting programs that provide support and resource access to new mothers have been found to create cost savings in four primary areas:

- increased maternal employment and productivity
- decreased reliance on the public welfare system
- decreased spending on health care and related services
- decreased intervention by the criminal justice system

Using these four points as a guideline, most home-visiting programs create a cost savings of $5.70 for every prevention dollar spent on high-risk groups, and savings of $1.26 for every prevention dollar spent on low-risk groups. However, two national programs were found to lose money. Healthy Families America, which provides various resources to expectant and new mothers, shows a loss of 4.8 cents for every program dollar spent. Similarly, Early Head Start, which works to improve family functioning and positive health outcomes, loses 7.7 cents for every dollar spent (Howard & Brooks-Gunn, 2009). These programs continue to receive funding due to the question of the human cost.

Chronically Ill and Disabled Persons

There is a movement toward creating cost savings by increasing the amount of home-based care, as opposed to clinic and residential-based care, for chronically ill and disabled people. Home-based care programs involve a team of doctors and nurses who engage and support the patients in seeking their own positive health outcomes. These programs have the most promise of increasing wellness among this population while reducing their total cost of care.

Cost analysis of the Johns Hopkins Guided Care model, an integrated system of care that trains nurses in primary care settings to manage care coordination for high-risk patients with chronic illnesses or disabilities, indicates that integrated care approaches offer significant savings. Data on the Guided Care program shows that patients enrolled in the program experienced 21% fewer hospital readmissions, which translates to significant financial savings (Holahan, Schoen, & McMorrow, 2011).

Equally promising is data from the Intermountain Healthcare Primary Care Medical Home (PCMH) model, which focuses on high-risk elderly patients. In addition to nurse care managers, PCMH uses electronic health records to streamline coordination of care. A two-year study of the PCMH model found that it created a total hospitalization reduction of 10% (Holahan et al., 2011).

Courtesy of Getty Images/Thinkstock

Money that would otherwise be spent on clinic and residential care could be saved by increasing home-based care for chronically ill and disabled people.

Both examples offer encouraging evidence in favor of managed care models that engage patients, take advantage of technology, and use trained nurses to provide a higher level of patient care coordination.

Persons Diagnosed With HIV/AIDS

Cost analysis of HIV/AIDS testing and treatment programs should include consideration for indirect human cost of quality of life in addition to expanded life expectancy and direct costs. The CDC considers a treatment program cost effective if the cost per **quality-adjusted life year (QALY)**, an outcome measure that weighs both the quality and quantity of life, is at or below $100,000 per QALY gained.

Determining the cost-efficacy of HIV prevention programs relies on informed estimates as to the number of new infections that likely would have occurred in a set period. Considering that number with the cost of treatment provides a view of the cost-efficacy of prevention programs in the United States. The CDC reports that HIV prevention programs prevented an estimated 361,878 new HIV infections from 1991 to 2006. That translates to a savings of $129.9 billion during that same period (CDC, 2012d).

Persons Diagnosed With Mental Conditions

Much of what is spent on mental conditions in the United States is on social services and in the criminal justice system. In 2002, then Chair of the President's New Freedom Commission on Mental Health, Dr. Michael Hogan, commented, "We are spending too much on mental illness in all the wrong places" (as cited in Insel, 2008). A decade later, his point still stands in that most of the direct and indirect costs of mental illness are not directly related to health care for the individuals involved but are instead spent on items like public income assistance (welfare) and in addressing homelessness (Insel, 2008).

Managed care models may hold the most hope for cost-effective reduction of the overall cost of mental conditions. Improving the coordination of physical and mental health care can reduce the likelihood of negative health outcomes. Mental health conditions often present together with other issues, such as alcohol or drug dependence, a situation termed mentally ill chemical abuse (MICA). Addressing multiple needs at the same time reduces length and number of treatments sought. Though it is difficult to measure the direct and especially the indirect costs of mental health issues, evidence suggests that improved programs within the health care system can reduce overall costs in terms of social services, criminal justice, and productivity loss (National Institute of Mental Health [NIMH], 2009).

Suicide- and Homicide-Liable Persons

Violence prevention programs are most effective when disseminated through the school system and other organizations that directly reach young people. Suicide and homicide prevention are closely tied to mental health and substance abuse prevention. Among those implemented in schools, the **Signs of Suicide (SOS) program** is perhaps most widespread. SOS trains educators and program facilitators who then run the SOS program in schools; the program teaches students how to recognize signs of suicide in themselves and others and how to respond to suicide indicators (Signs of Suicide, 2012). Studies of the SOS program have found it to be one of the most effective and cost-efficient suicide prevention programs in the United States (Aseltine, James, Schilling, & Glanovsky, 2007).

Alcohol and substance abuse are most often treated through outpatient therapy, allowing the patient to preserve productivity at home and at work.

Persons Affected by Alcohol and Substance Abuse

Outpatient therapy is the most popular treatment program for alcohol and substance abuse. Outpatient therapy is not only more cost effective than residential treatment but it also allows the patient to maintain productivity both at work and at home. Evidence exists that outpatient therapies can improve cost-efficacy by combining multiple therapies that address both physical and psychological factors in a managed care plan (Beaston-Blaakman, Shepard, Horgan, & Ritter, 2007).

Prevention programs are even more cost effective in that they lower the incidence rate of alcohol and substance abuse. In doing so, prevention programs reduce the amount spent on substance abuse treatments, emergency medical needs, and in the criminal justice system. Substance abuse prevention programs aimed at youth have the dual effect of mitigating suicide and homicide rates. As such, many violence prevention programs have a built-in substance abuse avoidance message.

Indigent and Homeless Persons

There are many great programs that address the different needs of the homeless population. Some provide food, others provide shelter, and others provide medical care. The exact work and goal of a program must be considered in a cost-benefit analysis of any program serving homeless people. An organization providing multiple services under one roof should consider each program separately in order to ascertain where funds are best allocated.

Evidence supports the theory that critical time intervention programs that immediately respond to the needs of homeless people with mental health conditions is cost effective in that these programs reduce the number of shelterless nights per individual served (Jones et al., 2003). Supported housing programs that integrate clinical care and sheltering have also been found to be cost effective in serving homeless people with mental health conditions. Although they are expensive to run, supported housing programs are found to significantly reduce the number of shelterless nights (Rosenheck, Kasprow, Frisman, & Liu-Mares, 2003).

Immigrants and Refugees

Health care access for noncitizen immigrants and refugees continues to be a hot-button topic in the United States. An argument can be made that disqualifying immigrants from social welfare programs such as Medicaid would save said programs billions of dollars. On the other hand, denying health care coverage and access to immigrants creates a significant financial liability to care providers, as well as state and federal governments, in the form of uninsured health care costs.

Courtesy of Gerry Boughan/Shutterstock

Noncitizens and refugees continue to campaign for affordable access to basic health care.

The long debate over the Patient Protection and Affordable Care Act (PPACA) included voiced concerns over allowing noncitizen immigrants increased access to social welfare programs, particularly Medicaid. The law was written to offer lawfully present noncitizen immigrants the same qualifying access to Medicaid as native-born citizens; but the long-standing five-year waiting period is still active under PPACA. The law also includes lawfully present immigrants (those who have immigrated through the proper channels) in the mandate to maintain health insurance coverage and gives them equal access to the new health insurance marketplace developed under PPACA. Lawfully present immigrants are also eligible under the other requirements for tax credits for health insurance premiums, as created by PPACA (Siskin, 2010). Undocumented immigrants are exempted from the mandate and are also denied access to the new insurance marketplace (Siskin, 2011).

Critical Thinking

Cost-benefit analysis and cost-effectiveness both have different applications and uses. Can you think of two ways each type of analysis might be used?

Self-Check

Answer the following questions to the best of your ability.

1. Cost analysis of abuse prevention is complicated by what difficulties?
   a. reaching victims and potential victims
   b. cost-effectiveness of the program
   c. finding participants 10 years later
   d. social stigma of victims of abuse

2. The CDC considers a treatment program cost effective if the cost per quality-adjusted life year (QALY) is at or below _____ per QALY gained.
   a. $50,000
   b. $75,000
   c. $100,000
   d. $125,000

3. Prevention programs are more cost effective in that they lower the incidence rate of what types of abuse?
   a. alcohol and substance abuse
   b. emotional abuse
   c. verbal abuse
   d. domestic partner abuse

Answer Key

1. a   2. c   3. a

Case Study: The Argument Over Data Representation: Planned Parenthood Federation of America

In 2011, Planned Parenthood Federation of America (PPFA) (2012) found itself in the middle of a debate over the way medical service providers should collect and report data on services rendered. Amidst a political firestorm over funding, PPFA released annual data on the total number of services, separated by type, which the entire organization had rendered in 2010. PPFA claimed that the data showed that abortion services accounted for 3% of the total number of services.

The data was questioned because it did not reflect the number of patients who received abortion services; it reflected the total number of abortion services rendered. Concerns were also voiced that a patient seeking abortion services received multiple services as part of the abortion services (counseling, pregnancy tests, other medical tests, contraception, and breast exams, to name a few). The PPFA data counted each service separately, instead of as a package with the abortion services. It was posited that abortion services might account for significantly more than 3% of PPFA's total business, were the data reported differently.

In the end, it was decided that there was no proof of data misrepresentation by PPFA. This is because PPFA reports services data in accordance with Section 1001 of Title X of the Public Health Service Act. Title X is the federal program under which many family planning resource centers, including PPFA, health departments, and other community-based programs receive state and federal funding for reproductive health and family planning services. Title X is administered by the U.S. Department of Health and Human Services, Office of Population Affairs (2011). Under the administrative guidelines, all participating organizations must count services rendered and report data using the same definitions and data reporting practices. This allows the administrative offices of Title X to provide standardized data that enables objective cost analysis and program reviews that determine future funding to grantees under Title X. In this way, Title X has contributed to standardized data reporting across all programs receiving government funds for family planning services.

Chapter Summary

The cost of medical care is more than what physicians charge to treat patients. Direct costs of care are tangible and include the cost of medication and treatment, including operational items such as staffing costs. Indirect costs of care include intangible items that are more difficult to measure. Time off work, productivity loss at work and at home, and quality of life are all indirect costs of care.

Treatment and prevention programs must prove that the money spent is worthwhile in order to gain funding from grants, from donors, and from within the organizations themselves. Cost analysis considers direct and indirect costs along with intended outcomes and actual outcomes. The least expensive program may not actually offer the most cost-effective treatment method. Many times, prevention programs are more cost efficient than treatment programs because preventing negative outcomes is usually less expensive than reversing them.

Critical Thinking

The chapter states that prevention is a better way to spend money than curing people after they have contracted a disease or illness. Can you think of examples of certain health issues that would benefit from this approach and how prevention can reduce the associated costs?

Self-Check

Answer the following questions to the best of your ability.

1. To determine how an organization should best use its resources, it must determine the true cost of health care.
   a. True
   b. False

2. For the purposes of this chapter, how are direct costs defined?
   a. those costs associated with providing health care
   b. how much a specific procedure costs
   c. if it is tangible, it is a direct cost
   d. by how much direct benefit a patient receives from the procedure

3. When determining resource allocation to care for vulnerable populations, what must be considered? (Select two.)
   a. patient benefits
   b. direct costs
   c. indirect costs
   d. social approval

4. The United States experienced a record-breaking birthrate of 4,316,233 total births in what year?
   a. 1998
   b. 2007
   c. 2009
   d. 2012

5. Primary prevention programs focus on what?
   a. public education and awareness
   b. social relationships
   c. responsibility
   d. peer pressure

6. Treatment and prevention programs must prove that the money spent is _____ in order to gain funding from grants, from donors, and from within the organizations themselves.
   a. worthwhile
   b. accessible
   c. accounted for
   d. placed in a strong financial institution

Answer Key

1. a   2. c   3. b, c   4. b   5. a   6. a

Additional Resources

Visit the following websites to learn more about the topics covered in this chapter:

Patient Centered Medical Home, which advocates a continuum of care

http://www.ncbi.nlm.nih.gov/pmc/articles/PMC1466763/?tool=pmcentrez

The Signs of Suicide website

http://www.mentalhealthscreening.org/programs/youth-prevention-programs/sos/

The Office of Population Affairs website about Title X

http://www.hhs.gov/opa/title-x-family-planning/

Web Exercise

This chapter has discussed the unseen costs of health care services, including everything from physicians' salaries to the cost of medical supplies such as tongue depressors and gloves. It has also discussed and given examples of cost-benefit and cost-effectiveness analyses. Choose a position that is for or against the statement, "Is any program worth the cost if only a single human being benefits from the program?" Research that position and write a three- to five-page paper outlining your position. Be sure to use reliable sources and cite them in APA format. Wikipedia and YouTube should not be used in this assignment. Your paper must meet the following requirements:

- three to five pages, double-spaced
- 12-point Times New Roman font
- APA formatting for quotes, citations, and sources

In your paper, be sure to address the following:

- explanation of your position as for or against
- examples supporting your position
- why you chose those particular examples
- did you change your stance when researching and why?

Key Terms

absenteeism The missing of days of work by employees.

cost-benefit analysis (CBA) Determines the likelihood of the project producing a positive outcome and a good return on the financial investments of the project.

cost-effectiveness analysis (CEA) A method of comparing two or more programs.

direct costs Tangible costs that can be measured by totaling the financial prices of all of the resources used to treat a patient.

indirect costs Abstract costs that are difficult to measure in economic terms.

monetary inflation Loss in currency value.

monetary value Cost in terms of a dollar total.

neonatal Just-born, generally considered to be the first day or two after birth.

postnatal Infancy after the first few days postdelivery.

presenteeism Wherein workers show up for work but have severely lowered productivity over a length of time.

quality-adjusted life year (QALY) An outcome measure that weighs both the quality and quantity of life.

Signs of Suicide program A nationwide program that trains educators and other facilitators to educate youth on recognizing the signs and symptoms of suicide and the appropriate ways to respond.

8

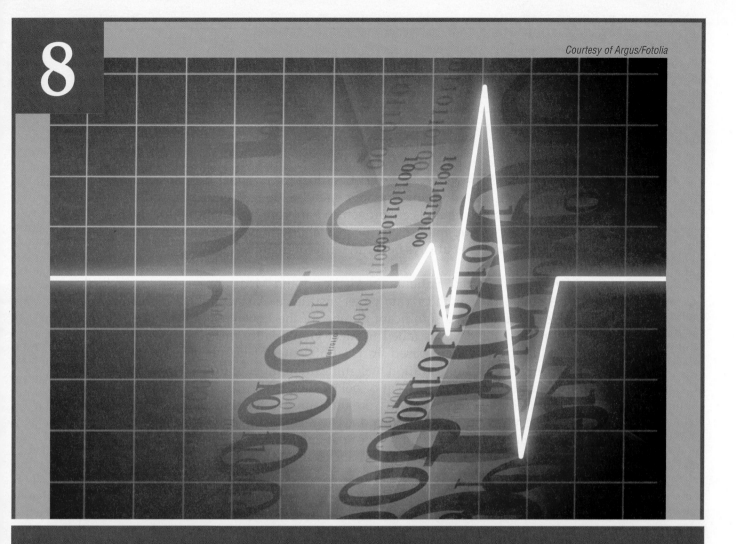

Monitoring the Quality of Care

Learning Objectives

After reading this chapter, you should be able to:

- Identify the criteria used to measure the quality of care received by vulnerable populations.
- Examine the quality of health care received by vulnerable populations.
- Evaluate program quality.
- Identify the issue of establishing universal care protocols.
- Find resources for establishing best practices and protocols.

Introduction

Cost-based analysis provides a method to determine where resources are best spent, but it does not do enough to measure the quality of care received. The quality of care is measured in terms of treatment results (does the patient fully recover or improve quality of life?), provider characteristics (does the provider fully answer patients' questions? how much time does the provider spend with each patient?), and treatment standards (what treatment methods are proven and appropriate for individual illnesses?). Access affects quality of care in terms of the availability of new technologies and medicines. However, "new" is not always better in terms of treatment quality.

Some evidence indicates that patients on Medicaid and Medicare receive lower quality health care than those with private payer insurance. An April 2012 report by Kaiser Health News found that a significant number of the 12,000 federally funded health care centers in the United States failed to meet vital quality measures (Kaiser Health News, 2012a). The findings are based on Health Center Data collected by the Health Resources and Services Administration. A significant number of the patients seen at federally funded health care centers live at or below the poverty line. The data shows that 38% of patients treated at these centers were uninsured at the time of treatment (Health Resources and Services Administration, n.d.). The relationship between a failure to meet quality of care standards and the number of patients on Medicaid, Medicare, and with no insurance may not be a direct link, but it does indicate a problem with quality of care for America's most vulnerable populations.

Critical Thinking

How would you measure quality of care? Do you think treatment results, provider characteristics, and treatment standards tell everything?

Self-Check

Answer the following questions to the best of your ability.

1. What knowledge is best obtained from cost-based analysis?
   a. where resources are best spent
   b. quality of care received
   c. mortality rates
   d. patient satisfaction

2. Although federally funded health care centers treat people at all income levels, a significant number of the patients seen live where in relation to the poverty line?
   a. slightly above the poverty line
   b. well above the poverty line
   c. at or above the poverty line
   d. at or below the poverty line

3. What indicates a problem with quality of care for America's most vulnerable populations?
    a. the link between a failure to meet quality of care standards and the number of patients on Medicaid and with no insurance
    b. the increased costs of pharmaceuticals (drugs)
    c. the expense of diagnostic imaging (CAT, MRI, PET, etc.)
    d. the mandate of electronic health records in every health care facility

Answer Key

1. **a**   2. **d**   3. **a**

8.1 Monitoring the Quality of Care

Several factors must be considered to create a full picture of the quality of care received by a given population. Quality of care, for example, can be measured by the characteristics of care providers, such as whether or not they are licensed, whether they have maintained their credentials with continuing education, and so on. These kinds of external requirements are known as **structure considerations**. Quality of care is also measured with treatment standards and protocols used to treat certain conditions or types of patients, which are referred to as **process considerations**. The result of a particular treatment is known as its **outcome**. The outcome of a particular treatment, procedure, or health care service is another way to measure quality of care. For example, a good outcome for wisdom tooth surgery would mean that the tooth was extracted without undue pain to the patient; a bad outcome would mean that the surgery did not go well and the patient experiences undue pain and infection at the surgical site. All three factors (structure considerations, process considerations, and outcome) are considered in tandem using the Donabedian Model to measure quality of care.

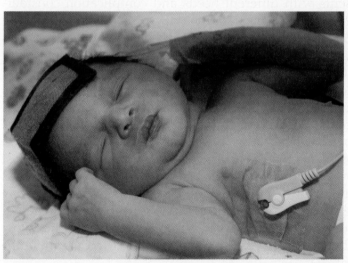

Courtesy of Reflektastudios/Fotolia

Quality of care is influenced by structure, process, and outcomes.

Different health care sectors tend to focus quality measurements on different factors. Residential treatment centers, such as nursing homes for the chronically ill, disabled, and elderly, often use structure considerations to measure quality. The idea behind this methodology is that ensuring appropriately trained staff and maintaining all necessary licenses will result in high-quality care. The mental health sector tends to measure quality by the use of treatment standards and protocols, such as prescribing sleep aids to insomniacs, to reach treatment objectives. Alternatively, those in the fields of obstetrics, gynecology, and neonatology tend to focus on treatment outcomes, like delivering a healthy baby, to gauge quality of care. It is important to note that quality of care consists of many aspects of evaluation and measurement. One is the patient's perspective, and that tends to be subjective. For example, one mother may be comfortable with a physician's decision to perform a Cesarean delivery while another mother may feel angry about her own Cesarean delivery. Those charged with measuring the quality of care must be prepared to consider different factors and reevaluate measurement practices as needs arise and situations change.

Vulnerable Mothers and Children

Structure and process considerations for caring for high-risk mothers and newborns focus on two distinct concerns: prenatal care and neonatal care. As discussed in previous chapters, regular and timely prenatal care has been shown to reduce negative outcomes at birth. Process-oriented questions arise regarding the role of technology in delivery and postnatal care of newborns. When deciding on a treatment plan, medical staff must consider both standardized treatment protocols and the individual patient's situation, and the two are not always in sync. Sometimes, the newest mode of treatment is not always the best option, complicating the task of creating protocols of care for specific problems.

This issue is particularly apparent in decisions concerning ventilation, or assisted breathing, of low birth weight babies. There are many assisted breathing options, and every patient and every treatment presents with different needs and complication considerations. For example, high-frequency oscillatory ventilation (HFOV) is preferred by some physicians because it has been found to decrease injury from chronic lung disease and is acceptable to use with surfactant, a substance that stabilizes the alveoli in the lung and improves functionality. Most full-term, normal birth weight babies are born with natural surfactant; however, preterm babies often lack this substance, which is vital to lung function and health. Synthetic surfactant is used when the infant's lungs have not matured enough to make their own surfactant. However, HFOV may cause lung damage by overextending the lungs. Concern also exists regarding clinical staffs' familiarity with HFOV. Improper use may create more problems than it cures, and HFOV may not be the best option for all situations (Courtney, Durand, Asselin, Eichenwald, & Stark, 2003; Benitz, 2008). HFOV offers an illustration of the way structure and process quality controls may not always create the best outcomes. Administrators and physicians need to work together within a provider organization to determine the best process recommendations that allow providers to follow protocol while using their training and judgment to determine the best treatment plan for each patient.

Abused Individuals

Structural and process quality considerations for addressing the needs of abused individuals begin with training physicians, social workers, teachers, and others who work in direct contact with the public on how to recognize the signs of abuse as well as how to identify particular bruising patterns, how to distinguish injuries caused by accidents from injuries caused by physical abuse, and also to distinguish bruising patterns caused by abuse from bruises caused by certain medical conditions or chronic diseases. Many people lack appropriate training in recognizing abuse, though educators, health care workers, and social workers do have mandated training on recognizing and reporting abuse.

Still others might shy away from the topic for fear of offending a client or of incurring liability for reporting their suspicions. However, all people who report suspicions of abuse are protected from liability by the Good Samaritan laws.

As shown in Chapter 7, abuse prevention programs offer the best outcomes in terms of cost efficiency and human cost. Social service programs that provide support and home visits to new parents have been found to decrease the risk of child abuse. Training nursing home staff and home health aides in dealing with elderly patients and stress may reduce the incidence of elder abuse. Programs that provide training and support for adult caretakers of elderly parents also work to reduce the incidence of abuse in private care settings. However, the goal to "reduce the incidence of elder abuse" may be too general to act as a quality measurement or quality control mechanism. Instead, mini-objectives can be created under the larger goal to reduce the incidence of elder abuse; then, programs can be measured against the mini-objectives on the way to assessing the larger goal.

Chronically Ill and Disabled Persons

The quality of care for the chronically ill and disabled varies based on a number of factors, not the least of which is whether the patient has private payer insurance or is on Medicare or Medicaid. Hurdles to maintaining quality of care on an individual basis include the patient's ability to get to and from doctor and rehabilitation appointments, as well as the patient's ability and willingness to make lifestyle choices that improve the chances of positive health outcomes.

In medical settings, whether home health medical care or residential care centers such as nursing homes, quality measurement and control are focused on structure and protocol considerations more than outcomes. This is because outcomes are best determined on an individual basis, but structure and protocols offer care providers guidelines to ensure smooth operation. There is also difficulty in getting providers to follow guidelines and quality control measures. In a 2012 survey from the John A. Hartford Foundation, one-third of older Americans reported that their primary care physicians failed to review all of their medications. Two-thirds of those polled reported that medical care providers failed to inquire about recent falls, a problem that puts many elderly in the hospital annually. The study also found that of the 35 million older Americans on Medicare, only 2.3 million had wellness visits with their physicians (Kaiser Health News, 2012b). The purpose of the study was to show physicians where the gaps in elder care are so that they may better address them.

Courtesy of Monkey Business/Fotolia

To maintain quality of care and improve the chances of positive health outcomes, a patient must have the ability to get to and from doctor appointments and be willing and able to make positive lifestyle choices.

The nursing home industry is highly regulated in almost every department, including nursing, dietary, maintenance, and housekeeping. In fact, each department, and the nursing home as a whole, has its own regulatory body. The federal government regulates nursing home facilities through the Centers for Medicare and Medicaid Services (CMS). This regulatory body serves the 1.1 million people served by care organizations throughout the United States (Centers for Medicare and Medicaid Services [CMS], 2012). It serves as a watchdog for the industry, and every six months it puts out a book titled *The Long Term Care Survey*, which outlines changes in laws and interpretive guidelines for facilities to follow. These guidelines and interpretations of current laws in long-term care are enforced by the states during **annual survey**, a process in which a team of industry-specialized experts visits a facility and determines its compliance with applicable laws. In nursing facilities, this process is carried out through each state's Office of the Inspector General (OIG). In hospitals, this survey is carried out by the Joint Commission on the Accreditation of Healthcare Organizations (JCAHO). Depending on whether the facility is in compliance with industry regulations, the facility receives a statement of compliance or a statement of deficiency.

The **statement of compliance** shows that a facility is in compliance with all applicable laws and regulations, whereas a **statement of deficiency** shows different levels of noncompliance. Isolated instances of deficiency are rare occurrences that are noticed and need to be corrected, such as one resident not having a cup of water readily available. Systemic deficiencies, on the other hand, are ongoing problems that require more immediate correction to return to compliance, such as mobility-challenged residents being left in bed half the day because the staff is busy with mobile residents. The range of noncompliance is noted in the statement of deficiencies with a letter code from A to G. The A rating is the worst, with widespread, systemic failures, whereas the G rating is minor, indicating isolated incidents with the potential to harm few residents. The A–D deficiencies carry monetary penalties per day, per deficiency, with fines up to $250,000 dollars per day. Some deficiencies that cause widespread injury, like broken stairs that have caused injuries but haven't been repaired, and injuries that have been covered up by staff, are considered "Immediate Jeopardy," and can cause the immediate closing of a facility.

A facility that receives a statement of deficiency has to become compliant within a certain period (industry standard is less than a month) and write OIG a statement of corrections that identifies the deficiency and explains both the process the facility will employ to correct the deficiency and the ongoing process they will use to keep it from reoccurring. This process typically includes staff, department head, and administrator sign-off for a period of three months to one year, where the process is examined, and the facility can be sure to correct the deficiency. If the statement of corrections is accepted by the regulatory body (OIG or the Joint Commission), a statement of compliance is issued after the paying of any monetary penalties incurred.

A report with all information on facilities that take federal or state money for long-term care is located at http://medicare.gov/nhcompare/. This website is easy to understand and hosts each nursing home's last three surveys, dietary health inspections, staffing ratios, implementation of quality measures within the facility, fire safety inspections, penalties incurred through the compliance survey process, and complaints and incidents investigated by each community's long-term care ombudsman, OIG, or Joint Commission. This website is updated frequently with new information.

Persons Diagnosed With HIV/AIDS

There is currently no cure for HIV/AIDS, but new therapies and drugs can improve the quality of life and prolong the lives of HIV/AIDS patients. As such, the focus of health care for HIV/AIDS patients is on care, not cure. Though the intended outcomes are the same for all treatments (prolonging life, improving or maintaining quality of life), the process and structural considerations can differ widely. Different HIV/AIDS patients need different drugs at different times over the courses of their lives, and different care providers meet patient needs differently. The problem is further exacerbated by access to care problems in terms of the price tag of HIV/AIDS treatments and by care providers who are not well trained to treat this vulnerable population or to provide prevention counseling and care to groups most at risk of contracting the disease, as evidenced by the significantly high number of African Americans who represent new cases of HIV each year (Kaiser Permanente, n.d.).

Courtesy of AlexRaths/iStockphoto

Because HIV/AIDS has no cure, health care professionals focus, instead, on caring for patients and managing their symptoms.

In an effort to decrease the number of new HIV infections each year, the United States government launched the National HIV/AIDS Strategy. Key components of the strategy include expanding access to care for HIV/AIDS patients and improving the quality of care received by HIV/AIDS patients (U.S. Department of Health and Human Services, n.d.). In 2012, Kaiser Permanente launched the HIV Challenge, with the goal of providing physicians and other health care providers with the knowledge and tools to improve the quality of care they give their HIV/AIDS patients. The challenge focuses on HIV prevention, early testing for HIV, and early intervention for HIV/AIDS patients. Launched with the National HIV/AIDS Strategy in mind, the program encourages health care providers to make structure and process improvements as a means of improving outcomes (Kaiser Permanente, 2012).

Persons Diagnosed With Mental Conditions

Great disparities exist in the quality of mental health care services received by different populations. Many private insurance plans cover some amount of mental health treatment. In addition to quality of coverage problems, mental health providers are found in an enormous array of settings, specializing in a great many facets of mental health. This disjointed structure of the mental health provider network creates both structure and process quality issues. Structurally, practitioners with private practices may have quality measured only in terms of maintaining proper licensing. Process-wise, these practitioners are free to use their own preferred methods. Sometimes, quality is measured primarily by a doctor's ability to maintain patient relationships. Outcomes-based measurements of quality are tailored more on individual patients' needs and so can be difficult to track across providers and patients. However, some insurers, including the Children's Health Insurance Program (CHIP), have policies and programs in place to track the quality of health care, including mental health care, to which participating providers must adhere (Agency for Healthcare Research and Quality, 2010).

The Substance Abuse and Mental Health Services Administration's (SAMHSA) Office of Behavioral Health Equity (OBHE) works to coordinate mental health care across agencies to create a higher quality, more uniform mental health care structure. OBHE focuses on reducing the disparities experienced by vulnerable groups in the mental health care arena. The outcomes goal of OBHE is to improve access to quality mental health care for vulnerable populations as a means of reducing the strain put on those populations by substance abuse and mental health problems (SAMHSA, OBHE, n.d.).

The World Health Organization (WHO) addressed the need for quality control mechanisms in the mental health sector in a 2003 report titled "Quality Improvement for Mental Health." The report outlines ways for mental health providers to establish care processes and set outcome goals. It encourages going beyond accreditation standards and consulting regularly with organizations that work with and for people with mental conditions, as well as regular information gathering to help provide a clear view of what is working in the structure and processes to create the best possible outcomes. This report offers administrators and other organizational policy makers an easy-to-implement quality assurance plan to reduce disparities and improve quality of mental health care delivery.

Suicide- and Homicide-Liable Persons

The outcomes-oriented goals of treatment for violence-prone individuals are to prevent violence from occurring. More specific goals are based on individual patients' needs and situations. Cost-efficacy studies indicate that prevention programs may have the most impact on reducing suicide and homicide, though community impact programs that improve the wealth and health of violence-prone communities at large are perhaps most effective. As for structure and process, treatment for violence-prone individuals is most common in mental health settings. As such, the same quality concerns and recommendations apply.

Persons Affected by Alcohol and Substance Abuse

Structure and process quality assurance for substance and alcohol abuse are created under guidelines for best practices, called **treatment improvement protocols (TIPs)**, set forth by the SAMHSA's Center for Substance Abuse Treatment (CSAT) (n.d.). These protocols offer information, guidance, and tools, including checklists for care providers to use in recognizing and treating alcohol and substance abuse. The protocols are extensive and are broken down by subject. For example, some protocols for "Substance Abuse Treatment for Persons with Co-Occurring Disorders" include the following (Center for Substance Abuse Treatment [CSAT], 2005):

- Apply CSAT's "no wrong door" policy by ensuring that patients receive appropriate treatment regardless of where they entered the system (for example, being recognized as a substance abuser by the family doctor should not be a barrier to the proper substance abuse therapy).

- Perform a thorough assessment.
- Achieve integrated treatment (for example, include pharmaceutical and psychological therapies to recovering substance abusers).
- Ensure continuity of care.

Although the overall intended outcome of alcohol and substance abuse treatments is to get the patient to stop his or her maladaptive behavior as well as limit reoccurrence, universally defined treatment outcomes are lacking in the field, and instead may vary from practitioner to practitioner.

Indigent and Homeless Persons

The problem of establishing quality control and procedural standards for homeless individuals is directly linked with the problem of establishing access to care for this vulnerable group. Outcome standards for caring for homeless and indigent people should go beyond responding to existing ailments to encourage wellness visits to clinics. Wellness visits enable the homeless to take advantage of prevention programs such as vaccinations and sexually transmitted disease (STD) counseling. **Inoculations**, or preventive shots, against illnesses that are common among people who regularly sleep outdoors include those for influenza and pneumonia. These inoculations can reduce the likelihood of a homeless person needing emergency medical care for lung infections.

Courtesy of Sframe/Fotolia

Rather than responding to preexisting conditions when caring for homeless and indigent people, it should be a goal to encourage preventative measures toward maintaining good health.

SAMHSA's Homelessness Resource Center (HRC) attempts to address the need for process standards and care norms for the homeless population. HRC publishes "Best Practices for Providers" to provide tools, information, and encouragement for those individuals and health care organizations that provide medical treatment to the homeless population. HRC ranks cultural understanding high on the list of best practices because understanding how a homeless individual experiences the world is key to creating individualized treatment goals and providing quality care to each patient. HRC covers an expanding variety of topics specific to treating the homeless population, including best practices for community reentry (such as finding permanent housing for a homeless person who has been in jail and establishing treatment under appropriate physicians, both before the individual is released into the community), best practices for parent-child interaction therapy (such as having the parent engage the child in a play session to strengthen their relationship), and best practices for implementing an evidence-based practice (such as using the "Seeking Safety" manual to implement programs for homeless females with sexual abuse experiences) (SAMHSA HRC, n.d.).

Immigrants and Refugees

Much as with homeless people, quality of care for immigrants and refugees begins with cultural awareness. Some cultures and religions may not accept some treatment methods and processes. Language barriers further frustrate patients and care providers alike. The ability to communicate paired with an understanding of cultural beliefs that may affect a patient's compliance with selected treatments can improve the likelihood of selecting a mode of treatment that will provide the best possible outcomes.

Structural quality improvements for treating immigrant and refugee populations should include maintaining a multilingual staff. When a patient enters who does not speak English, and a multilingual staff member is not available to translate, professional interpreters should be made available. This is most important in situations of grave health matters, such as cancer diagnoses. Administration concerned with quality control should be aware of the languages and cultures most often seen in the practice and provide relevant staff training. Doing so reduces access barriers and gives providers better tools with which to treat patients.

Critical Thinking

Structures and processes can be used as a means to improve care to patients. One method includes tailoring care to an individual's needs. How could this method impact both the quality of care and access to that care? What new structures and processes would you consider to improve quality of care?

Self-Check

Answer the following questions to the best of your ability.

1. Process-oriented questions arise regarding the role of technology in delivery and postnatal care of newborns.
   a. True
   b. False

2. Hurdles to care include the patient's ability and willingness to make _____ changes that improve the chances of positive health outcomes.
   a. transportation
   b. medicinal
   c. lifestyle choice
   d. employee insurance

3. What outcome objective may be too general to act as a quality measurement or quality control mechanism?
   a. establish single-payer system
   b. reduce the incidence of elder abuse
   c. increase early prevention
   d. provide education

Answer Key

1. **a**   2. **c**   3. **b**

Case Study: Improving Quality of Care

Agnes is an 89-year-old resident of a long-term care community. She is ambulatory with the assistance of a walker, continent, and maintains a high level of socialization within her community and family life. Agnes has a problem, however. She lives in a community that caters to the nonambulatory resident, with limited socialization opportunities. Agnes does not feel she is receiving quality care in her current facility. Should she move to a different long-term care community, or can she convince the facility to work within the care plan process to help her receive the type of care she deserves?

Agnes decides to work with her facility's personnel to improve her own care. She casually suggests some changes through her monthly resident council meeting, which starts each of the facility's department heads thinking about improvement and quality of care for ambulatory residents like Agnes. Specifically, Agnes makes the following suggestions:

- more activities for ambulatory residents
- fresher food choices for those residents with a more discerning palette, including more fresh fruits and vegetables
- more access to outside areas around the home

The facility's department heads are bound by the care plan process in the home to respond to each suggestion or recommendation, even if that means saying to that resident that something is not currently possible. The facility is a responsive one, so they come up with the following plan of action:

- The facility adds two activities per week for ambulatory residents. The activity director invites a workout instructor to come in once a week; this instructor specializes in both standing-up and sitting-down routines. The activity director has also had dealings with numerous dance instructors over her career, so she brings in another instructor in a different discipline and changes the weeks' planning and calendars to allow more mobile residents the ability to "show their moves."
- The dietary director works through her suppliers to guarantee more seasonal fresh fruits and vegetables. The substitution comes at a minimal cost to the facility and guarantees a higher quality of life for those who will enjoy it, including Agnes.
- The facility has some staff members who are willing to spend some time during their shifts outside with the residents, walking and sitting on the grounds. The director of nursing and the administrator also volunteer to spend some time with those residents wanting to take in some fresh air, and the dietary department suggests the addition of a lemonade stand on the grounds to pass out beverages to keep the residents hydrated.

Agnes got her wish. The quality of care she receives, and thus her quality of life as a whole, is improved because she communicated with the staff. The facility is pleased because they were able to fulfill the needs of an underserved group within their facility at a minimum of cost, but a maximum of benefit, to the facility.

In this case, as in many others related to quality of care in a long-term care setting, quality stems from what the residents want. Agnes did not have huge, earth-shattering needs. She simply wanted to feel like a member of a community, so she voiced her opinions. Most issues with quality of life and quality of care are a matter of common sense.

Chapter Summary

Monitoring and improving the quality of care received by patients of varying populations must be viewed in terms of structure, process, and outcomes. Improving quality on the structure level often involves training staff and reducing barriers to access. Improving quality on the process level involves creating treatment standards that offer providers guidance on best practices but leaves room for physicians to make decisions based on individual patient needs. The goal of structure and process quality improvement is to improve the quality of health care outcomes for every patient.

Evidence suggests that vulnerable populations, especially those with public payer insurance or no insurance, receive lower quality health care than that enjoyed by patients with private health insurance. This points to structural problems in the health care system, but access barriers to care should not be ignored as part of the overall problem of providing high-quality health care to vulnerable groups.

Critical Thinking

Consider three issues of establishing universal care protocols. What are these issues, and what challenges stand in the way of correcting them?

Self-Check

Answer the following questions to the best of your ability.

1. Abuse prevention programs offer the best outcomes in terms of cost efficiency and human cost.
   a. True
   b. False

2. What is the process whereby a team of industry-specialized experts visits and determines a facility's compliance with applicable laws?
   a. process analysis
   b. client feedback
   c. annual survey
   d. charting compliance

3. Health care for HIV/AIDS patients focuses on _____.
   a. cure
   b. care
   c. education
   d. prevention

4. What department of the Substance Abuse and Mental Health Services Administration focuses on reducing the disparities experienced by vulnerable groups in the mental health care arena?
   a. the administrative department
   b. Office of Client Services
   c. Office of Political Lobbying
   d. Office of Behavioral Health Equity (OBHE)

5. Structure and process quality assurance for substance and alcohol abuse are known as which of the following?
   a. treatment improvement protocols
   b. provisions of care
   c. treatment plans
   d. palliative care

6. Quality of care for immigrants and refugees begins with what?
   a. cultural awareness
   b. in-home visits
   c. immigration
   d. a complete medical history

Answer Key

1. a   2. c   3. b   4. d   5. a   6. a

Additional Resources

Visit the following websites to learn more about the topics covered in this chapter:

Results from an April 2012 report by Kaiser Health News about health care failing to meet standards

http://www.kaiserhealthnews.org/stories/2012/april/18/community-health-centers-under-pressure.aspx

Results from a 2012 survey in which patients report doctors' failures to inquire after medications or falls

http://capsules.kaiserhealthnews.org/index.php/2012/04/doctors-fall-short-in-helping-many-seniors/

A description of health disparities

http://info.kp.org/communitybenefit/html/our_work/global/our_work_5_a.html

Web Exercise

Let's say you have an elderly family member who needs to be placed in a skilled facility. You are not sure which facility is the best choice, so you need to conduct some research. Go to the following website that provides evaluations of nursing home facilities: http://medicare.gov/nhcompare/. Perform a search to locate three facilities in your area, and gather the following information for each facility:

- What are the overall results of the last survey performed on the facility?
- What is their staffing ratio (the number of staff to each patient)?
- Were there any penalties within the last two years? What was the violation, and what were the results (fines, loss of funding, staff discipline)?
- Have there been any complaints filed against the facility? What was the complaint and what was the resolution?

Write a three-page report that summarizes the research and explain which facility you would put your family member in and why you chose that facility.

Key Terms

annual survey A process in which a team of industry-specialized experts visits a facility and determines its compliance with applicable laws.

inoculations Preventive shots administered to prevent the spread of illness.

outcome The result of treatments.

process considerations Treatment standards and protocols used to treat certain conditions or types of patient.

statement of compliance A statement showing that a facility is in compliance with all applicable laws and regulations.

statement of deficiency A statement showing different levels of noncompliance with applicable laws and regulations.

structure considerations Characteristics of care providers such as licensure and other external requirements.

treatment improvement protocols (TIPs) Guidelines for best practices created by the Substance Abuse and Mental Health Services Administration's (SAMHSA) Center for Substance Abuse Treatment (CSAT). These guidelines offer information and tools for care providers to effectively treat alcohol and substance abuse.

9

Studying Vulnerable Populations

Learning Objectives

After reading this chapter, you should be able to:

- Recognize the three types of research needed to identify, understand, and address the needs of vulnerable populations.

- Identify vulnerable populations using descriptive research.

- Identify vulnerability using analytic research.

- Assess program efficacy using evaluative research.

Introduction

To understand how to best address the needs of vulnerable populations, research must be conducted. The type of research used to study special populations in America's health care system falls into three broad categories. **Descriptive research** focuses on identifying those most at risk and the methods of identifying these groups and their needs—for example, identifying which youth are most at risk for violent behavior.

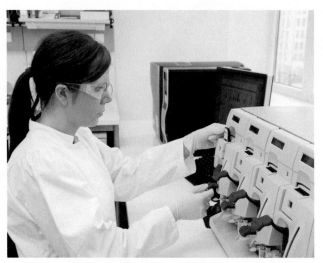

Courtesy of Gina Sanders/Fotolia

Descriptive, analytic, and evaluative research are all essential types of research used to study special populations in America's health care system.

Analytic research focuses on identifying the reasons for vulnerability and ways to prevent and remediate vulnerability, so it is used to identify why certain youth have higher risks of violent behavior than others. **Evaluative research** helps determine the success of existing programs that aim to provide services to vulnerable groups—meaning that evaluative research asks such questions as, "What programs are effective at addressing the needs of youth identified as being at risk for violent behavior?"

Each research category serves an important purpose; However, more integration between research types and studies would help improve the understanding of vulnerability as well as the programs that serve America's most vulnerable. The research associated with vulnerable populations is often fragmented, in that studies often look at one particular issue or group but do not always consider the connections that exist across issues and populations.

Critical Thinking

The three types of research all have advantages in certain situations and disadvantages in others. Do you think there would there be a benefit in using only one type of research in all situations to ensure consistency and accuracy?

Self-Check

Answer the following questions to the best of your ability.

1. Which type of research focuses on identifying those most at risk and the methods of identifying these groups and their needs?
    a. descriptive research
    b. analytic research
    c. evaluative research
    d. collaborative research

2. Which type of research focuses on identifying the reasons for vulnerability and the ways to prevent and remediate vulnerability?
    a. descriptive research
    b. evaluative research
    c. analytic research
    d. electronic research

3. Which type of research works to determine the success of existing programs that aim to provide services to vulnerable groups?
    a. evaluative research
    b. descriptive research
    c. analytic research
    d. qualitative research

Answer Key

1. **a**   2. **c**   3. **a**

9.1 Descriptive Research: Identifying the Vulnerable

Studies that work toward identifying vulnerable groups fall into the descriptive research category, which means that they seek to describe which groups are most vulnerable. Unfortunately, efforts to identify and count America's vulnerable populations are disjointed, with the result that there is little uniformity in terms of the definitions being used. Furthermore, lack of consistency when defining the characteristics of vulnerable groups causes data to become skewed—such as in some studies where specific groups are over- or underrepresented—and difficult to compare across studies. Issues of data collection necessary to study high-risk populations further complicate this problem. For example, one study may ask care providers to define patients by race while another study asks patients to define themselves by ethnicity. It would be much easier and more accurate if the two studies used the same terminology and definitions. Though using the same source for data is not always needed (for example, if the studies want to see the difference in how providers and patients define patients' races), using standardized data sources and data collecting methods (paper survey vs. computerized data mining) helps in performing cross-comparisons of the studies. Even as definitions begin to form, the length of time taken to interpret and report data leads much of it to be obsolete before a report is written.

Research into the descriptive characteristics of vulnerable populations should pay attention to the definitions used in prior research studies and use them where they can or address the changes in the reporting so that terminology is consistent across the various studies. In general, best practices that establish common terminology and provide for uniformity in data collection and reporting are necessary.

Vulnerable Mothers and Children

Traditionally, birth and death records were the main source of data available to those working on descriptive research of vulnerable mothers and children. The **National Vital Statistics System (NVSS)** is maintained by the Centers for Disease Control and Prevention's National Center for Health Statistics (NCHS). NVSS is a reporting system that tracks birth, death, and health data to provide a picture of what the American population looked like in the past and what it looks like now; NVSS uses that data to estimate future birth, death, and health trends.

Courtesy of Alena Kovalenko/Fotolia

Future birth, death, and health trends can be estimated based on current data from the National Vital Statistics System.

NCHS frequently reviews data reporting methods. Lack of registered births and incomplete registrations continue to be problematic for NVSS and the researchers who rely on its data. Previous efforts to remedy this problem have included updating classifications and surveying households (Hetzel, 1997). NCHS also provides standardized reporting forms, training, and an instruction manual to help those charged with reporting to ensure complete and accurate information.

Abused Individuals

Two issues plague data regarding child abuse, intimate partner abuse, and elder abuse. The definitions of abuse are somewhat subjective, and it is suspected that a considerable number of incidents go undetected and unreported. Data for descriptive research into abused individuals usually comes from clinical studies, household surveys, interviews with victims and perpetrators of abuse, and protective service agency reports.

The Administration for Children and Families conducts the National Incidence Study (NIS) on Child Abuse and Neglect about once per decade. The study was created as a requirement of the Child Abuse Prevention and Treatment Act. NIS contributes to the field of descriptive research not only by compiling data but also by creating standardized terminology and a framework for classifying and reporting child abuse by severity, maltreatment type, and demographics (Administration for Children and Families, n.d.b). Researchers conducting clinical studies and interpreting official reports should consider using the standards set forth by the NIS. Doing so would help create a network of research on the subject that would improve research accuracy.

Chronically Ill and Disabled Persons

Descriptive research on the chronically ill and disabled is relied on when determining health care program eligibility. The primary problem with this research is that much of it is subjective. For example, two patients with similar arthritis symptoms may report different amounts of pain on a scale of 1 to 10. What one patient finds uncomfortable, say bending over to tie shoelaces, may be impossibly painful for another patient with a similar amount of inflammation. Should the second patient receive more physical therapy paid for by insurance or have his or her medication costs subsidized while the patient reporting less pain is deemed ineligible for such programs?

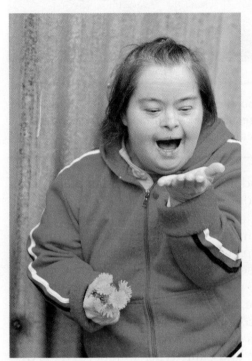

Courtesy of muro/Fotolia

Health care program eligibility for the disabled and chronically ill is determined by descriptive research, which is largely subjective.

The broadest information set available covering the chronically ill and disabled in the United States is the National Health Interview Survey (NHIS) conducted annually by the U.S. Census Bureau. The bureau selects households to participate in the survey and asks the participants to meet with interviewers to answer questions about race, living situation, diagnosed health issues, and perceived health issues and wellness. Survey participation is about 90% of selected households; of those that refuse the survey, replacements are not selected (Centers for Disease Control and Prevention, 2012f). By conducting the survey through live interviews, participants are encouraged to provide complete and accurate information. However, much of a person's perceived health is subjective, and accuracy cannot be guaranteed.

Persons Diagnosed With HIV/AIDS

Descriptive research helps to identify those groups that are most at risk for contracting the HIV virus so that preventive programming can be directed in appropriate ways. In the 1980s, HIV was thought of as a "gay man's" disease. However, HIV is also prevalent among intravenous drug users and can be transmitted through bodily secretions regardless of sexual preference. It is therefore important to determine who in the population has HIV, who in the population is most likely to contract HIV, and through what means the disease is most often contracted among different groups. Socioeconomic characteristics are also important in determining which groups are most at risk.

In the early stages of the epidemic, studies lacked uniformity in the way they defined HIV/AIDS cases. Some looked at HIV in the early stages, while others did not define HIV/AIDS until the point when AIDS actually set in. In 1985, the CDC and the World Health Organization (WHO) published a case definition for AIDS with the intention of improving testing and diagnoses procedures and creating a standardized definition to be used in research. In 1987, the official definition changed to make it easier to diagnose AIDS in Africa and other underdeveloped countries where medical technology is lacking. The last CDC/WHO definition of HIV/AIDS was published in 1993 and led to earlier diagnosis of HIV in women and children (Center for Disease Control, 1993).

Courtesy of franckreporter/iStockphoto

Contrary to early popular thought, HIV is not a specifically "gay man's" disease, but can be transmitted through bodily secretions regardless of sexual preference.

Many local health departments and physicians' offices participate in the CDC **seroprevalence** surveys. Seroprevalence is the incidence of infection, based on blood serum testing and the presence of antibodies for a specific disease in a given population. Though these surveys track new HIV diagnoses, they usually do not include much demographic information. Changes have been made in the last decade, however, to the CDC's reporting program to help reporters include nonpersonal socioeconomic and demographic information, such as race, gender, and insurance type. Some states and cities have mandatory reporting laws that compel physicians at specified locations and clinic types to report HIV/AIDS cases and provide counseling for diagnosed patients. The New York City Department of Health and Mental Hygiene has one such program under a New York state law (New York City Department of Health and Mental Hygiene, 2012).

Persons Diagnosed With Mental Conditions

Research that attempts to identify populations with mental conditions and those at risk of developing mental conditions faces obstacles from questions regarding what constitutes a mental illness and what methods are used to classify mental illness. Furthermore, the issue of **primacy**—whether the mental condition is the primary health factor or whether it is a secondary symptom of something else—is particularly important. Counting the number of people treated for mental conditions is also complicated by the wide variety of physicians who treat a wide variety of problems. For example, a person with severe mental illness may see a psychiatrist, but someone who is feeling blue might be more likely to see his or her general practitioner, who is less likely to participate in reporting programs that seek to study the population diagnosed with mental conditions.

The Substance Abuse and Mental Health Services Administration (SAMHSA) publishes reports on the state of mental health in the American population and on mental health services in the country. Beginning with the 2008 report, "Mental Health, United States, 2008," SAMHSA began including data from a variety of sources instead of just information from the administration. The inclusion of various sources provides for a broader look at mental health in the United States (Substance Abuse and Mental Health Services Administration [SAMHSA], 2010b).

Suicide- and Homicide-Liable Persons

The vital statistics system reports data on suicides and homicides. However, many attempted suicides go unreported, and medical examiners report that many achieved suicides are not reported as such due to the stigma associated with suicide (Bureau of Justice Statistics, 2011). Official records and coroner reports are the main sources of data on suicide numbers.

The main sources of data on homicide numbers come from police reports, the Federal Bureau of Investigation (FBI), and other areas of the criminal justice system. The FBI publishes multiple reports that include information on homicide, including Uniform Crime Reports and the Homicide Reports supplement and the National Crime Victimization Survey (formerly the National Crime Survey). The National Crime Victimization Survey is taken on an ongoing basis from a sampling of U.S. households and asks about experienced crime events such as rape and burglary (Bureau of Justice Statistics, 2011). As such, underreporting of personally traumatic events (like rape) and underrepresentation of the groups most affected by crime due to nonparticipation skew the numbers. In addition to sources from the FBI, the CDC offers access to the National Violent Death Reporting System (NVDRS). The NVDRS gathers data from multiple sources for each reported incident. By doing so, the NVDRS helps create a more accurate picture of suicide and homicide in the United States.

Persons Affected by Alcohol and Substance Abuse

The network of data available on the prevalence of alcohol and substance abuse is incohesive because different reports focus on different aspects of the problem and on different populations. Social surveys, like the National Household Survey on Drug Abuse and the Monitoring the Future survey, are subject to the same underreporting issues that nearly all social surveys are subject to. SAMHSA works through the Center for Mental Health Services (CMHS) to develop and publish standards for reporting on mental health and substance abuse services. The CMHS Uniform Reporting System (URS) provides standardized data that is easily compared. Even with the URS in place, there remains a need for research into the prevalence and nature of alcohol and substance abuse that uses reporting standards that make using the data for program implementation faster, easier, and more universal.

The CDC's Behavioral Risk Factor Surveillance System is an ongoing survey that tracks behaviors associated with poor health outcomes, including the prevalence of alcohol, tobacco, and drug use. The survey is conducted by phone and is used to measure the current health status and the current risk behaviors in the country, as well as monitor the

Courtesy of delkoo/fotolia

Collecting comprehensive data on alcohol and substance abuse can prove difficult due to issues of underreporting and variations of focus among data collection services.

ties between risk behaviors like alcohol abuse and health (Centers for Disease Control and Prevention, 2012g). The CDC tracks similar information on risk-associated behaviors, including alcohol use, drug use, tobacco use, seat belt use, and eating habits among America's youth using the ongoing Youth Risk Behavior Surveillance System (YRBSS). YRBSS is conducted utilizing many resources to reach youth, including schools; state, local, and tribal agencies; and health organizations (Centers for Disease Control and Prevention, 2012h). The CDC's efforts to collect data on risk-associated behavior on an ongoing basis are essential to studying and predicting America's health, identifying vulnerable populations, and recognizing risk factors that contribute to vulnerability.

Indigent and Homeless Persons

As discussed in earlier chapters, studying the prevalence of and risk factors for homelessness is challenging because the homeless population is transient and therefore difficult to quantify. Also, homelessness does not necessarily mean that a person is sleeping on the street. Shelters and other temporary housing programs are able to provide some information, such as a nightly count of the number of people staying there. Some places offer additional services, such as counseling and medical services, and are therefore able to offer some amount of information regarding the reasons for homelessness and common medical issues.

Courtesy of Aaron Kohr/shutterstock

Due to the transient nature of the homeless population, it is difficult to analyze the rate of occurrence and risk factors for homelessness.

Another method used to gather data on the incidence rate of homelessness in a given area is the **point-in-time count**. A point-in-time count seeks to determine the total number of homeless people sleeping outdoors in a specific area during a specific period. Counters walk the streets looking for homeless individuals and count the number found and note where they were located. Point-in-time counts, however, do not provide a thorough assessment of a city's homeless needs because the scope is so small.

Immigrants and Refugees

Though the U.S. Census Bureau, Program for Research on Immigration Policy, U.S. Immigration and Customs Enforcement, and other independent organizations have tried, no exact count of the number of undocumented workers in the United States currently exists. Reports on current estimates categorize undocumented workers into three groups: those making a permanent move to the country (settlers), those making a temporary trip to the country (sojourners), and those who enter the United States to work but who return home after the growing season or other work season is done (commuters). However, there are no strongly supported counts for any category.

The Immigration and Naturalization Service (INS), Current Population Survey, and census do supply some data on the number of documented immigrants and refugees seeking asylum in the United States. The Office of Refugee Resettlement conducts surveys of the demographics, socioeconomics, and use of public services by refugees. Other than the data from these surveys, little cross-disciplinary, cohesive research exists on the subject.

Critical Thinking

The very nature of many populations, like homeless and commuters, make them inherently difficult to accurately measure. How do you think this lack of knowledge impacts public funding for health care and services? Consider a descriptive research study that can examine the needs of these populations without measuring the populations directly. What variables could this study measure? What knowledge could be obtained from the data gathered?

Self-Check

Answer the following questions to the best of your ability.

1. What reporting system tracks birth, death, and health data to provide a picture of what the American population looks like?
   a. National Vital Statistics System
   b. United States Census
   c. electronic health records
   d. Center for Health and Human Services

2. Descriptive research on the chronically ill and disabled is relied on when determining health care program eligibility. What is the primary problem with this research?
   a. it is informal
   b. it is anecdotal

    c.   it is subjective
    d.   it is objective

3. Which of the following is one of the problems with research into identifying populations with mental conditions?
    a.   identifying what constitutes a mental illness
    b.   privacy regulations such as HIPAA
    c.   lack of overall data
    d.   poor record keeping

Answer Key

1. **a**   2. **c**   3. **a**

9.2 Analytic Research: Understanding Vulnerability

Analytic research of vulnerable populations attempts to explain why vulnerability occurs and to identify programs that address the problem of vulnerability and the needs of existent high-risk populations. Much analytic research fails to consider how issues from other academic fields affect the points and people being studied. For example, analytic research on health care quality may not necessarily consider research on poverty. Examining **cross-disciplinary research** concerns, like the way poverty affects the quality of health care received, broadens the scope of the research and sheds light on the interconnectedness of the macro- and microlevel characteristics that cause vulnerability.

The characteristics that create vulnerability and the consequences of vulnerability to individuals and society at large are best measured and reported in **longitudinal studies**. Longitudinal studies consider the data in terms of large spans of time, such as a high-risk individual's lifetime or years of policy results. Take, for example, a longitudinal study of children in foster care. Interviews were conducted of both the children and their caregivers regarding the children's risk behaviors during a period termed "Time 1." Those same children and caregivers were interviewed again six years later during a period termed "Time 2." The study results indicate that the risk behaviors identified in Time 1 were directly tied to the risk behavior outcomes found in Time 2 (Taussig, 2002).

Comparative studies that consider the characteristics of one group with those of other groups are useful in identifying the causes of vulnerability. An example is a study that identifies work disability outcomes between health care workers in urban areas and health care workers in rural areas. The study found that rural health care workers are more susceptible to poor work disability outcomes and identified factors including heavy workloads and increased overtime as contributing to the problem (Franche et al., 2010). Researchers conducting comparative studies often find that it is difficult to collect similar data across many populations, especially those identified as vulnerable. This is because many of America's vulnerable people are transient both in where they live and in the services they use. A cross-disciplinary approach can help with data collection. By including data available from studies outside a given discipline, researchers are given more to work with to present a broader understanding of the issues surrounding vulnerability.

Vulnerable Mothers and Children

Analytic research on the vulnerability of mothers and children tends to either rely on outdated data or to be outdated itself. The National Maternal and Infant Health Survey (NMIHS) and the corresponding longitudinal follow-up surveys are among the most frequently cited data sets on maternity outcomes; unfortunately, the NMIHS was conducted in 1988. As such, the oft-cited NMIHS is an insufficient source for researchers who want to know the current state of health care for vulnerable mothers and children, though it is useful for longitudinal study comparison purposes.

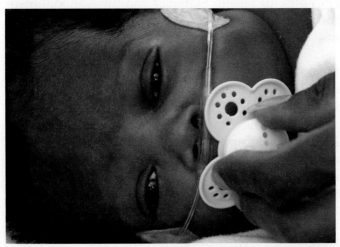

Courtesy of Sabryna Washington/Fotolia

Expanded birth records provide a more comprehensive picture of a person by including detailed data on the mother, such as her behavioral risk factors and history of pre- and postnatal care.

Expanded birth records offer more updated information. In addition to the standard birth certificates that are available, which list parents' names, birth dates, and birth location, expanded birth records collect data on behavioral risk factors of the mother as well as information on the medical handling of births and postnatal care. Similarly, revised death certificates are useful resources for collecting data on causes of death, including causes of infant mortality. Linked birth and death records are also available, which provide a more complete picture of the risk factors that contribute to vulnerability.

Abused Individuals

A 2005 study by the World Health Organization (WHO) found a link between intimate partner violence and physical and mental health. Victims surveyed reported health problems, including suicidal thoughts, dizziness, and vaginal discharge. Many reported having such symptoms years after the abuse had ended (World Health Organization [WHO], 2005). The WHO study relied on survey participant answers and included longitudinal questions regarding when and for how long participants were in abusive situations.

However, while the WHO study sheds light on the effects of abuse, the data does not seek explanations for the abuse. Researchers attempting to identify causal factors would do better to take a multidisciplinary view of the problem and make sure to always avoid forcing the data to match a theory. Although household factors, such as economic struggles within the family, are important to consider, the macrolevel factors—like the social ideology that informs relationship dynamics—that can contribute to abuse must not be overlooked when determining who is most at risk for abuse. Data can be mined from police and protective services reports; however, incidence rates are believed to be lower than the reality because many incidents of abuse go unreported.

Chronically Ill and Disabled Persons

Analytic models are useful in identifying the needs of chronically ill people, how those needs are met, and the utilization rates of programs for the chronically ill and disabled. Standards for analytic research on topics associated with this particular vulnerable group have been published by the National Center for Health Statistics and the National Institute on Aging. These standards outline the basic data sets needed and analysis necessary to guide policy and program decisions.

Analytic research also helps identify the population-based factors associated with the development of chronic diseases. One such study found a link between consuming sugary beverages and type 2 diabetes diagnoses (Malik et al., 2010). With analytic research, descriptive research is pooled to create a macrolevel view of the chronic illnesses and programs for such in a given population or geographic area. This research is useful for measuring risk factors' contributions to the problem of chronic illness and for analyzing programs on both a microlevel and a macrolevel, which indicates how well a given community is responding to the needs of the chronically ill and disabled.

Persons Diagnosed With HIV/AIDS

Analytic research into the epidemiology of HIV/AIDS necessitates a cross-disciplinary approach with the social sciences. HIV presents a particularly interesting epidemic because the majority of HIV transmission is caused directly by human behavior, as opposed to diseases like cholera that can transmit through the water supply. The National Institute of Allergy and Infectious Diseases (NIAID) supports research into HIV/AIDS epidemiology, including the search for a vaccine against HIV, efficacy of HIV/AIDS treatment and prognosis improvement, and behavioral risk factors and social issues that contribute to the epidemic. NIAID makes much of the research available to policy makers, other researchers, and the public through its website and publications (NIAID, 2012). The U.S. military also has an HIV research program, with a focus on preventing U.S. troops from contracting the disease while traveling on assignment. The military's HIV research program studies the HIV/AIDS epidemic across the globe and translates those findings into data to help create programs to decrease the incidence of HIV within the military (U.S. Military HIV Research Program, 2012). Both of these organizations use multidisciplinary approaches to learn more about treating and preventing HIV.

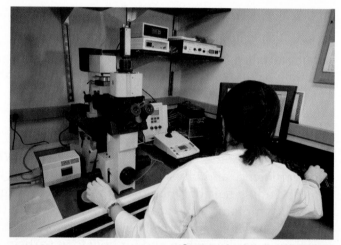

Courtesy of emin kuliyev/shutterstock

In addition to supporting the search for a vaccine against HIV, the National Institute of Allergy and Infectious Diseases (NIAID) supports research into behavioral risk factors and social issues that contribute to the epidemic.

Persons Diagnosed With Mental Conditions

Analytic research into the mind focuses on both the physical brain and the emotional psyche. For example, pharmaceutical companies need to know not only whether a drug works but also how it works on the brain. After all, a drug must accomplish what it is designed to do without causing irreparable physical or psychological damage. Different organizations conduct and fund analytic research for different reasons.

The National Institutes of Health (NIH) supports research into the human brain through a program called the Human Connectome Project. The goal of the project is to map the brain and neurons that affect human behavior and emotion. Two projects funded through the Human Connectome Project are the WU-Minn Consortium and the Harvard/MGH-UCLA Project. Altogether, the Human Connectome Project is working to create a better understanding of neurological and psychiatric disorders. However, the Connectome Project is mostly focused on physical mapping of the brain. More research is needed into the social factors that contribute to mental conditions (National Institutes of Health [NIH], 2012).

Suicide- and Homicide-Liable Persons

Attempts at researching the reasons for death in suicide cases are often conducted post-mortem through psychological autopsies, wherein researchers attempt to find a cause for the suicide through interviewing people who knew the victim. This approach provides useful information on the risk factors of suicide, and research on the topic has helped to inform policy makers and program administrators on the best methods to try to prevent suicide in high-risk groups.

Analytic research into homicide rates and the social and emotional factors that contribute to homicide is sparse, and research projects are disconnected. A cross-disciplinary approach that considers both the micro- and macrolevel contributing factors of homicide is needed. Data resources for analytic research into homicides come mainly from the same sources where descriptive researchers find their information. Additionally, analytic researchers seeking information on homicides can turn to criminal records and court records for extended information that might shed more light on the problem.

Persons Affected by Alcohol and Substance Abuse

Analytic research into the causes of alcohol and substance abuse is often theory-driven. This is one field of research wherein the subjects are generally available for interviews and can be studied longitudinally. Additionally, new research mapping the physical attributes of the brain may be considered in tandem with research into other risk factors, thereby providing a better understanding of why some people are more prone to alcohol and substance abuse than others. For example, the National Institute on Drug Abuse (NIDA) (2011b) confirms that a combination of factors ranging from biology to socioeconomic situations cause drug addiction.

Research into alcohol and substance abuse must overcome the obstacle of lack of program data. Lack of standardization for measurements of program and patient success, unclear outcome expectations, and personal biases are contributing factors to the gap in information regarding the efficacy of programs addressing the needs of people affected by alcohol and substance abuse.

Courtesy of Tubol Evgeniya/shutterstock

A standardized reporting system for collecting information on homelessness would enable researchers to utilize schools to glean insight about the effects of homelessness on children.

Indigent and Homeless Persons

Longitudinal research into the outcomes of homelessness and indigence is lacking due mostly to the transience of this group and the fact that many indigent and homeless people move in and out of homelessness. Of particular importance is research into the effects of homelessness on children and how that experience will shape their adult lives. Shelters have reported increased numbers of homeless families, but many lack programs for continued tracking of homeless children. Schools could be of use in gathering information about the effects of homelessness on children, but there is no standardized reporting system for collecting this type of information.

Analytic research into the economic factors that contribute to homelessness does exist through organizations such as the National Institute of Mental Health (NIMH) and the National Alliance to End Homelessness (NAEH) (n.d.). There have been studies that attempt to recognize the micro- and macrolevel risk factors that lead to homelessness, including mental illness (micro) and economic recessions (macro). However, research projects that focus on one issue pertaining to indigence and homelessness, such as the prevalence of substance abuse, would do well to consider their own research in relation to work done on other topics and in other disciplines.

Immigrants and Refugees

Studies on the lives of immigrants and refugees in the United States need to be designed with cultural sensitivity. For example, when analyzing the lack of service usage by certain immigrant or refugee populations, it is not enough to simply say "they don't use this service"; rather, the socioeconomic and cultural reasons that services are not used need to be found.

More longitudinal research is also needed that follows immigrant children in the United States as they develop into adults. Some of this work is done in educational settings, as schools work to better serve the needs of immigrant children as they grow. Schools can be instrumental in helping outside researchers gather data and contact immigrant families. The Longitudinal Immigrant Student Adaptation (LISA) study conducted by researchers at NYU Stienhardt School of Culture, Education, and Human Development (2012) followed the social and educational development of immigrant children and their families for five years and identified risks and needs associated with educating immigrant children. (For more information on this study, read *Learning in a New Land* by Carola Suarez-Orozco, Marcelo Suarez-Orozco, and Irina Todorova.) Many of the community services available to immigrants and refugees are independently operated, and many rely on volunteers. These outreach programs could provide useful information on the ways in which these families integrate and develop once in the United States, but a standardized, centralized reporting system is needed for the data to be comparable.

Critical Thinking

Assume that you want to do a cross-disciplinary study on abused individuals. How would you take a cross-disciplinary approach to investigate this population? At what other fields would you look?

Self-Check

Answer the following questions to the best of your ability.

1. A 2005 WHO study sheds light on the effects of abuse, but what does it *not* seek to find?
   a. the causal factors of abuse
   b. how long abuse lasted
   c. the household factors involved
   d. a link between intimate partner abuse and mental health

2. What are the causes of the majority of HIV transmissions?
   a. mental illness
   b. domestic violence
   c. human behavior
   d. violent crime

3. When researchers interview people who knew a suicide victim in an attempt to find a cause for the suicide, they are performing _____.
   a. psychological autopsies
   b. forensics
   c. crime scene investigation
   d. analytical research

Answer Key

1. a   2. c   3. a

9.3 Evaluative Research: Studying Program Efficacy

Evaluative research seeks to determine the value of existing programs that address the needs of vulnerable groups and offer guidance on ways to improve services to these groups. Evaluative research often relies on service providers for data. This means that much of the data collected is ambiguous and, in some cases, skewed.

Evaluative researchers studying the needs of vulnerable populations frequently find themselves dealing with funding cuts. In addition to limiting the size and scope of these studies, funding shortages can prolong the amount of time taken to collect information and report findings. As with all other types of research into vulnerability, evaluative research is often outdated before results are even made available. Combining research efforts across disciplines and organizations pools resources and improves the likelihood that an evaluative study will be completed in a timely manner.

Vulnerable Mothers and Children

Biases sometimes skew research results on the efficacy of programs aimed at reducing risks for vulnerable mothers and children. Many studies exist that focus on specific children's health issues associated with prematurity and low birth weight. For example, a study done by the University of Rhode Island found that children born premature experience poorer health as they grow, experience more social struggles than their full-term peers, and have an increased risk of heart health as adults (University of Rhode Island, 2011). However, not as much research has been conducted into the health and social outcomes for vulnerable mothers. Research into the barriers of access to prenatal and preventive care for mothers is scarce. As such, it is difficult to define which programs are most effective, though research indicates that early and regularly scheduled prenatal care is linked to lowered health risks for infants.

Courtesy of lilly 3/iStockphoto

The scarcity of research into the barriers of access to prenatal care for mothers makes it difficult to gauge the efficacy of various programs.

Abused Individuals

Evaluative research into programs for addressing the needs of abused individuals and for preventing abuse indicates that preventive programs are more cost effective than responsive programs. Still, research into these programs would be improved by conducting studies that involve both control and test groups in a given program. Then, the results could be compared against clearly outlined program objectives. Barriers to this research include an uncoordinated system of programs aimed at this vulnerable population.

The Administration for Children and Families (n.d.a) provides some guidance on appropriate responses to child abuse and treating child victims of abuse. This information can be used to help standardize research into program viability.

Chronically Ill and Disabled Persons

Chronic illnesses and disabilities are costly to patients, the nation, and insurance companies. Because of this, much research has been conducted into program outcomes for treating this vulnerable group, like the many ongoing research programs conducted by the Agency for Healthcare Research and Quality (2012). These programs seek to improve health care outcomes while minimizing health care costs. Whereas too much reliance on theories often plagues research into other fields, research into programs for the chronically ill and disabled often has a problematic lack of theory behind it. More research is needed into the ways in which public policy affects this vulnerable group, as public policy decisions trickle down through the health care delivery system. More emphasis on the health outcomes for individuals is also important for creating programs that respond to the needs of chronically ill and disabled people instead of just the need to reduce costs.

Persons Diagnosed With HIV/AIDS

Research intended to evaluate programs for people diagnosed with HIV/AIDS should also include research into the behaviors of this group of patients. Research results should be compared with clearly stated program outcome goals and then consideration given as to why some patients exhibit behaviors that lead to negative health outcomes after an HIV diagnosis. This research should not be conducted in a bubble; treatment programs should be compared with data on other treatment programs to find the best possible ways in which to influence positive patient behavior and treatment compliance, as well as to establish the efficacy of programs in relation to each other.

Persons Diagnosed With Mental Conditions

Just as the network of programs to address the needs of people diagnosed with mental conditions, including private practitioners and mental health wards in short- and long-term inpatient settings, is disjointed and nonstandardized, so too is the research into said programs. Program objectives need to be clearly defined to create programs that work and encourage patients to continue treatments. As with HIV/AIDS, patient behavior affects compliance and program outcomes. Clearly defined test groups and control groups may offer insight into the ways in which patient behavior can be altered to encourage improved outcomes. Other problems exist with the reporting of mental health data due to the stigmatization of mental illness and the protections put into place through the Health Insurance Portability and Accountability Act (HIPAA) and other privacy laws.

Studies of existing program evaluations offer insight into how research in this field should be conducted and understood. Research comparing programs via existing evaluations has found that prevention programs for children, like those focusing on preventing physical abuse and drug abuse, do have a positive impact on the recipients' risk of developing mental disorders. Yet cost is always a factor in health care, and more research is needed to establish which existing programs are most cost effective and how mental health programs can improve to become more cost efficient and to better patients' health outcomes.

Suicide- and Homicide-Liable Persons

Research is needed to improve existing programs that respond to the needs of people who are prone to violence against themselves or others. Not every program is most effective for every vulnerable subgroup. Studies need to consider the subgroups addressed by prevention programs and match the programs with the right subgroups. For example, suicide prevention hotlines may be more effective at reducing suicide attempts among adolescents than among the elderly. The Center for Elderly Suicide Prevention & Grief Counseling (CESP) (n.d.) offers a suicide prevention program aimed specifically at the elderly, and portions of the program may not translate well for use with adolescents. External evaluation of existing programs is needed because internal program evaluation is not always unbiased. Research is under way that is currently investigating the efficacy of existing programs, how public policy affects such programs, and ways in which providers can improve mental health treatment and respond to the needs of suicide-liable individuals. The Services Effectiveness Research Program (SERP) at Duke University studies mental health prevention and treatment services and works to improve standardization of the health care field and create new

Courtesy of Diego Cervo/Shutterstock

Additional research, specific to each vulnerable subgroup, is necessary in order to more effectively meet the needs of people with a predisposition for violent behavior.

prevention and treatment methods to reach more people (Duke University, Department of Psychiatry and Behavioral Sciences, 2011).

Persons Affected by Alcohol and Substance Abuse

In the 1980s, federal and state governments responded to drug abuse rates by funding research and prevention programs, but funding dwindled into the 1990s and on into the 2000s. However, that is not to say that research has ceased entirely. The National Institute on Drug Abuse (NIDA) continues to support research into the causes of alcohol and drug dependence and the best ways to treat patients and mitigate the problem in the country. Prevention programs are thought to be most cost effective in the field of substance abuse. Many school systems continue to utilize the Drug Abuse Resistance Education (DARE) (2012) program to teach elementary- and middle-school students ways and reasons to avoid drug use.

Though DARE and other preventive programs have been around for decades, research into the overall outcomes of these programs is problematic. Many such programs lack clearly stated measurable goals, a problem that complicates measuring outcomes and program integrity. In fact, it has been alleged that DARE is not as effective at preventing drug abuse as was once believed (Fitzgerald, 2006; Hanson, n.d.; Perri, 2010). More research is needed into the influencing factors associated with alcohol and drug abuse and into ways in which prevention and treatment programs can respond to them.

Indigent and Homeless Persons

Problems with standardization of information and an overall lack of program evaluation make it difficult to compare services and programs that address the needs of indigent and homeless people. This is because many services are community based, located in churches and private organizations. Resources, including funds and manpower, are at a premium in these organizations. As such, little is left for research and documentation.

Courtesy of sonne07/Fotolia

Researchers can utilize resources such as the U.S. Department of Housing and Urban Development (HUD) and the Homelessness Resource Center to gather information on and compare programs for low-income individuals.

The U.S. Department of Housing and Urban Development (HUD) (n.d.) is a resource for information on public policy affecting programs for low-income and homeless individuals. As discussed earlier, the Homelessness Resource Center, a program administered by SAMHSA, has used research to provide recommendations for standardization and best practices for programs that address the needs of the homeless. Researchers can use these resources as a basis for comparison when evaluating programs.

Immigrants and Refugees

Research into the unintended consequences of public policy regarding immigration, such as increased racism against certain immigrant groups, is needed to inform future policy decisions. Research is also needed that assesses the ramifications of policy decisions on the physical and mental health of both documented and undocumented immigrants. Furthermore, research into direct correlations between public policy and immigration rates would be useful in determining what future goals should be.

Organizations like the Pew Research Center (2012) and the National League of Cities (2010) perform and support research into the effects of public policy on the lives of immigrants and into the efficacy of existing programs. Information from third-party research sources may also offer interesting insights and a knowledge foundation that can inform future research efforts.

Critical Thinking

Much of the evaluative data on services for special populations comes from service providers and is usually skewed and inaccurate. Why would this be the case? Why wouldn't a service provider provide complete and accurate information?

Self-Check

Answer the following questions to the best of your ability.

1. What do many programs such as DARE lack?
   a. clearly stated measurable goals
   b. participation
   c. corporate sponsors
   d. administrative staff

2. What factor contributes to the lack of information standardization and program evaluation of indigent and homeless populations?
   a. the transient nature of the population
   b. the unwillingness of researchers to be exposed to unclean environments
   c. the lack of funding for documentation and record keeping
   d. the unwillingness of the indigent population to communicate due to embarrassment

3. Identify one unintended consequence of public policy regarding immigration mentioned in the text.
   a. increased racism against certain immigrant groups
   b. reduction of funding by states to immigrant groups
   c. harsher anti-immigration laws
   d. reduction in admissions of immigrants to higher education

Answer Key

1. a   2. c   3. a

Case Study: Health Surveys Are Subjective

Much of the research that seeks to define and project numbers of vulnerable populations is subjective. Survey respondents may decide not to participate, which creates a situation wherein some social groups are over- or underrepresented in the surveys. Of those who do choose to participate, absolute honesty is not guaranteed. Face-to-face surveys often have better participation rates, but respondents may feel uncomfortable disclosing private health and financial information to surveyors.

An example of one such health survey was recently conducted by the health department in the city of Louisville, Kentucky. The survey sought information on the way residents used health care providers throughout the city, with the intention of learning how citizens perceive the current health system in Louisville. All Louisville residents were invited to participate. However, one limiting factor of the survey was that it was available online and not mailed or otherwise made available. The online nature of the survey meant that certain groups, particularly immigrants and low-income individuals who did not have Internet access at home, were likely to be underrepresented in the survey results. The multiple-choice answer selection also limited the survey by forcing participants into a set response, not allowing for answers outside the multiple-choice selection or for further information regarding a particular incident.

Some of the survey questions were objective, such as the participant's zip code, gender, and age range. Some questions were purposefully subjective, and answers were likely to be skewed by respondents' understanding of the questions and possible answers. Examples of subjective questions from the survey include the following:

The last time you had to use the emergency room, what was the reason?

  a. nonemergency issue (rash, prescription refill, etc.)
  b. urgent issue (cut, injury to joint, fever, etc.)
  c. emergency (difficulty breathing, chest pain, seizures)
  d. not applicable

This question relies on the respondent and the questioner having the same idea of what constitutes an emergency. Suggestions are included in parentheses, but not every possibility is listed. Another example of subjective survey questioning is the rating scale:

Using the scale below, please check the box for each issue that you think is a big barrier to health care in Louisville Metro/Jefferson County.

	Strongly agree	Agree	Neither agree nor disagree	Disagree	Strongly disagree	No opinion
1. Doctor's office hours						
2. Trans-portation						
3. Knowing where to go in a health care facility						
4. Cost or expenses						*(continued)*

Case Study: Health Surveys Are Subjective *(continued)*

	Strongly agree	Agree	Neither agree nor disagree	Disagree	Strongly disagree	No opinion
5. Discrim- ination/bias						
6. Health knowledge						
7. Health beliefs						
8. Insurance issues						
9. Stigma						
10. Culture and language						
11. Medi- caid rules						
12. Fear of depor- tation						

Source: LouisvilleKY.gov. (2012). 2012 Community Health Needs Assessment Survey. http://www.surveymonkey.com/s/HealthNeeds Survey

Researchers are often aware that sliding scale questions like this are subjective, and in this case patient perception (which is subjective by nature) was exactly what researchers wanted to know. Subjectivity in survey questions is not always a barrier to quality research, but readers should be aware of it when reading research results.

Chapter Summary

Though descriptive, analytic, and evaluative research does exist that seeks to improve the ways in which vulnerability is mitigated and managed in the United States, much of that research needs improvement. Improving research outcomes involves improving reporting systems in order to gather information from an unconnected system of providers and programs that serve vulnerable populations. Much more research is needed into the causes of vulnerability and how to best limit negative outcomes that come from high-risk situations and behaviors. Public policy has a large effect on program viability and overall outcomes for many groups within the country. Research into the causes of vulnerability and the needs of the vulnerable can work to better inform policy makers. Similarly, research into the effects of public policy on programs can help shape the future of vulnerability in America.

Critical Thinking

Previous chapters in this text have discussed many of the vulnerable groups and the issues associated with them. You have also performed some basic research on your own to expand your knowledge. Based on what you have read and done thus far, do you perceive a research method or technique that will consider the connections that exist across issues and populations?

Self-Check

Answer the following questions to the best of your ability.

1. The definitions of abuse are somewhat objective.
    a. True
    b. False

2. The last CDC/WHO definition of HIV/AIDS was published in what year?
    a. 1982
    b. 1987
    c. 1993
    d. 2001

3. Studies on the lives of immigrants and refugees in the United States need to be designed with what consideration?
    a. older generations
    b. cultural sensitivity
    c. major political funding
    d. future employment eligibility

4. What type of research also helps identify the population-based factors associated with the development of chronic diseases?
    a. qualitative
    b. evaluative
    c. analytical
    d. quantitative

5. It is possible that suicide prevention hotlines may be more effective at reducing suicide attempts among _____ than among the _____.
    a. adolescents, elderly
    b. elderly, homeless
    c. low-income, high-income
    d. new mothers, elderly

6. Reports on current estimates categorize undocumented workers into which three groups?
   a. settlers, sojourners, commuters
   b. students, residents, migrants
   c. hostile, friendly, neutral
   d. employable, nonemployable, disabled

Answer Key

1. **b**   2. **c**   3. **b**   4. **c**   5. **a**   6. **a**

Additional Resources

Visit the following websites to learn more about the topics covered in this chapter:

National Vital Statistics System

http://www.cdc.gov/nchs/nvss.htm

The Services Effectiveness Research Program

http://serp.mc.duke.edu/

Office of Refugee Resettlement

http://www.acf.hhs.gov/programs/orr/

Centers for Disease Control

http://www.cdc.gov/minorityhealth/populations.html

Web Exercise

Create a fictional character that falls into at least one of the special populations covered in this chapter. For example:

An immigrant to the United States, who has a job but does not have health benefits, discovers on a visit to a local health clinic that he has type 2 diabetes.

Be reasonable and make sure it is a logical scenario.

Create a presentation that identifies the following:

- who your subject is
- what special population your subject falls into

- two to three pieces of existing research that have been done regarding the spe population
- two to three examples of what cross-disciplinary research could be done with th information

Be sure that your sources of information are reliable and professional. Remember that you cannot use or cite publicly editable sites/articles such as Wikipedia, YouTube, or blogs. All content and sources must be in APA format.

Key Terms

analytic research Studies that focus on identifying the reasons for vulnerability and the ways to prevent and remediate vulnerability.

comparative studies Research that compares the characteristics of one group with those of other groups.

cross-disciplinary research Collecting and examining data from multiple academic fields.

descriptive research Studies that focus on identifying those most at risk and the methods of identifying these groups and their needs.

evaluative research Studies that work to determine the success of existing programs that aim to provide services to vulnerable groups.

longitudinal studies Research that considers the data in terms of large spans of time.

National Vital Statistics System (NVSS) A reporting system that tracks birth, death, and health data to provide a picture of what the American population looked like in the past and what it looks like now; NVSS uses that data to estimate future birth, death, and health trends.

point-in-time count A method used to determine the total number of homeless people sleeping outdoors in a specific area during a specific period of time.

primacy Whether the condition is the primary health factor or whether it is a secondary symptom of something else.

seroprevalence The incidence of infection, based on blood serum testing, in a given population.

Where Do We Go From Here?

Learning Objectives

After reading this chapter, you should be able to:

- Discuss the importance of collaboration between policy makers and vulnerable populations.

- Explain the community-oriented approach to health care.

- Define the market-oriented approach to health care.

- Specify the role that vulnerable populations should play when developing health care programs.

- Identify policies (social and economic) for health care reform that will improve health care services accessibility, cost, and quality.

Introduction

Policy makers and program administrators must realize that there is often a lack of communication between those creating the programs aimed at vulnerable populations and the individuals who make up those populations. Programs won't be useful if they do not directly address the needs of the vulnerable in ways that are accessible to the vulnerable. The best way to achieve useful program design or reform is to collaborate with the population you are trying to serve. Program designers and medical practitioners can learn a lot about the needs of those they are serving simply by asking them. By having conversations with patients and community leaders, and even by asking patients and patrons to complete surveys, policy makers, program administrators, and practitioners gain insight into the needs and wants of the vulnerable populace. Only through a coordinated, collaborative effort to address the serious issues confronting vulnerable populations can the health and wellness of said population increase to resemble those who are not classified as vulnerable.

Courtesy of Digital Vision/Thinkstock

Effective program planning must include communication between policy makers and the individuals who make up the vulnerable populations meant to benefit from a particular program.

Critical Thinking

Communication can take many different forms. Communication can include everything from formal town hall meetings to informal conversations between two people. Communication does not necessarily even need to involve talking. Describe three special populations and specify a form of communication that could be used to gather information on each group.

Self-Check

Answer the following questions to the best of your ability.

1. The best way for program administrators to achieve useful program design or reform is to collaborate with whom?
    a. the population they are trying to serve
    b. legal counsel
    c. government advisors
    d. academic researchers

2. Declarations from those in charge will be useless because _____.
    a. no one will listen
    b. there is no food
    c. those in charge have not sought the council of the masses
    d. those in charge do not care

3. Only through a coordinated, _____ effort to address the serious issues confronting vulnerable populations can the health and wellness of said populations increase to resemble those who are not classified as vulnerable.
    a. collaborative
    b. grassroots
    c. organized
    d. revolutionary

Answer Key

1. **a**   2. **c**   3. **a**

10.1 The Community-Oriented Approach

Courtesy of iStockphoto/Thinkstock

Several social and interpersonal factors influence a person's sense of well-being.

The key to a **community-oriented approach** to health policy is remembering that a person's well-being is greatly affected by family, friends, and other social factors. In other words, discharged patients will fare better or worse depending on their individual support networks. On a larger scale, this means that health policy needs to look beyond the microlevel and consider the macrolevel factors that affect the populations being served. There are five levels of focus in community engagement: (a) the individual, (b) the social and network systems, (c) the influences of organizations to bring change, (d) the community collaborative relationships, and (e) the state and federal policies and regulations. Concepts that summarize social ecology theories relating to the efforts of community engagement in addressing this need are as follows:

• health status, emotional well-being, and social cohesion, which are influenced by the physical, social, and cultural status of the individual or his or her environment
• different effects of the individual's health, which includes perception and financial resources available
• the influence by others on the individual or group

Community-oriented health policy works to improve health outcomes by making changes on a community level. To do this, community members should be consulted about the needs of their communities and the daily risks encountered there. This goes beyond patients to include consulting those who work directly with patients, and consulting community leaders and organizers on what issues they consider important in the identified community. Once policy makers understand what the contributing factors are, they can begin to form policy to address those factors. Problems with participation often trouble these efforts. Instead of creating focus groups, policy makers can work with physicians to build relationships with patients that encourage discourse and disclosure. Improving the physician-patient relationship not only offers a way to learn the needs of the patients but is in itself an improvement of patient care.

Cross-Disciplinary Solutions

Inadequate housing, high poverty levels, and low education levels can all contribute to ill health and poor health outcomes. Housing issues may include exposed asbestos that leads to lung infections, poverty reduces accessibility to health care, and low education levels contribute to poor lifestyle habits. Though they may appear to be outside the realm of health policy, the effects these and other factors discussed in this book have on health is considerable. As such, community-oriented health policy must address all such factors.

Courtesy of nathings/fotolia

Contributing factors to poor health can include poverty, substandard housing, and low education levels.

The community-oriented approach involves cross-disciplinary planning and programming in order to address individual patient needs as well as to address the community factors that contribute to vulnerability. Health policy that takes a community-based approach should bring together agencies from many different specialties and fields. Health care providers, care management teams, social services officers, and community-based resource programs can be brought together to design programs and policies that improve patients' chances of positive treatment outcomes. This can be accomplished through an ideology of comprehensive collaboration and sharing of pertinent health information across what had previously been silos or territories where information was held close to the vest.

An example of one such program would be a hospital that discharges high-risk youth with a referral to a social worker at a local youth center. The social worker could encourage the youth to participate in the activities offered at the youth center, thereby improving the youth's social capital and ultimately improving his or her chance of positive outcomes in life as well as health. This example illustrates the care continuum from treatment (hospitalization for illness) to long-term services (youth center involvement) and addresses some needs of the vulnerable youth population. Programs at the youth center should be designed to address the needs of the people it serves. One of the best sources for information about those needs is the people being served and, in this case, adults from the relevant community.

Critical Thinking

The community-oriented approach involves cross-disciplinary planning and programming in order to address individual patient needs as well as to address the community factors that contribute to vulnerability. What this means from the perspective of the individual is that discharged patients will fare better or worse depending on their personal support networks. On the other side of the coin, how does improved patient health benefit the greater community? Do you believe the community has a vested interest in ensuring improvements in health at the level of the individual? If so, why?

Self-Check

Answer the following questions to the best of your ability.

1. Community-oriented health policy works to improve health outcomes by making changes on what level?
   a. community
   b. macro
   c. micro
   d. individual

2. Problems with participation often trouble the efforts of policy makers. What is one of the best ways to raise participation levels?
   a. Talk to focus groups.
   b. Look at housing data (sales, property values, etc.).
   c. Work with physicians to build relationships within the community.
   d. Look at how many voters are in the area.

3. Health care providers can be brought together to design programs using what ideology?
   a. comprehensive collaboration
   b. business as usual
   c. keep the information we have to ourselves
   d. continuum of care

Answer Key

1. **a**   2. **c**   3. **a**

10.2 The Market-Oriented Approach

As discussed in earlier chapters, the United States' economy is built on the concept of the ideal free market, unlike the single-payer systems found in countries such as Canada and Great Britain. In other words, the U.S. health care system is **market-oriented**, meaning it relies on competition between care providers to strive for quality and control cost. However, it must also meet the needs of health care consumers, who may not be knowledgeable enough to know what they need because of uncertainty of health and outcomes, as well as a sense that asking questions means questioning doctors' authority.

One disadvantage of a market-oriented health care system is that because health care is often a necessity, people have little opportunity to shop around for the best service and prices. This issue is particularly pronounced in economically depressed areas where access to health care is limited. To address this, America's health care delivery system is evolving and may have never been so prominent an issue as during the lengthy debates over the Patient Protection and Affordable Care Act of 2010 (PPACA). Even if the health care system is part of the free market economy, governments have an interest in ensuring affordable access to all citizens for two reasons: (a) Federal and state governments fund public payer insurance plans, and (b) an unhealthy population costs the country money. As such, the way Americans finance health care, both now and in the future, is at the fore-front of the debate over health care reform.

Changing the Health Care System

One of the many goals of health care reform is to achieve near-universal coverage for all U.S. citizens and a safety net for accessing health care for all people. In an attempt to do this while managing costs, state and federal governments have tried implementing incentive plans to help employers cover the cost of health insurance with tax cuts and other rewards. Other attempts have disincentivized employers from not offering health insurance to employees by fining certain businesses that don't have employee health coverage. Business owners often rail against both methods, arguing that it should not be the responsibility of employers to ensure universal care coverage.

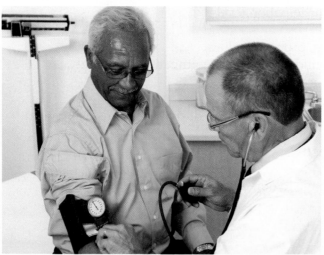

Courtesy of gchutka/iStockphoto

Health care reform strives to achieve adequate access to and coverage of health care for all people, regardless of citizenship status.

Program plans should be evaluated based on these coverage concerns, as well as how they close the coverage gaps from public to private payers by equalizing the provider reimbursement structure and the use of large risk pools to determine pricing. Plan coverage and need and effectiveness norms and definitions that dictate what procedures and services are covered at what levels for which conditions should consider the care continuum model and provide coverage for services across the entire continuum. Plans that use a **community rating**, which is broad population grouping for computing risks and premiums, allow for more coverage for more people at less cost. The alternative, **experience rating**, uses a small group of eligible people and encourages denying coverage to the most vulnerable, as they are most likely to cost the insurer money. Some plans use **carve outs** to cover high-risk patients and pay for some patients' disproportionately high costs. The difficulty with these plans comes when trying to find a fair way to cover patients' needs and offer fair reimbursement for service providers without driving up premiums.

The use of insurance premiums as a means of paying for health care is problematic. Premiums fail to consider varying economic abilities of enrollees to pay premiums and service co-pays. Under the current methodology, health insurance premiums do little to minimize financial barriers to health care, especially in ways that seem tangible to the consumer. As health insurance premiums rise, more and more Americans are allowing their coverage to lapse. Many have also seen their office visit and pharmacy co-pays increase simultaneously. The monthly costs associated with maintaining insurance coverage often seem more immediate than the risk of a catastrophic health event. People living on fixed incomes and those living in poverty have been found to be the most affected by increasing insurance premiums and co-pay costs. Payer systems that include progressive payment scales based on financial need and ability provide more equitable financial access to health care. In fact, cost sharing has been found to limit access to preventive care more than limiting the need for treatment.

While patients are struggling to afford health care coverage and services, providers are struggling to stay open or to make profits. The free market system encourages all service providers in every field to strive for profitability, often to the point of diminishing services to raise profit margins, as in the case of physician practices limiting the number of Medicaid patients they will treat because Medicaid often does not reimburse at as high a level as private payer insurance. Even health care providers who still focus on serving patients find it difficult to run a facility when insurance companies and public payers are constantly negotiating prices. Many among America's most vulnerable who use public payer health coverage have experienced a significantly diminished number of care providers who will accept public payer coverage. This is because many states have lowered the physician reimbursement rates well below what private payers have negotiated. Under these terms, it is in the providers' best interests to limit the number of public payer–enrolled patients and maximize the number of private payer–enrolled patients to increase profits. The American public payer system relies on micro-oriented means to limiting reimbursement. As America struggles to solve problems with the medical care delivery system, policy makers should consider the macro-oriented means used to limit reimbursements in other countries that boast more universal coverage and accessibility.

Physician reimbursement isn't the only area where service costs are rising. It is generally believed that it is not patients but rather physicians who create high demand for expensive procedures and services. Because they are responsible for writing the orders, physicians are also consumers of health care services. **Cost containment** includes managing increasing physician fees and also minimizing the number of expensive services called for by physicians. Policy makers may find it difficult to balance cost containment without disincentivizing the necessary treatments of patients on Medicare and Medicaid.

Health maintenance organizations (HMOs) are a type of insurer that uses a prepaid system to arrange care for covered patients. Because they make prepaid agreements with providers, HMOs are often a less expensive insurance option. Prepaying helps with cost containment by insuring against rising costs for a specified amount of time, because the services are paid for before they are rendered. Because HMOs have a reasonable idea of their revenue for the year (premium dollars per member) and how many members they have to serve, prepaying allows them to keep costs down in order to make profits. Though consumers of HMO plans have reported satisfaction with the premiums and co-pay costs associated with HMOs, they have reported less satisfaction with the standard of care received. Annual numbers on HMOs usually show that they lead in preventive care and reduced number and lengths of hospital stays. Whether that is because HMO patients use more preventive care or because providers are less likely to recommend expensive therapies for HMO patients is unclear.

The PPACA attempts to create universal coverage balanced with affordability. The law includes a mandate that every person must have health insurance by 2014 or pay penalties. Penalty monies should be used to help cover the costs associated with uninsured patients seeking emergency medical attention. Such cases drive up the cost of health care and health insurance for every person in the United States. With the cost of health insurance climbing, universal coverage can be achieved only if premiums are affordable for all people. In an attempt to harness the power of the free market and increase health insurance coverage across the nation, the PPACA created the **American Health Benefit Exchanges** (Henry J. Kaiser Foundation, 2010c). These marketplaces will be administrated by state governments and will provide standardization and competition in the health insurance market. The point is to make it both more affordable and easier for individuals to purchase their own health insurance instead of relying on employers and government programs. This is a market-oriented approach that relies on the free market ideal. At the time this book was written, the insurance exchanges were not yet open; it will be many years before their overall effectiveness can be measured in terms of efficiency, openness of the marketplace, and cost containment.

Critical Thinking

The text says that government should be highly interested in solving the health care crisis because an unhealthy population costs the country money. If individuals pay for their own health care, how does an unhealthy population cost the country money?

Self-Check

Answer the following questions to the best of your ability.

1. Premiums fail to consider varying economic abilities of enrollees to pay for what?
   a. premiums and service co-pays
   b. direct costs of health care
   c. emergency transportation fees (ambulance, etc.)
   d. indigent persons who use health care services

2. Because they make prepaid agreements with providers, what type of organization is often a less expensive insurance option?
   a. labor unions
   b. family health centers
   c. PPOs
   d. HMOs

3. The PPACA law includes a mandate that every person must have health insurance by what year or pay penalties?
   a. 2014
   b. 2016
   c. 2018
   d. 2020

Answer Key

1. **a**   2. **d**   3. **a**

10.3 Improving Accessibility, Cost, and Quality

Taking a community-oriented approach to health care policy means including community members in discussions of change and in the decision-making process. This approach also recognizes that changes need to be made in the affected communities, not only in insurance and medical care provider settings. Increasing social status, social capital, and human capital also works to improve access, cost, and quality of health care received by individual patients.

Minorities and females generally make less money and receive fewer employment benefits than do Caucasian males. Additionally, many females, children, and the elderly find themselves lacking social power in relation to males—Caucasian males in particular. Policy changes that work to minimize vulnerability should focus on changing the social status differences between these groups, like improving housing conditions and attracting businesses to create jobs in poor urban areas. Improving the ability of minorities and women to hold higher-paying jobs by improving educational opportunities is an ongoing challenge. Many low-income communities lose their best educated and most community-minded inhabitants to areas with more economic opportunities. Public policy that incentivizes businesses to locate in low-income areas in order to change a region's economic viability improves the lives of all members of the community as more females and minorities find more opportunities within these companies.

As public policy is often lacking in improving social status for America's most vulnerable, many minority groups have found power through **grassroots social movements**, which are community changes that begin with the people. The Women's Suffrage movement is an example of a grassroots movement that affected public policy change in favor of the group who initiated it. The Women's Suffrage movement in the United States caused the addition of the Nineteenth Amend-

Courtesy of Hemera/Thinkstock

Salary and employment benefits are just one area in which minorities and females receive less than their Caucasian male counterparts.

ment to the U.S. Constitution, which gives all women the same eligibility and right to vote that were previously only enjoyed by men. Similarly, the Civil Rights movement improved the social status of minorities by outlawing racial segregation and discrimination. The Occupy Wall Street of 2012 movement offers an example of a contemporary social movement that worked to raise the social status of all Americans who cannot boast large amounts of wealth. Policy makers can learn from these grassroots movements and use that information to improve social status and thereby health care access for America's most vulnerable populations.

Policy Changes to Improve Social Capital

Social capital is also linked to health care cost, quality, and access. Policies are needed that respond to the changing American family. Increasing numbers of households have only one parent or two parents of the same gender. Legal marriage is being replaced for many couples with cohabitation, sometimes called **mingling**—living with a sexual partner without getting married, often still having children together. For some groups, such as same-gender couples, public policy has focused more on restricting social capital than on improving it, with states making state constitution amendments that ban marriage between people of the same gender.

Public policy does best when it focuses on improving social capital rather than diminishing it. Strengthening family units builds stronger communities. But social capital doesn't end at the front door. Social capital extends well into the community and includes all the people that make up a person's support network, whether extended family, friends, or neighbors. Public policy that works to strengthen families and communities through improved family medical leave, parental leave, improved access to child care services, and improved access to caregiver resources makes it easier for individuals to contribute to their communities. Policy investments in social capital double as investments in access to health care, as social capital is a major factor in overall health and access to care. As with efforts to improve social status, efforts to improve social capital are most successful when community residents are actively involved in identifying the needs present in the community and in program development. Not only does this involvement offer insight that program developers may otherwise lack, but involving community members in the development process also helps energize the community to use the program once it is established.

Social capital levels are directly tied to investment in human capital. Strong family ties help keep children in school and help parents maintain employment. Multi-adult households have more working power to contribute to the household income, and increased income opens doors to health care access as well as education and other opportunities.

Policy Changes to Improve Human Capital

Public policy focusing on investing in the growth of human capital is lacking. By nature, community-oriented policies support programs and institutions that provide for growing human capital. Early childhood education programs are an example of school-based investments in human capital. These programs, like Head Start, have been found to greatly improve the chances of students continuing through high school by improving early literacy scores and providing access to other resources, including some health care services. Basing family resource centers and clinics in schools increases access to these resources and improves the human capital of the entire family. Simply increasing funding for public education works to narrow the gaps in education available in different community settings. Programs that improve the education received at public schools in economically depressed areas invest in the human capital of the students, as better education provides for better job opportunities later in life.

Courtesy of iStockphoto/Thinkstock

Public policy is needed to focus on investing in the growth of human capital. Early childhood education programs like Head Start are examples of school-based investments in human capital and offer educational, health care, and nutritional resources.

Better opportunities are key to building human capital on an individual level. However, many American families find that it is increasingly difficult to raise a family on one income and that the salaries commanded by high school diplomas are no longer enough to lift a family out of poverty. Economic development partnerships—like those in which state and local governments offer business incentives in terms of tax breaks and even investment cash to businesses willing to locate within their geographic regions—can help improve the overall economy of an area and provide more opportunities for higher income. Such partnerships are often forged between city governments and businesses, but these partnerships do not prosper if they aren't supported by the community. Policy makers should invite the active participation of community residents and leaders to make sure that community interests are properly represented when such partnerships are formed.

Policy and program recommendations for improving human capital include encouraging low-income housing development by the private sector, as opposed to low-income housing being the sole responsibility of government. In this way, local businesses can grow while providing for a community need. Similarly, improving access to supportive housing for people experiencing homelessness, people diagnosed with HIV/AIDS, the chronically ill and disabled, refugees, and others in need creates a safety net for these individuals that enables them to increase their own human capital by holding jobs and accessing other resources.

Paradigm shifts are also still needed in order to create true equality between Caucasian men, minorities, and women in the workplace. The minimum wage is reviewed on an ongoing basis by state and national governments. Raising the minimum wage usually meets with resistance, and has both positive and negative economic ramifications. Other economically based changes that would improve human capital for America's most vulnerable include improving enforcement of child support payments and expanding the earned income tax credit for families.

Critical Thinking

When communities invest in the growth of human capital, they provide avenues to elevate social status and social capital for not just the very poor, but the entire community. How does increasing social status, social capital, and human capital increase the benefits to special populations? How can helping one or two special populations in a community lead to the betterment of the community as a whole?

Self-Check

Answer the following questions to the best of your ability.

1. Minorities and females generally make less money and receive fewer employment benefits than whom?
   a. Caucasian males
   b. Asian females
   c. Pacific Islanders
   d. Native Americans

2. Many minority groups have found power through what type of movement?
   a. ethnic support group movement
   b. labor movement
   c. grassroots social movement
   d. professional organization

3. Early childhood education programs are an example of school-based investments in what type of product?
   a. human capital
   b. social capital
   c. social status
   d. social networking

Answer Key

1. **a**   2. **c**   3. **a**

Case Study: Changes in Health Care as a Result of Gender Neutrality

How long does a woman normally stay in a hospital after giving birth to a child?

In 1980, the average stay was 3.8 days, according to the Centers for Disease Control and Prevention (CDC) (2010c). This average dropped to 2.1 days in 1995, but rose again to 2.4 days in 1997. The Organization for Economic Cooperation and Development (OECD) tracks the same data and reported that in 2010, the average stay was again at 2.1 days, after dipping to 1.9 for much of the latter 2000s (Organization for Economic Cooperation and Development [OECD], 2011). Given the historically short duration of the average hospital stay for pregnant women, it may be difficult to imagine a woman giving birth and then staying in the hospital for over a month. But that's just what happened to a woman named Wendy during World War II.

Wendy checked herself in to the hospital with symptoms of childbirth and went through 16 hours of labor. Her son, Rob, was born on a bright Monday morning but would not see the outside world until he was a month old because Rob's father Harold, who was fighting in the South Pacific at the time, was not able to check Wendy and Rob out of the hospital. The law of the land during that period stated that the father, or a male relative, had to check a new mother out of the hospital. A frantic search for Harold's brother began, but the brother had just started boot camp in Florida, and the Army did not release him until after the four-week training process had concluded. After that, Harold's brother drove from Florida to the hospital in Kentucky and signed the papers releasing Wendy and Rob from the hospital.

Could this happen today? Of course not. The current laws and public policies related to health and health choices have changed to such a degree that women's rights and the rights of other groups have evolved and been established to empower them to make decisions, both medical and legal, for themselves.

Chapter Summary

Policy and program designers fare best when they incite and encourage community involvement in recognizing the needs present in a given community and plan for ways to address those needs. Market-oriented approaches to improving health care access and quality focus on the way Americans purchase health care. This can be a useful tactic, as America's health care system is based on a free market. Community-oriented programs and policies focus on mitigating the factors that contribute to vulnerability. Grassroots movements have proven effective in the past as ways for individuals to work together to incite the change and social improvements needed.

America's health care system presents unique challenges for policy makers and consumers alike. Those seeking to effect positive change do best when they include the people they intend to help in the planning process. Improving health care quality, access, and affordability for every person saves lives in more ways than one, and the entire country benefits from improving the lives of the people.

Courtesy of edbockstock/fotolia

Community involvement is integral to the success of a program in a given community because those individuals are most familiar with their own needs.

Critical Thinking

Top-down and bottom-up change can both effectively improve societies. Top-down changes tend to originate at the federal or state government level, whereas bottom-up changes can originate at the community or even individual levels. Can you think of examples of a top-down and bottom-up change? Consider one special population and a challenge that they face. Which type of change (top-down or bottom-up) do you think would be the most effective catalyst of social improvement for this group?

Self-Check

Answer the following questions to the best of your ability.

1. The worst way to achieve useful program design or reform is to collaborate with the population you are trying to serve.
   a. True
   b. False

2. Unfit housing, poverty, and low education levels can all contribute to what?
   a. crime
   b. food deserts
   c. ill health
   d. early childhood programs

3. One of the many goals of health care reform is to achieve _____ for all U.S. citizens and a safety net for accessing health care for all people.
   a. financial stability
   b. near-universal coverage
   c. full employment
   d. religious freedom

4. The monthly costs associated with maintaining insurance coverage often seem more _____ than the risk of a catastrophic health event.
   a. distant
   b. immediate
   c. relevant
   d. difficult

5. America's health care system presents unique _____ for policy makers and consumers alike.
   a. challenges
   b. opportunities
   c. programs
   d. discussions

6. Grassroots movements have proven _____ in the past as ways for individuals to work together to incite the change and social improvements needed.
   a. effective
   b. ineffective
   c. illegal
   d. difficult

Answer Key

1. b   2. c   3. b   4. b   5. a   6. a

dditional Resources

t the following websites to learn more about the topics covered in this chapter:

An article on the study of a community-based participatory research (CBPR) on health care and the growing Hispanic population in North Carolina (published 2011):

http://www.implementationscience.com/content/6/1/38

An article on managed consumerism in the health care industry:

http://content.healthaffairs.org/content/24/6/1478.full

Web Exercise

Create a seven-minute presentation explaining the pros (advantages) and the cons (disadvantages) of the two different systems discussed in this chapter. You are encouraged to start with the two websites listed in the Additional Resources section, but you must use at least three reputable sources for each side of the discussion.

Key Terms

American Health Benefit Exchanges Marketplaces created by the PPACA that will be administered by state governments and will provide standardization and competition in the health insurance market.

carve outs Special insurance planning used to cover high-risk patients and pay for some patients' disproportionately high costs.

community-oriented approach An approach that takes into consideration that a person's well-being is greatly affected by family, friends, and other social factors.

community rating A rating utilized by insurance companies that uses a broad population grouping for computing risks and premiums.

cost containment The process of managing increasing physician fees and also minimizing the number of expensive services called for by physicians.

experience rating A rating utilized by insurance companies that uses a small group of eligible people.

grassroots social movements Community changes that begin with the people.

health maintenance organizations (HMOs) A type of insurer that uses a prepaid system to arrange care for covered patients.

market-oriented An approach that relies on competition between care providers to push for quality and affordability.

mingling The act of living with a sexual partner without getting married, often still having children together.

Glossary

absenteeism The missing of days of work by employees.

alcoholism Overuse and dependence on alcohol.

American Health Benefit Exchanges Marketplaces created by the PPACA that will be administrated by state governments and will provide standardization and competition in the health insurance market.

analytic research Studies that focus on identifying the reasons for vulnerability and the ways to prevent and remediate vulnerability.

annual survey A process in which a team of industry-specialized experts visits a facility and determines its compliance with applicable laws.

binge drinking Five or more drinks per occurrence.

carve outs Special insurance planning used to cover high-risk patients and pay for some patients' disproportionately high costs.

childbearing age The age range of highest fertility, which is 15 to 44.

Children's Health Insurance Program (CHIP) Administered under the Medicaid services umbrella, CHIP provides extended eligibility and coverage for qualifying children up to age 19.

commodity A product available for purchase.

common good Social theory based on reciprocity and doing good for all society members.

community-oriented approach An approach that takes into consideration that a person's well-being is greatly affected by family, friends, and other social factors.

community rating A rating utilized by insurance companies that uses a broad population grouping for computing risks and premiums.

comparative studies Research that compares the characteristics of one group with those of other groups.

compulsory Forced by legal or physical means.

continuum of care The combination of preventive health services, treatment services, and long-term care services that spans a patient's lifetime and provides for the best health outcomes.

co-pay The portion of a patient's bill for which he or she is responsible at the time a medical service is provided.

cost-benefit analysis (CBA) Determines the likelihood of the project producing a positive outcome and a good return on the financial investments of the project.

cost containment The process of managing increasing physician fees and also minimizing the number of expensive services called for by physicians.

cost-effectiveness analysis (CEA) A method of comparing two or more programs.

cross-disciplinary research Collecting and examining data from multiple academic fields.

curative medicine Medical practices focusing on curing existing diseases and conditions.

deductible The portion of expenses a person must pay out of pocket before an insurer pays any expenses.

descriptive research Studies that focus on identifying those most at risk and the methods of identifying these groups and their needs.

differential vulnerability hypothesis The theory that some people have more adverse reactions than others to negative life events.

direct costs Tangible costs that can be measured by totaling the financial prices of all of the resources used to treat a patient.

documented immigrant An immigrant who has come to the United States through legal channels but has not had to undergo the rigorous level of screening experienced by refugees or overdocumented immigrants.

duplicate victim rate The number of child abuse incidents counted.

eldercide The killing of persons age 65 and older.

electronic health records Digital databases that store patient health information, making it accessible to all of a patient's approved providers.

enrollees Insurance plan participants.

epidemiology The study of how a disease moves through populations.

episodic homelessness Recurring, frequent, or ongoing homelessness.

equity Access and coverage being the same for all people.

evaluative research Studies that work to determine the success of existing programs that aim to provide services to vulnerable groups.

experience rating A rating utilized by insurance companies that uses a small group of eligible people.

externalizing disorders Mental conditions that lead to outward activities of destruction such as drug abuse and violence.

food deserts Residential areas without readily available access to grocers who carry fresh fruits, vegetables, and meats.

free market economy An economy based on open competition among corporations with a lack of government regulation.

gestational hypertension High blood pressure during pregnancy.

grassroots social movements Community changes that begin with the people.

gynecological care Medical care specializing in the female reproductive system.

health maintenance organizations (HMOs) A type of insurer that uses a prepaid system to arrange care for covered patients.

human capital The amount of investment in a person's potential.

indirect costs Abstract costs that are difficult to measure in economic terms.

individual rights Social theory based on individuals' choices and freedoms.

infanticide The killing of children age 5 and under.

inflation Loss of currency value.

inoculations Preventive shots administered to prevent the spread of illness.

insurance claims Bills sent to the insurance company to pay for a covered patient's health care services rendered.

insurance underwriters Companies that evaluate the risk and exposure of potential clients, decide how much coverage the client should receive, and determine how much the client should pay for it.

internalizing disorders Mental health conditions that cause emotional responses, such as anxiety disorders and depression.

longitudinal studies Research that considers the data in terms of large spans of time.

long-term care Care that focuses on constant, ongoing health care needs.

macro influences Larger social and environment influences on our lives.

manslaughter Killing another person due to negligence.

market-oriented An approach that relies on competition between care providers to push for quality and affordability.

Medicaid A health insurance program funded with state monies, which provides health insurance to qualifying low-income adults.

Medicare A federally run health insurance program for people age 65 and over, and those unable to work due to permanent disabilities.

micro influences Personal decisions and influences on our lives.

mingling The act of living with a sexual partner without getting married, often still having children together.

monetary inflation Loss in currency value.

monetary value Cost in terms of a dollar total.

murder The purposeful, malicious killing of another person.

National Vital Statistics System (NVSS) A reporting system that tracks birth, death, and health data to provide a picture of what the American population looked like in the past and what it looks like now; NVSS uses that data to estimate future birth, death, and health trends.

neonatal Just-born, generally considered to be the first day or two after birth.

obstetricians Doctors who treat pregnant women for pregnancy.

Occupational Safety and Health Administration (OSHA) Established by the Occupational Safety and Health Act of 1970, this group was created to ensure safe and healthful working conditions for working men and women by setting and enforcing standards and providing training, outreach, education, and assistance.

outcome The result of treatments.

overdocumented immigrant A legal immigrant to the United States that has official refugee status.

Pareto principle The theory that 80% of the outcome is caused by 20% of the effort.

parity Access and coverage being the same across health service types.

pathology The history of a disease.

per capita For each person.

physiological Having to do with the physical body.

point-in-time count A method used to determine the total number of homeless people sleeping outdoors in a specific area during a specific period of time.

postnatal Infancy after the first few days postdelivery.

prenatal care Care of the mother and baby during pregnancy, including ultrasounds, gestational diabetes screening, and obstetric and gynecological care.

presenteeism Wherein workers show up for work but have severely lowered productivity over a length of time.

preventive care services Medically related and medically based services that focus on maintaining health.

preventive medicine Medical practice focusing on education and lifestyle choices with the intention of minimizing the risk of illness.

primacy Whether the condition is the primary health factor or whether it is a secondary symptom of something else.

private payer sector Programs that provide financial access to health care, which includes insurance companies, employer-run health coverage programs, and patients who pay for health care out of pocket.

process considerations Treatment standards and protocols used to treat certain conditions or types of patient.

psychological Having to do with the mind.

public payer sector Government-funded programs that provide financial access to health care.

public policy Laws, regulations, and other government activities that dictate how society should function.

quality-adjusted life year (QALY) An outcome measure that weighs both the quality and quantity of life.

real median income The middle average income level for the United States, adjusted for inflation.

relative risk The potential of imperfect health in groups exposed to risk factors in relation to the potential of imperfect health in groups not exposed to the same risk factors.

Ryan White HIV/AIDS Program A federal program administered by the Health Resources and Services Administration that provides funding to states and community-based organizations to improve health care access and provide life-saving medications for HIV/AIDS patients in low-income areas.

serious mental illness (SMI) Any mental disorder that significantly interferes with daily life.

seroprevalence The incidence of infection, based on blood serum testing, in a given population.

Signs of Suicide program A nationwide program that trains educators and other facilitators to educate youth on recognizing the signs and symptoms of suicide and the appropriate ways to respond.

social attitudes Positive or negative evaluations of people, places, things, and events that are shared by a majority of the community as a whole.

social capital The measurement of personal relationships in an individual's life.

Social Security and Disability Insurance (SSDI) program A federal government that provides a financial safety net, in the form of monthly income checks, for people who become disabled and who have worked enough to contribute to the SSDI program before becoming disabled.

social selection theory The argument that mental illness causes people to fall into low socioeconomic status.

social status A person's place in society as created by personal characteristics, opportunities, and rewards.

social stress theory The argument that the stressors experienced by low socioeconomic groups cause mental health conditions.

socioeconomic classes A combined economic and social measure of a person's work experience and family economic position in relation to others.

statement of compliance A statement showing that a facility is in compliance with all applicable laws and regulations.

statement of deficiency A statement showing different levels of noncompliance with applicable laws and regulations.

sudden infant death syndrome (SIDS) The unexplainable death of an infant any time before the first birthday.

Supplemental Security Income program (SSI) A federal program administered by the Social Security administration that provides financial support for disabled citizens.

surfactant A substance that stabilizes the alveoli in the lung and improves functionality.

transient homelessness A state of homelessness wherein the affected individuals move from home to home, often staying with various family or friends for short periods of time before moving on.

transitional homelessness Short-term homelessness.

treatment improvement protocols (TIPs) Guidelines for best practices created by the Substance Abuse and Mental Health Services Administration's (SAMHSA) Center for Substance Abuse Treatment (CSAT). These guidelines offer information and tools for care providers to effectively treat alcohol and substance abuse.

treatment services Services intended to restore health to ailing individuals.

undocumented immigrant Often referred to as "illegal aliens," immigrants from countries outside the United States or its territories who have not completed the official immigration process.

unique victim rate The number of victimized children counted in child abuse cases.

vulnerability A person's risk level, based on factors such as environment, education, resources, and finances.

workers' compensation A form of insurance that provides wage replacement, medical treatment, and rehabilitation services to employees injured in the course of employment.

References

Administration for Children and Families. (n.d.a). National incidence study of child abuse and neglect (NIS-4); Overview. Retrieved from http://www.acf.hhs.gov/programs/opre/research/project/national-incidence-study-of-child-abuse-and-neglect-nis-4-2004-2009

Administration for Children and Families. (n.d.b). Reporting child abuse and neglect. Retrieved from http://www.childwelfare.gov/responding/reporting.cfm

Agency for Healthcare Research and Quality. (2010). Findings on children's health care quality and disparities. *AHRQ Pub. No. 10-P006.* Retrieved from http://www.ahrq.gov/qual/nhqrdr09/nhqrdrchild09.pdf

Agency for Healthcare Research and Quality. (2012). Retrieved from http://www.ahrq.gov/browse/outcome.htm

American Psychological Association (APA). (2012). Retrieved from http://www.apa.org/pi/aging/resources/guides/elder-abuse.aspx#

Armstrong, G. L. (2007). Injection drug users in the United States, 1979–2002: An aging population. Retrieved from http://archinte.ama-assn.org/cgi/reprint/167/2/166.pdf

Aseltine, R. H., James, A., Schilling, E. A., & Glanovsky, J. (2007). Evaluating the SOS suicide prevention program: A replication and extension. *BMC Public Health,* 7(161). Retrieved from http://www.biomedcentral.com/1471-2458/7/161 doi:10.1186/1471-2458-7-161

Association of American Medical Colleges. (2010). AAMC president calls on Congress to address doctor shortage. Retrieved from https://www.aamc.org/advocacy/washhigh/highlights2010/161958/aamc_president_calls_on_congress_to_address_doctor_shortage.html

Barnes, L., Hall, P. A., & Taylor, R. CR. (2010). The social sources of the health gradient: A cross-national analysis. Retrieved from http://www.people.fas.harvard.edu/~phall/Gradient.pdf

Beaston-Blaakman, A., Shepard, D., Horgan, C., & Ritter, G. (2007). Organizational and client determinants of cost in outpatient substance abuse treatment. Retrieved from http://www.ncbi.nlm.nih.gov/pubmed/17417043

Benitz, W. (2008). NICU guide 2008: Mechanical ventilation. Retrieved from http://lane stanford.edu/portals/cvicu/HCP_Respiratory-Pulmoanry_Tab_2/Mechanical_ Ventilation.pdf

Bouchery, E. E., Harwood, H. J., Sacks, J. J., Simon, C. J., & Brewer, R. D. (2011). Economic costs of excessive alcohol consumption in the U.S., 2006. *American Journal of Preventive Medicine 41*(5), 516–524. Retrieved from http://www.ajpmonline.org/ article/S0749-3797%2811%2900538-1/abstract

Brown, K. E. (2011). Elder justice: Stronger federal leadership could help improve response to elder abuse. Retrieved from http://www.gao.gov/assets/130/125590.pdf

Browne-Miller, A. (2008). Making the case for domestic violence prevention through the lens of cost-benefit. San Rafael, CA: Transforming Communities Technical Assistance, Training and Resource Center. Retrieved from http://www.mcbw.org/files/ u1/Domestic_Violence_Prevention.pdf

Bureau of Justice Statistics. (2011). National crime victimization survey. Retrieved from http://bjs.ojp.usdoj.gov/index.cfm?ty=dcdetail&iid=245

Camarota, S. A. (2002). Immigrants in the United States: A snapshot of America's foreign-born population. Washington, DC: The Center for Immigration Studies. Retrieved from http://www.cis.org/articles/2002/back1302.pdf

Carey, L. A., Perou, C. M., Livasy, C. A., Dressler, L. G., Cowen, D., Conway, K., . . . Millikan, R. C. (2006). Race, breast cancer subtypes, and survival in the Carolina cancer study. Retrieved from http://ebd.lis.illinois.edu/INLS890-EBD/Papers/ Millikan.pdf

Center for Disease Control (CDC). (1992, December 19). 1993 Revised Classification System for HIV Infection and Expanded Surveillance Case Definition for AIDS Among Adolescents and Adults. *Morbidity and Mortality Weekly Report, 41*(RR-17).

Center for Elderly Suicide Prevention & Grief Counseling (CESP). (n.d.). Retrieved from http://www.ioaging.org/services/cesp_suicide_prevention_help.html

Center for Substance Abuse Treatment (CSAT). (2005). Substance abuse treatment for persons with co-occurring disorders. Retrieved from http://www.ncbi.nlm.nih .gov/books/NBK64197/

Centers for Disease Control and Prevention (CDC). (1996). Fetal mortality by maternal education and prenatal care, 1990. Retrieved from http://www.cdc.gov/nchs/ data/series/sr_20/sr20_030.pdf

Centers for Disease Control and Prevention (CDC). (2008a). Reported AIDS cases and persons reported living with AIDS, by area of residence, 2004–2008 and as of December 2008–eligible metropolitan areas and transitional grant areas for the Ryan White HIV/AIDS Treatment Extension Act of 2009. Retrieved from http://www.cdc.gov/hiv/surveillance/resources/reports/2010supp_vol17no1/pdf/2010_hiv_aids_ssr_vol17_n1.pdf#page=8

Centers for Disease Control and Prevention (CDC). (2008b). New estimates of U.S. HIV prevalence, 2006. Retrieved from http://www.cdc.gov/hiv/topics/surveillance/resources/factsheets/prevalence.htm

Centers for Disease Control and Prevention (CDC). (2010). Suicide: Facts at a glance. Retrieved from http://www.cdc.gov/ViolencePrevention/pdf/Suicide_Data Sheet-a.pdf

Centers for Disease Control and Prevention (CDC). (2010a). Teen pregnancy graphics data descriptions. Retrieved from http://www.cdc.gov/teenpregnancy/Long Descriptors.htm

Centers for Disease Control and Prevention (CDC). (2010b). CDC's HIV prevention progress in the United States. Retrieved from http://www.cdc.gov/hiv/resources/factsheets/PDF/cdcprev.pdf

Centers for Disease Control and Prevention (CDC). (2010c). Longer hospital stays for childbirth. Retrieved from http://www.cdc.gov/nchs/data/hestat/hospbirth/hospbirth.htm

Centers for Disease Control and Prevention (CDC). (2011). FastStats: Health expenditures. Retrieved from http://www.cdc.gov/nchs/fastats/hexpense.htm

Centers for Disease Control and Prevention (CDC). (2011a). Trends in current cigarette smoking among high school students and adults, United States, 1965–2010. Retrieved from http://www.cdc.gov/tobacco/data_statistics/tables/trends/cig_smoking/index.htm

Centers for Disease Control and Prevention (CDC). (2011b). High-impact HIV prevention: CDC's approach to reducing HIV infection in the United States. Retrieved from http://www.cdc.gov/hiv/strategy/dhap/pdf/nhas_booklet.pdf

Centers for Disease Control and Prevention (CDC). (2012a). Retrieved from http://www.cdc.gov

Centers for Disease Control and Prevention (CDC). (2012b). National suicide statistics at a glance. Retrieved from http://www.cdc.gov/ViolencePrevention/suicide/statistics/rates02.html

Centers for Disease Control and Prevention (CDC). (2012c). Summary health statistics for U.S. adults: National Health Interview Survey. Retrieved from http://www.cdc.gov/nchs/data/series/sr_10/sr10_252.pdf

Centers for Disease Control and Prevention. (2012d). HIV cost-effectiveness. Retrieved from http://www.cdc.gov/hiv/topics/preventionprograms/ce/index.htm

Centers for Disease Control and Prevention. (2012e). Smoking & tobacco use. Retrieved from http://www.cdc.gov/tobacco/data_statistics/fact_sheets/fast_facts/

Centers for Disease Control and Prevention (CDC). (2012f). National health interview survey. Retrieved from http://www.cdc.gov/nchs/nhis/participant.htm

Centers for Disease Control and Prevention (CDC). (2012g). Behavioral risk factor surveillance system. Retrieved from http://www.cdc.gov/brfss/

Centers for Disease Control and Prevention (CDC). (2012h). Youth risk behavior surveillance system. Retrieved from http://www.cdc.gov/HealthyYouth/yrbs/index.htm

Centers for Medicare and Medicaid Services. (2012). New Affordable Care Act program to improve care, control Medicare costs, off to a strong start. Retrieved from http://www.cms.gov/apps/media/press/release.asp?Counter=4333&intNumPerPage=10&checkDate=&checkKey=&srchType=1&numDays=3500&sr

Central Intelligence Agency (CIA). (2012a). The world factbook. Retrieved from https://www.cia.gov/library/publications/the-world-factbook/rankorder/2091rank.html

Central Intelligence Agency (CIA). (2012b). The world factbook. Retrieved from https://www.cia.gov/library/publications/the-world-factbook/index.html

Chang, H. F. (2000). A liberal theory of social welfare: Fairness, utility, and Pareto principle. Retrieved from http://www.yalelawjournal.org/pdf/110-2/changNEW.pdf

Child Welfare Information Gateway. (2012). Child maltreatment 2010. Retrieved from http://www.childwelfare.gov/pubs/factsheets/canstats.cfm

Ciabattari, T. (n.d.). Single mothers, social capital, and work-family conflict. *Upjohn Institute Working Paper no. 05-118*. Retrieved from http://www.upjohninst.org/publications/wp/05-118.pdf

Clean Needles Now. (n.d.). Retrieved from http://www.cleanneedlesnow.org/

Constitution of the United States of America and the Bill of Rights. (1787). Retrieved from http://www.archives.gov/exhibits/charters/constitution_transcript.html

Conway, J. (2011). Report of the Attorney General: 29 December 2011. Retrieved from http://www.taftlaw.com/linked_documents/0000/0913/Kentucky_AG_Report.pdf

Cooper, T. M., & Clayton, R. (2010). The Cooper/Clayton method to stop smoking. Retrieved from http://www.stopsmoking4ever.org/html/aboutus.html

Courtney, S. E., Durand, D. J., Asselin, J. M., Eichenwald, E. C., & Stark, A. R. (2003). Pro/con clinical debate: High-frequency oscillatory ventilation is better than conventional ventilation for premature infants. *Critical Care, 7*(6), 423–426. Retrieved from http://www.ncbi.nlm.nih.gov/pmc/articles/PMC374363/

Crosby, A. E., Ortega, L., & Stevens, M. R. (2011). Suicides—United States, 1999–2007. Retrieved from http://www.cdc.gov/mmwr/preview/mmwrhtml/su6001a11.htm

DeLisi, M., Kosloski, A., Sween, M., Hachmeister, E., Moore, M., & Drury, A. (2010). Murder by numbers: Monetary costs imposed by a sample of homicide offenders. *The Journal of Forensic Psychiatry & Psychology 21*(4), 501–513. Retrieved from http://www.soc.iastate.edu/staff/delisi/murder%20by%20numbers.pdf

DeNavas-Walt, C., Proctor, B. D., & Smith, J. C. (2011). Income, poverty, and health insurance coverage in the United States: 2010. *Current Population Reports: Consumer Income.* Washington, DC: U.S. Census Bureau. Retrieved from http://www.census.gov/prod/2011pubs/p60-239.pdf

Denning, P., & DiNenno, E. (n.d.). Communities in crisis: Is there a generalized HIV epidemic in impoverished urban areas of the United States? Retrieved from http://www.cdc.gov/hiv/topics/surveillance/resources/other/pdf/poverty_poster.pdf

Drug Abuse Resistance Education (DARE). (2012). About D.A.R.E. Retrieved from http://www.dare.com/home/about_dare.asp

Duke University, Department of Psychiatry and Behavioral Sciences. (2011). Services Effectiveness Research Program. Retrieved from http://serp.mc.duke.edu/

Durose, M., Harlow, C. W., Langan, P. A., Motivans, M., Rantala, R., & Smith, E. L. (2005). Family violence statistics, including statistics on strangers and acquaintances. Retrieved from http://bjs.ojp.usdoj.gov/content/pub/pdf/fvs02.pdf

Fang, X., Brown, D. S., Florence, C. S., & Mercy, J. A. (2012). The economic burden of child maltreatment in the United States and implications for prevention. *Child Abuse and Neglect, 36*(2). Retrieved from http://www.sciencedirect.com/science/article/pii/S0145213411003140

Fitzgerald, T. (2006). Is "Just Say No" an effective anti-drug approach? Retrieved from http://www.rps.psu.edu/probing/antidrug.html

Forum on Child and Family Statistics (Forum). (2011). Health insurance coverage. America's children: Key national indicators of well-being, 2011. Retrieved from http://www.childstats.gov/americaschildren11/care1.asp

Franche, R. L., Murray, E. J., Ostry, A., Ratner, P. A., Wagner, S. L., & Harder, H. G. (2010, October–December). Work disability prevention in rural healthcare workers. *Rural Remote Health, 10*(4), 1502. Retrieved from http://www.ncbi.nlm.nih.gov/pubmed/20964467

Friedman, S. H., & Resnick, P. J. (2007, October). Child murder by mothers: Patterns and prevention. *World Psychiatry, 6*(3), 137–141. Retrieved from http://www.ncbi.nlm.nih.gov/pmc/articles/PMC2174580/

Futures Without Violence. (2010). The health care costs of domestic and sexual violence. Retrieved from http://www.futureswithoutviolence.org/userfiles/file/Health Care/Health_Care_Costs_of_Domestic_and_Sexual_Violence.pdf

Garcia, T. C., Bernstein, A. B., & Bush, M. A. (2010). Emergency department visitors and visits: Who used the emergency room in 2007? *NCHS data brief, no 38.* Hyattsville, MD: National Center for Health Statistics. Retrieved from http://www.cdc.gov/nchs/data/databriefs/db38.pdf

Goodwin, P. Y., Mosher, W. D., & Chandra, A. (2010). Marriage and cohabitation in the United States: A statistical portrait based on Cycle 6 (2002) of the National Survey of Family Growth. *Vital Health Statistics, 23*(28).

Green, C. A. (n.d.). Gender and use of substance abuse treatment services. Retrieved from http://pubs.niaaa.nih.gov/publications/arh291/55-62.htm

Guttmacher Institute. (2012). Facts on publicly funded contraceptive services in the United States. Retrieved from http://www.guttmacher.org/pubs/fb_contraceptive_serv.pdf

Hamilton, B. E., Martin, M. P. H., & Ventura, S. J. (2011). Births: Preliminary data for 2010. *National Vital Statistics Reports, 60*(2). U.S. Department of Health and Human Services. Retrieved from http://www.cdc.gov/nchs/data/nvsr/nvsr60/nvsr60_02.pdf

Hanson, D. J. (n.d.). Drug Abuse Resistance Education: The effectiveness of DARE. Retrieved from http://www.alcoholfacts.org/DARE.html

Health Resources and Services Administration. (n.d.). Health center data. Retrieved from http://bphc.hrsa.gov/healthcenterdatastatistics/index.html

Healthy People.gov. (2012). Public health objectives for the nation, 2020. Retrieved from http://www.healthypeople.gov/2020/default.aspx

Henry J. Kaiser Family Foundation (KFF), & Health Research and Educational Trust. (2011). Employer health benefits: 2011 summary of findings. Retrieved from http://ehbs.kff.org/pdf/8226.pdf

Henry J. Kaiser Family Foundation (KFF), The. (2007). Physician shortage disproportionately affects rural, urban areas; Restrictions on foreign doctors could add to problem. Retrieved from http://dailyreports.kff.org/Daily-Reports/2007/July/23/dr00046410.aspx

Henry J. Kaiser Family Foundation (KFF), The. (2010a). Focus on health reform: Impact of health reform on women's access to coverage and care. Retrieved from http://www.kff.org/womenshealth/upload/7987.pdf

Henry J. Kaiser Family Foundation (KFF), The. (2010b). HIV/AIDS policy fact sheet: U.S. Federal Funding for HIV/AIDS: The President's FY 2011 Budget Request. Retrieved from http://www.kff.org/hivaids/upload/7029-06.pdf

Henry J. Kaiser Family Foundation (KFF), The. (2010c). Explaining health care reform: Questions about health insurance exchanges. Retrieved from http://www.kff.org/healthreform/upload/7908-02.pdf

Henry J. Kaiser Family Foundation (KFF), The. (2011a). Health care spending in the United States and selected OECD countries: April 2011. Retrieved from http://www.kff.org/insurance/snapshot/oecd042111.cfm

Henry J. Kaiser Family Foundation (KFF), The. (2011b). Primary care shortage. Retrieved from http://www.kaiseredu.org/Issue-Modules/Primary-Care-Shortage/Background-Brief.aspx

Henry J. Kaiser Family Foundation (KFF), The. (2012a). Retrieved from http://www.statehealthfacts.org/comparemaptable.jsp?ind=44&cat=2

Henry J. Kaiser Family Foundation (KFF), The. (2012b). Key facts on health coverage for low-income immigrants today and under health reform. Retrieved from http://www.kff.org/uninsured/upload/8279.pdf

Henry J. Kaiser Family Foundation (KFF), The. (2012c). United States: Medicare enrollment. Retrieved from http://www.statehealthfacts.org/profileind.jsp?sub=74&rgn=1&cat=6#notes-ind-290

Henry J. Kaiser Family Foundation (KFF), The. (2012d). Health coverage for children: The role of Medicaid and CHIP. Retrieved from http://www.kff.org/uninsured/upload/7698-06.pdf

Hetzel, A. M. (1997). History and organization of the vital statistics system. National Centers for Health Statistics. Retrieved from http://www.cdc.gov/nchs/data/misc/usvss.pdf

Hoefer, M., Rytina, N., & Baker, B. C. (2011). Estimates of the unauthorized immigrant population residing in the United States: January 2010. Retrieved from http://www.dhs.gov/xlibrary/assets/statistics/publications/ois_ill_pe_2010.pdf

Holahan, J., Schoen, C., & McMorrow, S. (2011). The potential savings from enhanced chronic care management policies. Retrieved from http://www.urban.org/uploadedpdf/412453-The-Potential-Savings-from-Enhanced-Chronic-Care-Management-Policies-Summary.pdf

Howard, K. S., & Brooks-Gunn, J. (2009, Fall). The role of home-visiting programs in preventing child abuse and neglect. *Journal Issue: Preventing Child Maltreatment*, *19*(2). Retrieved from http://futureofchildren.org/publications/journals/article/index.xml?journalid=71&articleid=514&sectionid=3510

HumanaVitality. (2012). Retrieved from http://www.humana.com/vitality/

Insel, T. R. (2008). Assessing the economic costs of serious mental illness. *American Journal of Psychiatry, 165*(6), 663–665. Retrieved from http://ajp.psychiatryonline.org/article.aspx?articleID=99862 doi: 10.1176/appi.ajp.2008.08030366

John A. Hartford Foundation. (2012). John A. Hartford Foundation poll: "How does it feel?" The older adult health care experience. Retrieved from http://www.jhart found.org/learning-center/hartford-poll-2012/

Jones, K., Colson, P., Holter, M., Lin, S., Valencia, E., Susser, E., & Wyatt, R. J. (2003). Cost-effectiveness of critical time intervention to reduce homelessness among persons with mental illness. *Psychiatric Services, 54*(6), 884–890. Retrieved from http://homelessness.samhsa.gov/%28X%281%29S%285vdhiu454dnonw325s1wgp55%29%29/Resource/View.aspx?id=25150&AspxAutoDetectCookieSupport=1

Juran, J. M. (1994). The non-Pareto principle; mea culpa. Retrieved from http://www.juran.com/downloads/Non-ParetoPrinciple-Mea Culpa_JMJuran 94.pdf

Kaiser Health News. (2012a). Community health centers under pressure to improve care. Retrieved from http://www.kaiserhealthnews.org/stories/2012/april/18/community-health-centers-under-pressure.aspx

Kaiser Health News. (2012b). Poll: Doctors fall short in helping many seniors. Retrieved from http://capsules.kaiserhealthnews.org/index.php/2012/04/doctors-fall-short-in-helping-many-seniors/

Kaiser Permanente. (2012). The HIV challenge. Retrieved from http://info.kp.org/communitybenefit/html/our_work/global/hivchallenge/hiv_challenge.html

Kaiser Permanente. (n.d.). What are health disparities? Retrieved from http://info.kp.org/communitybenefit/html/our_work/global/our_work_5_a.html

Kaplow, L., & Shavell, S. (2000). Notions of fairness versus the Pareto principle: On the role of logical consistency. Retrieved from http://www.law.harvard.edu/programs/olin_center/

Kiely, J. L., & Kogan, M. D. (n.d.). Reproductive health of women: Prenatal care. Retrieved from http://www.cdc.gov/reproductivehealth/ProductsPubs/DatatoAction/pdf/rhow8.pdf

Koyanagi, C., & Bazelon, D. L. (2007). Learning from history: Deinstitutionalization of people with mental illness as precursor to long-term care reform. Retrieved from http://www.kff.org/medicaid/upload/7684.pdf

Kung, H., Hoyert, D. L., Xu, J., & Murphy, S. L. (2008). Deaths: Final data for 2005. *National Vital Statistics Reports, 56*(10). Retrieved from http://www.cdc.gov/nchs/data/nvsr/nvsr56/nvsr56_10.pdf

Levit, K. R., Kassed, C. A., Coffey, R. M., Mark, T. L., McKusick, D. R., King, E., Vandivort, R., Buck, J., Ryan, K., & Stranges, E. (2008). Projections of national expenditures for mental health services and substance abuse treatment, 2004–2014. *SAMHSA Publication No. SMA 08-4326*. Rockville, MD: Substance Abuse and Mental Health Services Administration.

Lewin Group. (2004). Costs of serving homeless individuals in nine cities. Retrieved from http://www.lewin.com/~/media/Lewin/Site_Sections/Publications/2991.pdf

LouisvilleKY.gov. (2012). 2012 Community Health Needs Assessment Survey. Retrieved from http://www.surveymonkey.com/s/HealthNeedsSurvey

MacDorman, M. F., & Mathews, T. J. (2008). Recent trends in infant mortality in the United States. Retrieved from http://www.cdc.gov/nchs/data/databriefs/db09.pdf

MacDorman, M. F., & Mathews, T. J. (2011). Understanding racial and ethnic disparities in U.S. infant mortality rates. *NCHS Data Brief no. 74*. Hyattsville, MD: U.S. Department of Health and Human Services, CDC, National Center for Health Statistics; 2011. Retrieved from http://www.cdc.gov/nchs/data/databriefs/db74.htm

Macomber, J., & Pergamit, M. (2009). Vulnerable youth and the transition to adulthood. U.S. Department of Health and Human Services, Office of the Assistant Secretary for Planning and Evaluation. Retrieved from http://aspe.hhs.gov/hsp/09/VulnerableYouth/index.shtml

Malik, V. S., Popkin, B. M., Bray, G. A., Despres, J. P., Willet, W. C., & Hu, F. B. (2010, November). Metabolic syndrome and type 2 Diabetes: A meta-analysis. *Diabetes Care, 33*(11), 2477–2483. Retrieved from http://care.diabetesjournals.org/content/33/11/2477.full

Manchikanti, L., Caraway, D., Parr, A. T., Fellows, B., & Hirsch, J. A. (2011). Patient Protection and Affordable Care Act of 2010: Reforming the health care reform for the new decade. *Pain Physician, 14*, E35–E67. ISSN 2150–1149.

March of Dimes. (2008). The cost of prematurity to U.S. employers. Retrieved from http://www.marchofdimes.com/peristats/pdfdocs/cts/ThomsonAnalysis2008_SummaryDocument_final121208.pdf

March of Dimes Foundation. (2010). Census data on health insurance coverage of women and children. Retrieved from http://www.marchofdimes.com/censushighlights2009.pdf

Marcy, J. (2011). Doctor shortages under health law may depend on geography. *Kaiser Health News*. Retrieved from http://www.kaiserhealthnews.org/Stories/2011/March/17/primary-care-shortage.aspx

Martin, J. A., Hamilton, B. E., Ventura, S. J., Osterman, M. J. K., Kirmeyer, S., Mathews, T. J., & Wilson, E. (2011). Births: Final data for 2009. *National Vital Statistics Reports, 60*(1). Retrieved from http://www.cdc.gov/nchs/data/nvsr/nvsr60/nvsr60_01.pdf#table06

Martin, J. A., Osterman, M. J. K., & Sutton, P. D. (2010). Are preterm births on the decline in the United States? Recent data from the national vital statistics system. *NCHS Data Brief, No. 39*. Retrieved from http://www.cdc.gov/nchs/data/databriefs/db39.pdf

Mathews, T. J., & MacDorman, M. F. (2007). Infant mortality statistics from the 2004 period linked birth/infant death data set. *National Vital Statistics Reports, 55*(14). Retrieved from http://www.cdc.gov/nchs/data/nvsr/nvsr55/nvsr55_14.pdf

Mathews, T. J., & MacDorman, M. F. (2011). Infant mortality statistics from the 2007 period; linked birth/infant death data set. Retrieved from http://www.cdc.gov/nchs/data/nvsr/nvsr59/nvsr59_06.pdf

Mathews, T. J., Menacker, F., & MacDorman, M. F. (2003). Infant mortality statistics from the 2001 period linked birth/infant death data set. *National Vital Statistics Reports, 52*(12).

Medicare.gov. (2012) Retrieved from http://www.medicare.gov/

Milken Institute. (2007). An unhealthy America: The economic burden of chronic disease: Charting a new course to save lives and increase productivity and economic growth. Retrieved from http://www.milkeninstitute.org/healthreform/pdf/AnUnhealthyAmericaExecSumm.pdf

Mitchell, R. J., & Bates, P. (2011). Measuring health-related productivity loss. *Population Health Management, 14*(2), 93–98. Retrieved from http://www.ncbi.nlm.nih.gov/pmc/articles/PMC3128441/ doi: 10.1089/pop.2010.0014

Mohanty, S. A., Woolhandler, S., Himmelstein, D. U., Pati, S., Carrasquillo, O., & Bor, D. H. (2004). Health care expenditures of immigrants in the United States: A nationally representative analysis. *American Journal of Public Health, 95*(8). 1431–1438. Retrieved from http://www.ncbi.nlm.nih.gov/pmc/articles/PMC1449377/ doi: *10.2105/AJPH.2004.044602*

National Alliance on Mental Illness (NAMI). (2007). Fact sheet: The uninsured. Retrieved from http://www.nami.org/Template.cfm?Section=Uninsured&Template=/ContentManagement/ContentDisplay.cfm&ContentID=44609

National Alliance to End Homelessness (NAEH). (n.d.). Research council. Retrieved from http://www.endhomelessness.org/section/aboutus/working_groups/research_council

National Association of Community Health Centers. (2009). Primary care access: An essential building block of health reform. Retrieved from http://www.nachc.com/client/documents/pressreleases/PrimaryCareAccessRPT.pdf

National Center for Health Statistics (NCHS), National Vital Statistics System. (2012). America's children: Key national indicators of well-being, 2011. Retrieved from http://www.childstats.gov/pdf/ac2012/ac_12.pdf

National Center for Health Statistics (NCHS). (2011). *Health, United States, 2010: With special feature on death and dying*. Retrieved from http://www.cdc.gov/nchs/data/hus/hus10.pdf

National Center for Health Statistics (NCHS). (2012). Retrieved from http://www.cdc.gov/nchs/

National Center for Injury Prevention and Control. (2003). Costs of intimate partner violence against women in the United States. Atlanta, GA: Centers for Disease Control and Prevention. Retrieved from http://www.cdc.gov/ncipc/pub-res/ipv_cost/ipvbook-final-feb18.pdf

National Center for Victims of Crime. (2011). Crime victimization in the United States: Statistical overviews. Retrieved from http://ovc.ncjrs.gov/ncvrw2011/pdf/stat-overviews.pdf

National Center on Elder Abuse. (2006). 2004 survey of adult protective services. Retrieved from http://www.ncea.aoa.gov/Main_Site/pdf/021406_60FACTSHEET.pdf

National Coalition Against Domestic Violence (NCADV). (2007). Domestic violence facts. Retrieved from http://www.ncadv.org/files/DomesticViolenceFactSheet%28National%29.pdf

National Coalition Against Domestic Violence (NCADV). (n.d.). Domestic violence facts. Retrieved from http://www.ncadv.org/files/DomesticViolenceFactSheet%28National%29.pdf

National Coalition for the Homeless (NCH). (2007). HIV/AIDS and Homelessness. Retrieved from http://www.nationalhomeless.org/publications/facts/HIV.pdf

National Coalition for the Homeless (NCH). (2009). Mental illness and homelessness. Retrieved from http://www.nationalhomeless.org/factsheets/Mental_Illness.pdf

National Conference of State Legislatures (NCSL). (2011). State laws mandating or regulating mental health benefits. Retrieved from http://www.ncsl.org/issues-research/health/mental-health-benefits-state-laws-mandating-or-re.aspx

National Diabetes Education Program. (2012). The facts about diabetes: A leading cause of death in the U.S. Retrieved from http://ndep.nih.gov/diabetes-facts/index.aspx#gender

National Institute of Allergy and Infectious Diseases (NIAID). (2012). NIAID's HIV research program. Retrieved from http://www.niaid.nih.gov/topics/hivaids/Pages/Default.aspx

National Institute of Mental Health (NIMH). (2000). Women's mental health and gender differences research. Retrieved from http://grants.nih.gov/grants/guide/pa-files/PA-00-074.html

National Institute of Mental Health (NIMH). (2007). Suicide in the U.S.: Statistics and prevention. Retrieved from http://www.nimh.nih.gov/health/publications/suicide-in-the-us-statistics-and-prevention/index.shtml

National Institute of Mental Health (NIMH). (2009). Economic analysis estimates cost of providing comprehensive mental health care following disasters: Study clarifies public health value of large-scale mental health recovery efforts. Retrieved from http://www.nimh.nih.gov/science-news/2009/economic-analysis-estimates-cost-of-providing-comprehensive-mental-health-care-following-disasters.shtml

National Institute of Mental Health (NIMH). (2011). Director's blog: The economics of health care reform. Retrieved from http://www.nimh.nih.gov/about/director/2011/the-economics-of-health-care-reform.shtml

National Institute of Mental Health (NIMH). (2012a). Mental illness exacts heavy toll, beginning in youth. Retrieved from http://www.nimh.nih.gov/science-news/2005/mental-illness-exacts-heavy-toll-beginning-in-youth.shtml

National Institute of Mental Health (NIMH). (2012b). Suicide in the U.S.: Statistics and Prevention. Retrieved from http://www.nimh.nih.gov/health/publications/suicide-in-the-us-statistics-and-prevention/index.shtml

National Institute of Mental Health (NIMH). (2012c). Prevalence of serious mental illness among U.S. adults by age, sex, and race. Retrieved from http://www.nimh.nih.gov/statistics/SMI_AASR.shtml

National Institute of Mental Health (NIMH). (n.d.). Statistics. Retrieved from http://www.nimh.nih.gov/statistics/index.shtml

National Institute on Drug Abuse (NIDA). (2010). InfoFacts: Methamphetamine. Retrieved from http://www.drugabuse.gov/publications/drugfacts/methamphetamine

National Institute on Drug Abuse (NIDA). (2011a). Retrieved from http://www.drugabuse.gov/publications/drugfacts/drug-related-hospital-emergency-room-visits

National Institute on Drug Abuse (NIDA). (2011b). Retrieved from http://www.drugabuse.gov/

National Institute on Drug Abuse (NIDA). (2012). Retrieved from http://www.drugabuse.gov

National Institutes of Health (NIH). (2012). The Human Connectome Project. Retrieved from http://www.neuroscienceblueprint.nih.gov/connectome/

National League of Cities. (2010). Immigrant integration. Retrieved from http://www.nlc.org/find-city-solutions/center-for-research-and-innovation/immigrant-integration

National Prevention Information Network (NPIN). (2012). Retrieved from http://www .cdcnpin.org

National Safety Council. (2009). Retrieved from http://www.nsc.org/safety_work/Pages/ Home.aspx

New York City Department of Health and Mental Hygiene. (2012). HIV Reporting/Partner Notification Law. Retrieved from http://www.nyc.gov/html/doh/html/ah/ ahn1.shtml

NYU Stienhardt School of Culture, Education, and Human Development. (2012). Longitudinal immigrant student adaptation study. Retrieved from http://steinhardt .nyu.edu/immigration/lisa

Office of Substance Abuse Services (OSAS). (2004). Gender differences and their implications for substance use disorder treatment. Virginia: Virginia Department of Mental Health, Mental Retardation, and Substance Abuse Services.

One-Hundred Eleventh Congress. (2010). The Patient Protection and Affordable Care Act. Retrieved from http://burgess.house.gov/UploadedFiles/hr3590_health_ care_law_2010.pdf

Organization for Economic Cooperation and Development (OECD). (2011). Average length of stay: Childbirth. *Health: Key tables from OECD*, No. 52. doi: 10.1787/ l-o-s-childbirth-table-2011-1-en

Paquette, K. (2010). Unaccompanied youth experiencing homelessness. Homelessness Resource Center. Substance Abuse and Mental Health Services Administration. Retrieved from http://homeless.samhsa.gov/Resource/View.aspx?id=48807& AspxAutoDetectCookieSupport=1

Perri, J. (2010). D.A.R.E. generation wants marijuana legalized. *Los Angeles Times*. Retrieved from http://articles.latimes.com/2010/feb/01/opinion/la-oew-perri2-2010feb02

Peterson, C. L., & Burton, R. (2007). U.S. health care spending: Comparison with other OECD countries. *Federal Publications*. Paper 311. Retrieved from http://digital commons.ilr.cornell.edu/key_workplace/311

Pew Research Center. (2012). Publications on immigration. Retrieved from http://pew research.org/topics/immigration/

Planned Parenthood Federation of America. (2012). Affiliate medical services summary. Retrieved from http://www.plannedparenthood.org/files/PPFA/PP_Services.pdf

Post, R. E., Mainous, A. G., Gregorie, S. H., Knoll, M. E., Diaz, V. A., & Saxena, S. K. (2011). The influence of physician acknowledgment of patients' weight status on patient perceptions of overweight and obesity in the United States. *Archives of Internal Medicine, 171*(4), 316–321. Retrieved from http://archinte.ama-assn.org/ cgi/content/abstract/171/4/316/

Project Transitions. (n.d.). Retrieved from http://www.projecttransitions.org/ doi:10.1001/archinternmed.2010.549

Ranji, U., & Salganicoff, A. (2011). Women's health care chartbook: Key findings from the Kaiser Women's Health Survey. Retrieved from http://www.kff.org/women shealth/upload/8164.pdf

Reeves, W. C., Strine, T. W., Pratt, L. A., Thompson, W., Ahluwalia, I., Dhingra, S. S., et al. (2011). Mental illness surveillance among adults in the United States. *Morbidity and Mortality Weekly Report (MMWR), 60*(3), 1–32. Retrieved from http://www.cdc.gov/ mmwr/preview/mmwrhtml/su6003a1.htm

Rosenheck, R., Kasprow, W., Frisman, L. & Liu-Mares, W. (2003). Cost-effectiveness of supported housing for homeless persons with mental illness. *Archives of General Psychiatry, 60*(9). Retrieved from http://archpsyc.jamanetwork.com/article.aspx?artic leid=207801

Sampson, R. (2007). Domestic violence. *Problem-Oriented Guides for Police: Problem-Specific Guides Series no. 45.* Retrieved from http://www.cops.usdoj.gov/files/ric/public ations/e12061550.pdf

Schafft, K. A., Jensen, E. B., & Hinrichs, C. C. (2009). Food deserts and overweight children: Evidence from rural Pennsylvania. *Rural Sociology, 74*(2). Retrieved from http://www.dtc-wsuv.org/taverett/fooddesert/42009321.pdf

Schiller J. S., Lucas J. W., Ward B. W., Peregoy, J. A. (2012). Summary health statistics for U.S. adults: National Health Interview Survey, 2010. *Vital and Health Statistics, 10*(252).

Schnell, G., Joseph, S., Spudich, S., Price, R. W., & Swanstrom. (2011, October). HIV-1 replication in the central nervous system occurs in two distinct cell types. *PLoS Pathog, 7*(10), e1002286. Retrieved from http://www.nimh.nih.gov/science-news/ 2011/hiv-variants-in-spinal-fluid-may-hold-clues-in-development-of-hiv-related-dementia.shtml

Sen, A. K. (1970). The impossibility of a Paretian liberal. *Journal of Political Economy, 78*(1), 152–157.

Sharma, S. (2010). The need to serve rural America. Retrieved from http://www.ncbi.nlm .nih.gov/pmc/articles/PMC3008394/#b4-bth07_4_p024

Sharon, S. (2009). Ban lifted on federal funding for needle exchange. Retrieved from http://www.npr.org/templates/story/story.php?storyId=121511681

Signs of Suicide. (2012). Retrieved from http://www.mentalhealthscreening.org/ programs/youth-prevention-programs/sos/

Singh, G. K., & Yu, S. M. (1995). Infant mortality in the United States: Trends, differentials, and projections, 1950 through 2010. *American Journal of Public Health, 85*(7). Retrieved from http://www.ncbi.nlm.nih.gov/pmc/articles/PMC1615523/pdf/amjph00445-0063.pdf

Siskin, A. (2010). Questions about health reform and noncitizens. Retrieved from http://www.coburn.senate.gov/public/index.cfm?a=Files.Serve&File_id=ce7e55f4-4290-4442-8ae4-70ce96885171

Siskin, A. (2011). Treatment of noncitizens under the Patient Protection and Affordable Care Act. Retrieved from http://www.ciab.com/WorkArea/DownloadAsset.aspx?id=2189

St. Jude Children's Research Hospital. About St. Jude. Retrieved from http://www.stjude.org

Substance Abuse and Mental Health Services Administration (SAMHSA). (2011a). Results from the 2010 National Survey on Drug Use and Health: Summary of National Findings. *NSDUH Series H-41, HHS Publication No. (SMA) 11-4658*. Rockville, MD: Substance Abuse and Mental Health Services Administration.

Substance Abuse and Mental Health Services Administration (SAMHSA). (2011b). Current statistics on the prevalence and characteristics of people experiencing homelessness in the United States. Retrieved from http://homeless.samhsa.gov/ResourceFiles/hrc_factsheet.pdf

Substance Abuse and Mental Health Services Administration (SAMHSA). (2012). Results from the 2010 National Survey on Drug Use and Health: Mental Health Findings, NSDUH Series H-42, HHS Publication No. (SMA) 11-4667. Rockville, MD: Substance Abuse and Mental Health Services Administration.

Substance Abuse and Mental Health Services Administration (SAMHSA). (2010a). National expenditures for mental health services and substance abuse treatment, 1986–2005. *DHHS Publication No. (SMA) 10-4612*. Rockville, MD: Center for Mental Health Services and Center for Substance Abuse Treatment, Substance Abuse and Mental Health Services Administration.

Substance Abuse and Mental Health Services Administration (SAMHSA). (2010b). Mental Health, United States, 2008. HHS Publication No. (SMA) 10-4590, Rockville, MD: Center for Mental Health Services, Substance Abuse and Mental Health Services Administration.

Substance Abuse and Mental Health Services Administration's (SAMHSA) Center for Substance Abuse Treatment (CSAT). (n.d.). Treatment Improvement Protocols. Retrieved from http://www.samhsa.gov

Substance Abuse and Mental Health Services Administration's (SAMHSA) Homelessness Resource Center (HRC). (n.d.). Best practices for providers. Retrieved from http://homeless.samhsa.gov/Channel/View.aspx?id=17&AspxAutoDetectCookieSupport=1

Substance Abuse and Mental Health Services Administration's (SAMHSA) Office of Behavioral Health Equity (OBHE). (n.d.). SAMHSA's office of behavioral health equity. Retrieved from http://www.samhsa.gov/about/obhe.aspx

Sutton, P. D., Hamilton, B. E., & Mathews, T. J. (2011). Recent decline in births in the United States, 2007–2009. *NCHS Data Brief, No. 60*. Retrieved from http://www.cdc.gov/nchs/data/databriefs/db60.pdf

Taussig, H. N. (2002, November). Risk behaviors in maltreated youth placed in foster care: A longitudinal study of protective and vulnerability factors. *Child Abuse & Neglect, 26*(11), 1179–99. Retrieved from http://www.ncbi.nlm.nih.gov/pubmed/12398855

Thompson, M. (2008). Gender, mental illness, and crime. Retrieved from https://www.ncjrs.gov/pdffiles1/nij/grants/224028.pdf

Tjaden, P., & Thoennes, N. (2000). Extent, nature, and consequences of intimate partner violence. Retrieved from https://www.ncjrs.gov/pdffiles1/nij/181867.pdf

Torrey, E. F. (1997). *Out of the shadows: Confronting America's mental illness crisis*. New York: John Wiley & Sons.

Udall Center for Studies in Public Policy. (2006). Immigration and U.S. health care costs. Retrieved from http://udallcenter.arizona.edu/immigration/publications/fact_sheet_no_2_health_care_costs.pdf

United States Administration on Aging, National Center on Elder Abuse. (1997). Trends in elder abuse in domestic settings. Retrieved from http://www.ncea.aoa.gov/Main_Site/pdf/basics/fact2.pdf

United States Administration on Aging, National Center on Elder Abuse. (2005). Fact sheet: Elder abuse prevalence and incidence. Retrieved from http://www.ncea.aoa.gov/Main_Site/pdf/publication/FinalStatistics050331.pdf

United States Administration on Aging, National Center on Elder Abuse. (2006). The 2004 survey of Adult Protective Services: Abuse of adults 60 years of age and older. Retrieved from http://www.ncea.aoa.gov/Main_Site/pdf/021406_60PLUS_REPORT.pdf

United States Bureau of Justice Statistics. (2006). Mental health problems of jail and prison inmates. Retrieved from http://bjs.ojp.usdoj.gov/index.cfm?ty=pb detail&iid=789

United States Bureau of Justice Statistics. (2012). Homicide trends in the U.S. Retrieved from http://bjs.ojp.usdoj.gov/content/homicide/gender.cfm

United States Bureau of Labor Statistics. (2012). Retrieved from http://www.bls.gov/

United States Census Bureau. (1996). National survey of homeless assistance providers and clients. Retrieved from http://www.census.gov/prod/www/nshapc/NSHAP C4.html

United States Census Bureau. (2007). Population distribution in 2005. Retrieved from http://www.census.gov/population/pop-profile/dynamic/PopDistribution.pdf

United States Census Bureau. (2010). U.S. Census Bureau reports men and women wait longer to marry. Retrieved from http://www.census.gov/newsroom/releases/archives/families_households/cb10-174.html

United States Census Bureau. (2011a). Overview of race and Hispanic origin: 2010. Retrieved from http://www.census.gov/prod/cen2010/briefs/c2010br-02.pdf

United States Census Bureau. (2011b). Age and sex composition: 2010. Retrieved from http://www.census.gov/prod/cen2010/briefs/c2010br-03.pdf

United States Census Bureau. (2012a). Population profile of the United States. Retrieved from http://www.census.gov/population/www/pop-profile/natproj.html

United States Census Bureau. (2012b). Statistical abstract of the United States, 2012. Retrieved from http://www.census.gov/compendia/statab/cats/population.html

United States Census Bureau. (2012c). Substance abuse statistics. Retrieved from http://www.census.gov/compendia/statab/2012/tables/12s0207.pdf

United States Census Bureau. (2012d). America's families and living arrangements, current population reports: Family households by number of own children under 18 years of age. Retrieved from http://www.census.gov/compendia/statab/2012/tables/12s0064.pdf

United States Census Bureau. (2012e). Households and families: 2010. Retrieved from http://www.census.gov/prod/cen2010/briefs/c2010br-14.pdf

United States Census Bureau. (2012f). Profile America, facts for features: How many fathers? Retrieved from http://www.census.gov/newsroom/releases/archives/facts_for_features_special_editions/cb12-ff11.html

United States Centers for Medicare and Medicaid Services (CMS). (2012a). Assuring access to affordable coverage: Medicaid and the Children's Health Insurance Program final rule. Retrieved from http://www.medicaid.gov/AffordableCare Act/Provisions/Downloads/MedicaidCHIP-Eligibility-Final-Rule-Fact-Sheet-Final-3-16-12.pdf

United States Centers for Medicare and Medicaid Services (CMS). (2012b). What is CHIP? Retrieved from http://www.insurekidsnow.gov/chip/index.html

United States Conference of Mayors. (2010). Hunger and homelessness survey. Retrieved from http://www.usmayors.org/pressreleases/uploads/2010_Hunger-Homeless ness_Report-final%20Dec%2021%202010.pdf

United States Department of Health and Human Services (U.S. HHS). (2007). Maternal mortality and related concepts. Retrieved from http://www.cdc.gov/nchs/data/series/sr_03/sr03_033.pdf

United States Department of Health and Human Services (U.S. HHS). (2011a). Summary health statistics for U.S. adults: National health interview survey, 2010. Retrieved from http://www.cdc.gov/nchs/data/series/sr_10/sr10_252.pdf

United States Department of Health and Human Services (U.S. HHS). (2011b). Depressions higher in wealthier nations. Retrieved from http://healthfinder.odphp.iqsolutions .com/news/newsstory.aspx?docID=655161

United States Department of Health and Human Services (U.S. HHS). (n.d.). National HIV/AIDS strategy. Retrieved from http://www.aids.gov/

United States Department of Health and Human Services, Administration for Children and Families, Administration on Children, Youth and Families, Children's Bureau. (2011). Child Maltreatment 2010. Retrieved from http://www.acf.hhs .gov/programs/cb/stats_research/index.htm#can

United States Department of Health and Human Services, Administration for Children and Families. (2003). A coordinated response to child abuse and neglect: The foundation for practice. Retrieved from http://www.childwelfare.gov/pubs/user manuals/foundation/foundatione.cfm

United States Department of Health and Human Services, Administration for Children and Families, Administration on Aging. (1998). The national elder abuse incidence study. Retrieved from http://aoa.gov/AoA_Programs/Elder_Rights/Elder_Abuse/docs/ABuseReport_Full.pdf

United States Department of Health and Human Services, Agency for Healthcare Research and Quality. (2011). Health care costs and financing: HIV treatment costs much more when patients start treatment later in the disease. Retrieved from http://www.ahrq.gov/research/mar11/0311RA28.htm

United States Department of Health and Human Services, Centers for Disease Control and Prevention, National Center for Health Statistics. (2012). Summary health statistics for U.S. adults: National health interview survey, 2010. Retrieved from http://www.cdc.gov/nchs/data/series/sr_10/sr10_252.pdf

United States Department of Health and Human Services, Healthy People 2020. (2012). Retrieved from http://www.healthypeople.gov/2020/default.aspx

United States Department of Health and Human Services, Office of the Assistant Secretary for Planning and Evaluation. (2005). Overview of the uninsured in the United States: An analysis of the 2005 Current Population Survey. Retrieved from http://aspe.hhs.gov/health/reports/05/uninsured-cps/ib.pdf

United States Department of Health and Human Services, Office of Population Affairs. (2011). Title X family planning annual report: Forms and instructions. Retrieved from http://www.hhs.gov/opa/pdfs/fpar-forms-and-instructions-2011.pdf

United States Department of Homeland Security. (2006). Retrieved from http://www.dhs.gov/files/statistics/publications/LPR06.shtm

United States Department of Homeland Security. (2010). 2010 yearbook of immigration statistics. Retrieved from http://www.dhs.gov/xlibrary/assets/statistics/yearbook/2010/ois_yb_2010.pdf

United States Department of Housing and Urban Development (U.S. HUD). (2010). The 2009 annual homeless assessment report. Retrieved from http://www.hudhre.info/documents/5thHomelessAssessmentReport.pdf

United States Department of Housing and Urban Development (U.S. HUD). (2011). The 2010 annual homeless assessment report. Retrieved from http://hud.gov

United States Department of Housing and Urban Development (U.S. HUD). (2012). Retrieved from http://portal.hud.gov/hudportal/HUD

United States Department of Housing and Urban Development (U.S. HUD). (n.d.). HUD.gov. Retrieved from http://portal.hud.gov/hudportal/HUD?src=/program_offices/comm_planning/homeless

United States Department of Justice, Federal Bureau of Prisons. (2012). Substance abuse treatment. Retrieved from http://www.bop.gov/inmate_programs/substance.jsp

United States Department of Justice, National Drug Intelligence Center. (2011). The economic impact of illicit drug use on American society. Retrieved from http://www.justice.gov/ndic/pubs44/44731/44731p.pdf

United States Department of Justice, Office of Juvenile Justice and Delinquency Prevention. (2002). Drinking in America: Myths, realities, and prevention policy. Retrieved from http://www.udetc.org/documents/Drinking_in_America.pdf

United States Department of Justice. (2012). Uniform crime reporting statistics. Retrieved from http://www.ucrdatatool.gov/Search/Crime/State/RunCrimeTrendsInOneVar.cfm

United States Health Resources and Services Administration. (2012). Medically underserved areas and populations. Retrieved from http://bhpr.hrsa.gov/shortage/muaps/

United States Military HIV Research Program. (2012). About MHRP. Retrieved http://www.hivresearch.org/about.php

United States National Cancer Institute. (2008). Contents of the SEER cancer statistics review, 1975–2008. Retrieved from http://seer.cancer.gov/csr/1975_2008/sections.html

United States National Center on Elder Abuse. (2005). Fact sheet: Elder abuse prevalence and incidence. Retrieved from http://www.ncea.aoa.gov/main_site/pdf/publication/FinalStatistics050331.pdf

United States National Center on Elder Abuse. (2006). The 2004 survey of state adult protective services: Abuse of adults 60 years of age and older. Retrieved from http://www.ncea.aoa.gov/ncearoot/main_site/pdf/2-14-06%20final%2060+report.pdf

United States National Center on Elder Abuse. (n.d.). Trends in elder abuse in domestic settings. Elder Abuse information series no. 2. Retrieved from http://www.ncea.aoa.gov/Main_Site/pdf/basics/fact2.pdf

United States Public Health Service. (1999). Mental health: A report of the surgeon general. Retrieved from http://www.surgeongeneral.gov/library/mentalhealth/chapter4/sec6.html

United States Social Security Administration. (2011). What we mean by disability. Retrieved from http://www.ssa.gov/dibplan/dqualify4.htm

United States Social Security Administration. (2012a). Social Security program fact sheet. Retrieved from http://www.ssa.gov/OACT/FACTS/

United States Social Security Administration. (2012b). Ticket to Work: Overview of the Ticket program. Retrieved from http://www.chooseworkttw.net/about-program/faq.html

United States Social Security Administration. (2012c). Social security protection if you become disabled. Retrieved from http://www.ssa.gov/dibplan/index.htm

University of Rhode Island. (2011, June 16). Effects of premature birth can reach into adulthood. *ScienceDaily*. Retrieved from http://www.sciencedaily.com/releases/2011/06/110615171408.htm

Wiener, J. M., Hanley, R. J., Clark, R., & Van Nostrand, J. F. (1990). Measuring the activities of daily living: Comparisons across national surveys. U.S. Department of Health and Human Services. Retrieved from http://aspe.hhs.gov/daltcp/reports/meacmpes.htm

World Health Organization (WHO). (2003). Quality improvement for mental health. Retrieved from http://www.who.int/mental_health/resources/en/Quality.pdf

World Health Organization (WHO). (2005). Landmark study on domestic violence. Retrieved from http://www.who.int/mediacentre/news/releases/2005/pr62/en/index.html

World Health Organization (WHO). (2012). Retrieved from http://www.who.int

Xu, J., Kochanek, K., Murphy, S., & Tejada-Vera, B. (2010). Deaths: Final data for 2007. *National vital statistics reports, 58*(19). Hyattsville, MD: National Center for Health Statistics.

Index

public payers of health care for, 162–163

quality of care for, 226–227

social capital and, 91

social status and, 97

treatment services for, 132, 132*t*

Alcoholics Anonymous (AA), 132

Alcoholism, 48. *See also* Alcohol and substance abusers

American Health Benefit Exchanges, 266

American Health Care Association (AHCA), 136

American Housing Survey (AHS), 84

Analytic research, 234, 242–247

Annual Homeless Assessment Report to Congress (HUD), 33

Annual survey of health care facility, 224

APS (Adult Protective Services), 177

Arthritis, 47

Asians/Pacific Islanders, 84–85, 85*f*. *See also* Culture and ethnicity

Asthma in children, 25, 46

B

Baby boomer generation, 81

Barriers to health care, 175–189

    cultural/religious, 181, 182, 224

    financial, 174, 183–189. *See also* Financial barriers to health care

    organizational, 174, 175–182. *See also* Organizational barriers to health care

Behavioral Risk Factor Surveillance System (CDC), 25, 239–240

Best practices. *See also* Quality of care

    treatment improvement protocols (TIPs), 226–227

Bill of Rights, 4

Binge drinking, 48–49, 49*f*, 65, 66*f*

Birthrate, 20, 44, 60–61, 61*f*

Birth weight, 44–45, 60–61

Bullying, 90

C

Cancer, 47, 53

CARE Act (Ryan White Comprehensive AIDS Resources Emergency Act), 178

Carve outs in insurance plans, 265

Caucasians. *See also* Culture and ethnicity

    conditions contributing to vulnerability, 84–85, 85*f*

    infant mortality and, 12*f*, 13

    low birth weight and, 20–21

    single mothers and, 87, 88*f*

    social capital and, 88

Causes of vulnerability, 79–109

    case study, 106*b*

    human capital, 99–105

    population overview, 81–82

    social capital and, 86–93

    social status, 93–99

    U.S. way of life, 83–86

CBA (Cost-benefit analysis), 207

CDC. *See* Centers for Disease Control and Prevention

CEA (Cost-effectiveness analysis), 208

Census Bureau, 241

Center for Elderly Suicide Prevention & Grief Counseling (CESP), 250

Center for Immigration Studies, 73

Center for Mental Health Services (CMHS), 239

Center for Substance Abuse Treatment (CSAT), 226–227

Centers for Disease Control and Prevention (CDC)

    Behavioral Risk Factor Surveillance System, 25, 239–240

    on HIV/AIDS, 47, 203, 211, 238

    on mental health treatment costs, 203–204

    National Center for Health Statistics, 15, 244

    National Violent Death Reporting System (NVDRS), 239

Centers for Medicare and Medicaid Services (CMS), 156–157, 224

CESP (Center for Elderly Suicide Prevention & Grief Counseling), 250

Child abuse, 53. *See also* Abused individuals

Child Abuse Prevention and Treatment Act, 236

Childbearing age, 184

Child Protective Services (CPS), 176–177

Children and adolescents. *See also* Mothers and children

    alcohol use of, 31, 32*f*

    chronic illness and disabilities of, 25, 46–47, 100

    in family makeup, 83

    genetic predisposition to alcoholism, 91

    HIV/AIDS and, 27, 47

    homelessness of, 49–50, 91, 98, 246

    as immigrants and refugees, 50, 50*f*, 98

    mental conditions in, 47, 96

    mental disorder prevention programs for, 249–250

    Program for Children with Special Health Care Needs, 165

    social status of, 93, 95, 97

    substance abuse of, 30, 31–32*f*, 49, 49*f*, 97, 103*b*, 103*f*

    teen pregnancy/mothers, 20, 44, 60–61, 93, 94*f*

Children's Health Insurance Program (CHIP), 157, 226

Chronically ill and disabled people

    age of, 46–47

    analytic research on, 244

    cost of health care for, 201–203, 202*f*, 210–211

    culture and ethnicity of, 63

    defining as vulnerable, 24–26, 25*f*

    descriptive research on, 237

    education and income level of, 70–71

    evaluative research for, 249

    financial barriers to health care, 185–186

    gender differences of, 53

    human capital and, 100

    long-term care for, 138, 138*t*

    organizational barriers to health care, 177–178

    preventive care for, 119–120, 120*t*

M

Macro influences on health, 6, 35b, 117, 243, 261
Managed behavioral health care programs (MBHCPs), 154
Mandatory reporting, 222–223, 238
Manslaughter, 29
Market-oriented approach to pubic policy, 264–267
Marriage, 59–60, 268
Maternal mortality, 20, 60
MBHCP (Managed behavioral health care programs), 154
Medicare and Medicaid, 156–157, 184–188, 220. *See also* Public payers of health care
Men. *See* Gender differences
Mental disorder prevention programs, 249–250
Mental illness, defined, 28
Mentally ill patients
  age of, 47
  analytic research on, 245
  cost of health care for, 203–204, 211–212
  culture and ethnicity of, 65
  defining as vulnerable, 28–29, 29f
  descriptive research on, 238–239
  education and income level of, 71
  evaluative research for, 249–250
  financial barriers to health care for, 186–187
  gender differences of, 54
  human capital and, 101
  long-term care for, 140, 140t
  organizational barriers to health care for, 179
  preventive care for, 122, 122t
  private payers of health care for, 153–154
  public payers of health care for, 161–162
  quality of care for, 225–226
  social capital and, 90
  social status and, 96
  treatment services for, 131, 131t
Methadone clinics, 132
Methamphetamine use, 102, 103b, 103f
Micro influences on health, 6, 19, 35b, 117, 261
Military HIV research program, 244
Mingling (cohabiting), 268
Minimum wage, 270
Minorities. *See* Culture and ethnicity
Monetary inflation, 116, 201
Monetary value of direct and indirect costs, 207
Monitoring quality of care. *See* Quality of care
Mortality
  age-adjusted death rates, 24, 25f
  fetal mortality rates, 94
  infant mortality rates, 12f, 13, 19–20, 52, 60
  race and age and, 41–42, 42f
Mothers and children
  age of, 44–45
  analytic research on, 243
  cost of health care for, 198–200, 198–199f, 209
  culture and ethnicity of, 59–61, 61f
  defining as vulnerable, 19–21
  descriptive research on, 236
  education and income level of, 70

  evaluative research for, 248
  financial barriers to health care for, 184
  gender differences at birth, 52
  human capital and, 99–100
  long-term care for, 136, 137t
  organizational barriers to health care for, 175–176
  preventive care for, 117, 118t
  private payers of health care for, 152
  public payers of health care for, 158–159, 159f
  quality of care for, 222
  social capital and, 87–88, 88f
  social status and, 93–94, 94f
  treatment services for, 128, 128t
Multiple sclerosis (MS), 89
Murder, 29. *See also* Suicide- and homicide-liable people

N

National Alliance on Mental Illness (NAMI), 166, 179
National Alliance to End Homelessness (NAEH), 246
National Center for Health Statistics, 15, 244
National Center on Elder Abuse, 45
National Coalition Against Domestic Violence, 53
National Crime Victimization Survey, 24, 239
National Health Interview Survey (NHIS), 237
National HIV/AIDS Strategy (NHAS), 101b, 225
National Incidence Study (NIS) on Child Abuse and Neglect, 236–237
National Institute of Allergy and Infectious Diseases (NIAID), 244
National Institute of Health (NIH), 245
National Institute of Mental Health (NIMH), 48, 140, 246
National Institute on Aging, 244
National Institute on Drug Abuse (NIDA), 246
National League of Cities, 252
National Maternal and Infant Health Survey (NMIHS), 243
National Suicide Prevention Lifeline, 90
National Survey of Homeless Assistance Providers and Clients, 155
National Survey on Drug Use and Health (NSDUH), 28, 103b
National Violent Death Reporting System (NVDRS), 239
National Vital Statistics System (NVSS), 236
Native Americans. *See* Culture and ethnicity
NCHS (National Center for Health Statistics), 15, 244
Neglect as abuse, 23, 45, 46f, 53
Neonatal care, 198, 222
NHAS (National HIV/AIDS Strategy), 101b, 225
NHIS (National Health Interview Survey), 237
NIAID (National Institute of Allergy and Infectious Diseases), 244
NIDA (National Institute on Drug Abuse), 246
NIH (National Institute of Health), 245